The Great Teachers

The

Great

Teachers

by Frederick Mayer

The Citadel Press New York

To Benjamin Smith
—a great leader of our time

Acknowledgments

For permission to quote, I should like to thank the following publishers:

Beacon Press, Boston, for *Reconstruction in Philosophy* by John Dewey. Copyright 1948.

Harvard University Press, Cambridge, Mass., for *3000 Years of Educational Wisdom,* edited by Robert Ulich. Copyright 1947.

Sheed & Ward, New York, for *The Confessions of St. Augustine,* translated by F.J. Sheed. Copyright 1943.

Charles E. Merrill Books, Inc., Columbus, Ohio, for my *History of Educational Thought* (copyright 1960) and my *Ideas and Education* (copyright 1964).

American Book Company, New York, for my *History of Ancient and Medieval Philosophy* (copyright 1960) and my *History of Modern Philosophy* (copyright 1961).

F.M.

Contents

7

PART III

APPENDIX

Preface

In a period of mechanization and automation the importance of the teacher is especially great. We need not go to the extreme of Gandhi and Tolstoy to realize that technology will not solve the essential problems of man. What matters is the goal of society. Are we striving for adjustment or for creativity? Are our institutions guided by authoritarianism or the spirit of democracy? Is education merely an ornamental process or is it designed to transform the market place?

These are tormenting questions because so often in our century education had been perverted and has contributed to the cultural lag of modern man. Much of conventional education, especially in totalitarian countries, has been an empty ritual that has created the narrow mind and the fanatic who objects to the foundations of the twentieth century.

In American society, education is the main hope of democracy. Through education we hope to improve our intellects, our morals, and our institutions. Education thus has a dual function: It has to create responsible and inspired teachers and awakened followers; and, most important, it has to expand the open society that makes for progress and understanding.

To accomplish these goals, a reconstruction of education is

needed. There should be more emphasis on adult education, so that learning will not be limited to a few decades in the life of an individual. Furthermore, the humanities should occupy a central place. In every way, the teacher has to become the motivating force of our civilization. Above all, the idealism of our students and teachers must not be wasted in sterile endeavors that lead to an isolationist viewpoint regarding the crucial issues of our time.

The great teachers of the past can motivate the reforms of our age. We should realize that we honor the genius of the past best not by imitiation but by our own creativity. We can learn from them to be bold in our search and not to be discouraged by temporary reverses.

The great teachers can inspire us with genuine optimism. As Thoreau said, "We must learn to reawaken and keep ourselves awake, not by mechanical aids, but by an infinite expectation of the dawn."

The great teachers thus become forces of renewal for ourselves, for our neighbors, and ultimately for all mankind.

F.M.

The Great Teachers

PART I

1. The Aims of the Teacher

Significance

To be a teacher is to be part of the most constructive enterprise of mankind. In teaching we have the feeling that we are participating in a timeless undertaking. Since the beginning of mankind dedicated individuals have tried to improve others through the use of reason. Amidst the darkness of barbarian invasions, amidst the chaos of feudalism, the flame of learning could not be extinguished. In the twentieth century dictators like Hitler have tried to control freedom of thought but they failed, for man's love of learning is stronger than any despot.

The story of history ultimately is the story of education, of man's attempt to live by rationality rather than by prejudice, by enlightenment rather than by the ideas of the tribe; by perspective rather than by fragmentary immediacy.

Teaching means awakening. Most individuals are unaware of their own capacities. They live in a purgatory of indifference, and life to them is a very vague process in which an anticlimax prevails. Awakening in an intellectual sense is at first a painful process. It is so much easier to live by sensate means and not to challenge the standards of mediocrity. Plato's allegory of the cave has a perennial significance. At first, those who leave the cave of

15

ignorance are blinded by the light of knowledge. Real knowledge implies insecurity, even a conviction that our own standards and conclusions may be fallible.

Teaching leads to a feeling of transcendence. The ignorant man sees only the self, and the universe is mirrored in his own ego. The educated man feels related to his fellow man and to nature. He is impatient with the idols of his environment. He is a tireless traveler and he knows no frontiers. He finds comrades everywhere because there is no stronger bond than the bond of fellow-seekers. His desire is not merely to live for the moment, but to anticipate tomorrow and the day after tomorrow.

Teaching implies discipline. The universe is not a chaotic system but it is a law-abiding structure. The language of science has a technical vocabulary and it can be mastered only with severe effort. Interest is not always the basis of education and often is the by-product of insistent work. Without effort we remain on the surface and are mere dilettantes. No wonder that a great thinker like Marcus Aurelius was grateful to his teachers for instilling in him correct habits, especially the habit of rigorous investigation.

Teaching is a form of inspiration. Great educators, like Pestalozzi and Froebel, have shown how many possibilities human beings possess that they never explore. Man is defined not only by the actuality of history but by the dream of wisdom. This dream is the basis of progress. It is abstract; it is frequently unrelated to immediate challenges; yet it is an undertaking which ennobles humanity.

This spirit of idealism is represented in a letter written by a former student:

> I try to practice your methods of enthusiasm, friendliness, and interest in pupils.
> Here is a personal incident that may illustrate my attitude. During the first day of school an eleventh-grade student rushed up to me, hugged and kissed me, and said, "Gee, I'm glad to see you,

Mrs. O——!" My sister was with me, and she remarked, "I thought only first-graders loved their teachers."

Last weekend a couple from Arkansas whom my husband and I taught from grades eight to twelve came a hundred miles out of their way to see us. It has been ten years since they graduated. Do you think maybe we reached them?

From this same school we still get long letters at Christmas—not just cards—from thirty-seven students (remember, ten years ago, we left this community). I take their letters, combine the information, mimeograph it, and send each a copy.

Mission of the Teacher

The real function of the teacher is to explore life in all its dimensions. Most individuals, it appears, only exist in a fragmentary manner and they never explore their own potentialities or the richness of nature. A prototype of this attitude is portrayed in the main character in *The Stranger* by Albert Camus, one of the truly great novelists of the twentieth century. The hero of this book has no strong emotions; he scarcely shows any feeling when his mother dies; he goes with a girl, but he really does not care about her and uses her to provide for his physical needs.

Then he kills an Arab and his life changes drastically. During the trial he is pictured as an evildoer and a sadistic criminal, and is condemned to death. Still he is not moved. A priest tries to convert him to religion, but he is not moved. He does not believe in immortality. Are not all condemned to die? Are not all subject to the same merciless fate?

At last, when he knows that death is inevitable, he begins to appreciate the precious nature of life. Now he knows that every minute counts and that he has wasted so much time. Now he feels sympathy for his mother, who fell in love when she was in middle age. Why should not human beings try to prolong their existence? Was not death an interminable void out of which there was no escape?

Real education is a defiance of death. Both Aristotle and

Spinoza believed that the only immortality is the immortality of reason. The individual, they held, will pass away as a separate entity, but as a participant in the enterprise of reason he achieves reality.

In less philosophical terms, Wilder, in *Our Town*, pictures the fragile nature of life and man's major neglect of its possibilities. "Our Town" is a New England community, but it could be anywhere in the United States. It has its class system, its slum section, its political parties. It is a Republican community and somewhat suspicious of new institutions. Its churches follow orthodox lines, although new ideas are beginning to emerge. Against this background Wilder pictures the continuity of life, interrelating the dead and the living.

In the last act of the play, one of the characters who has passed away wants to return to life. Her desire is to live over one day of her former existence. Her wish is granted. As she meets her family again, as she becomes aware of the community, as she becomes conscious of the routine of most lives, she becomes extremely sad. Why do most human beings waste their best moments in triviality? Why are they motivated so often by hatred and antagonism?

In *Our Town*, Wilder maintains that only poets and saints really appreciate the dimensions of life. But we should not overlook the great teachers, who not only preserve and pass on to others a knowledge of past lives, but also help to make our present existence more meaningful.

The task of the teacher is to show that time is limited, and that in perspective human existence can be condensed into a few climactic moments. Man is a product of limitation and yet always yearns for transcendence. To know our limitations is the foundation of education; to transcend them is the vocation of the teacher.

2. Buddha

The Spirit of Indian Philosophy

Indian philosophy is primarily dominated by metaphysical interests. Most Indian thinkers are not satisfied with the consideration of superficial and transitory events; rather, they seek an unchanging and eternal essence. Unlike Chinese philosophy with its ethical interests, Indian philosophy deals above all with the problems of reality. Man, in Indian thought, is subordinated to the universe; life itself becomes a pilgrimage, almost an interlude in the cosmic process.

It has often been remarked that this interest in metaphysics destroys a truly ethical perspective on the part of the Indian thinker, and that it serves as a rationalization for existing social evils. However, this charge is only partially correct. It is true that much of Indian philosophy, especially Hinduism, has provided religious justification for the caste system. Other Indian philosophers, above all Buddha, vigorously attacked the prevailing social system, including the institution of the caste. The more we study Indian philosophy in its educational implications, the more we appreciate its bold ethical teachings and its sublime concept of the nature and destiny of man.

WORLD OF BEING   Noteworthy in Indian thinking is its *vast time perspective.* The destiny of the individual is not evaluated according to momentary considerations, or even according to historical factors; rather, again and again it is pointed out, especially in the *Upanishads,* that reality is beyond space and time. *Thus, the world of becoming is subordinated to the world of being.* It is difficult for the Westerner to appreciate this perspective, since he is so intensely conscious of historical events and, in most cases, has such a well-developed time-consciousness. The Indian thinker, on the other hand, tries to grasp reality as a whole. Imbued with the theory of reincarnation, he sees life on earth as only a fragmentary and partial process, as one step in a cosmic drama that has as its goal the extinction of all separateness and individuality.[1]

IMPERSONAL FORCE   This brings us to another salient factor of Indian philosophy—its impersonal basis. Whereas the Western mind usually regards personality as the highest category, and personal fulfillment as the ideal of existence, the Indian thinkers, from Buddha to Shankara, look upon selfhood as a lower category of being; they believe that the self is in a constant state of flux. According to most Indian thinkers, real education cannot be obtained if we abide by the demands of the individual ego, because real education demands the obliteration and absorption of the self in a larger unity.

In most cases, the Indian thinker does not worship God as a personal being; in fact, atheistic trends are strong in many systems, including Buddhism and Sankhya philosophy. This does not indicate a secular bent; instead, it appears that the Indian thinker is intoxicated with a detached, intellectual love of God. He feels, as Spinoza did, that the universe does not reveal personal features, but an impersonal force that transcends all limitations of space, time, and physical existence.

1. For an excellent introduction to Indian philosophy see P. Carus, *The Gospel of Buddha;* S. Radhakrishnan, *Indian Philosophy,* 2 vols.

LIFE OF THE SPIRIT   For real education, the Indian thinkers recommend, above all, emancipation from material goals and desires. Progress is not to be evaluated according to wealth, fame, or physical power. Social improvement is secondary, for the Indian thinker believes in the cultivation of the spirit and emphasizes cosmic values through which man realizes his essential self.

In fact, in Indian philosophy there is a definite contrast between the life of the senses and the life of the spirit. The life of the senses can gratify only our physical desires, brings about at best an animal happiness, and is essentially a superficial existence. The life of the spirit, which demands constant discipline and unending application, leads to true contentment, gives a knowledge of eternal life, and, in penetrating all appearances and all superficiality, reveals the illusion of multiplicity and the basic oneness of the universe.

TOLERANCE   Compared with Western philosophy, the Indian system of education permits more variety and tolerance when it treats philosophical conclusions.[2] Again and again, Indian thinkers point out that truth appears on various levels and that it is impossible for one man to have a monopoly on wisdom and scientific knowledge. A generous allowance is made for man's innate limitations; consequently, the categories of reason are frequently subordinated to the demands of intuition and insight. Thus, Indian thinkers do not accept the conclusion of science as absolutely valid, for in the highest stages of knowledge science is replaced by mysticism, and reason yields to an intuitive appreciation of reality.[3]

While religious controversies have cost millions of lives in the West, religious debates, at least in earlier times, were carried on

2. Many prominent schools of thought, especially the Buddhists and the Sankhya, presented vigorous arguments against the existence of God.
3. See Cyril Edwin Joad, *Counter-Attack from the East, The Philosophy of Radhakrishnan.*

in a far more broad-minded spirit in India. Hinduism, especially, was able to absorb a variety of other religious theories. The various gods of India intermingled and thus became extremely cosmopolitan.

PESSIMISM Indian philosophy has often been charged with being overly pessimistic. Schopenhauer derived much of his doloristic wisdom from the thinkers of the Upanishads and from Buddhism. The Indians certainly did not accept the optimistic belief that this is the best of all possible worlds. Indian pessimism, however, is not synonymous with a spirit of negativism and placidity. Rather, it is symbolic of a *profound dissatisfaction with the existing world*. The spirit of pessimism demands transcendence—the conquest of the lower self, of fame, of riches, and of the yearning for social approval. It reminds man of his eternal origin and his eternal destiny. In short, Indian thought presents us with a truly universal perspective. It demands that we turn away from the finite, from all that is transitory and perishable, and that we concentrate instead upon eternal ideas and the eternal verities.

Educational Ideals

The Indian educational ideal was a severe one. A student had to obey and follow his teacher in every way. Students were frequently subjected to corporal punishment, and were called on to practice asceticism. In the laws of Baudhayana a student is commanded to avoid light speech, dancing, and the playing of musical instruments; he is to assist the teacher, even when "the latter is making his toilet."

Various types of schools developed. There were private schools established by gurus ("venerable ones") who taught their disciples. There were also Parishads, which were assemblies of learned Brahmins, and Tols, which were one-room, one-teacher educational centers, surrounded by huts in which the students lived.

Forest colleges, which stressed the virtue of contemplation, attracted many famous scholars. Temple schools, which stressed religious instruction, arose after A.D. 500. Secular knowledge was cultivated by the court schools. Mathas and Vidyapathas were monastic centers that concentrated upon the knowledge of the *Vedas* and the *Upanishads*. The Mathas were orthodox centers of Brahmin learning, whereas the Vidyapathas were more liberal in their religious leanings.

Among the important Brahmin universities that were established in that era, the most famous were located at Benares, Nadia, and Taksasila. There the natural and physical sciences were studied, as well as logic, literature, philosophy, and religion. The teachers who were held in great respect, were supposed to be ascetic, learned, and gentle in their behavior. For them, scholarship was a way of life.

The Ideals of Buddha

In Gautama Buddha (563?–?483 B.C.) we find one of the most outstanding and provocative saints in history. He was not only a man of unusual religious insight, but also a philosopher and educator of great depth and penetration.[4]

Numerous legends surround his birth. Thus, we hear of many miracles, such as the healing of disease and blindness, and we hear of kings who came from all parts of the world to celebrate his birth. He was brought up amidst luxury and, as a member of the nobility, received an excellent education. Seldom had a man been so privileged; almost anything his heart desired was given him. He was happily married, adored his newborn child, and never lacked any material comfort.

Still, he was tormented by the evil that he saw around him. Evil appeared to him in three forms: old age, sickness, and death.

4. *See* E. J. Thomas, *The Life of Buddha;* E. Windisch, *Māra und Buddha;* Rhys Davids, *Buddhist India;* H. Oldenberg, *Buddha, sein Leben, seine Lehre;* H. Kern, *Manual of Indian Buddhism.*

Even with all the wealth and glory in the world, he felt that he would not be able to conquer death and find his essential self.

This crisis in his life produced a climactic decision. He resolved to leave his wife and child and became a hermit. For six years he mortified his body, ate very little, neglected his appearance; in fact, he even slept among corpses. To accustom himself to this type of existence, he clothed himself in haircloth. Living in this manner, he hoped to find salvation. Still, the enlightenment for which he was searching did not come.

Finally, disgusted with austerities, Buddha realized that neither asceticism nor self-indulgence could bring about true peace of mind, and that the middle road was the best solution. The key to his teachings lies in his formulation of the Four Truths:

I. *Life is sorrow and full of pain.* The great events of life, birth, sickness, old age, and death, are all equally painful.

II. *Sorrow is caused by desire.* Desire is exhibited in the pleasure that we find in this existence; it is manifested in the yearning for passion, in craving for existence, even in the craving for nonexistence.

III. *The pain that we observe is not ultimate and may be removed.* Instead of desire we must seek nonattachment. To Buddha, life is a virtual hell and escape from this hell can be found through moral means, not through metaphysical exercise.

IV. *The way of escape from sorrow is represented by the Eightfold Path:*

    1. *Right views* imply that we must understand the nature of the self and the nature of the universe. Those who believe that the self is eternal are utterly deluded, for the self is in a constant state of flux.

    2. Besides right views we need *right aspirations.* Thus, we must abandon the life of pleasure, and cultivate the resources of our inner spirit. We are not to bear malice toward any creature, animate or inanimate.

3. *Right words* demand that we abandon all lies. We are not to speak harshly of others, nor are we to engage in trivial gossip.

4. *Right conduct* emphasizes, above all, the rule of pacifism. Under no circumstances are we ever to take someone else's life. Furthermore, we are not to appropriate the goods of others. As for sensual indulgence and physical passion, such activities are expressly forbidden by Buddha.

5. *Right livelihood* deals with the occupations in which we are engaged. The choice of professions is to be guided by moral dictates. For example, we are to avoid the slave trade, and we are not to engage in the sale of harmful drugs.

6. *Right effort* demands that we cultivate the correct type of motives. We must guard against spiritual indifference and lethargy and earnestly search for truth. Like Kant, Buddha emphasized the importance of good will; for if our thoughts are pure we achieve happiness and true peace of mind.

7. *Right mindfulness* demands self-discipline. The great man is not one who conquers others but one who conquers his own self. The body, according to Buddha, is not autonomous; rather, it is to be guided by the mind.

8. The last link of the eightfold path is *right concentration*. Now we are emancipated from all transitory pleasures and from the life of the senses; the mind is in a state of ecstasy, and concentrates upon Nirvana.

Buddha constantly reminds us that we are to shun evil:

A man should hasten towards the good, and should keep his thought away from evil; if a man does what is good slothfully, his mind delights in evil. If a man commits a sin, let him not do it again; let him not delight in sin: the accumulation of evil is painful. If a man does what is good, let him do it again; let him delight in it: the accumulation of good is delightful.[5]

5. *The Dhammapada* (trans. by F. Max Müller), chap. IX.

Who is the wise man? Not one who has been born into a noble family or one who is blessed by riches:

> The man who wears dirty raiments, who is emaciated and covered with veins, who meditates alone in the forest, him I call indeed a Brahmana. . . . Him I call indeed a Brahmana who, even here, knows the end of his own suffering, has put down his burden, and is unshackled. Him I call indeed a Brahmana whose knowledge is deep, who possesses wisdom, who knows the right way and the wrong and has attained the highest end.[6]

Five moral rules are basic in Buddhism:

1. We are not to kill any living being.

2. We are not to covet or appropriate someone else's property.

3. We are not to engage in falsehood.

4. We are not to indulge in intoxicating drinks.

5. We are not to engage in unchastity.

Extremely significant is Buddha's concept of religious authority. While he did not deny the popular gods, and while he sympathized with the worship of the masses, he believed that salvation comes only through reliance upon our own powers. "Be ye a refuge unto yourself" is the keynote of Buddhist thinking.

Buddha stressed earnestness:

> Earnestness is the path of immortality (Nirvana), thoughtlessness the path of death. Those who are in earnest do not die; those who are thoughtless are as if dead already.
>
> Having understood this clearly, those who are advanced in earnestness delight in earnestness and rejoice in the knowledge of the elect.
>
> These wise people, meditative, steady, always possessed of strong powers, attain to Nirvana, the highest happiness.
>
> If an earnest person has roused himself, if he is not forgetful, if his deeds are pure, if he acts with consideration, if he restrains himself and lives according to law—then his glory will increase.

6. *Ibid.,* chap. **XXVI**.

By rousing himself, by earnestness, by restraint and control, the wise man may make for himself an island which no flood can overwhelm.

Fools follow after vanity. The wise man keeps earnestness as his best jewel.

Follow not after vanity. nor after the enjoyment of love and lust! He who is earnest and meditative, obtains ample joy.

When the learned man drives away vanity by earnestness, he, the wise, climbing the terraced heights of wisdom, looks down upon the fools: free from sorrow he looks upon the sorrowing crowd, as one that stands on a mountain looks down upon them that stand upon the lain.

Earnest among the thoughtless, awake among the sleepers, the wise man advances like a racer, leaving behind the hack.

By earnestness did Indra rise to the lordship of the gods. People praise earnestness; thoughtlessness is always blamed.

A Bhikshu (mendicant) who delights in earnestness, who looks with fear on thoughtlessness, moves about like fire, burning all his fetters, small or large.

A Bhikshu (mendicant) who delights in reflection, who looks with fear on thoughtlessness, cannot fall away from his perfect state—he is close upon Nirvana.[7]

Buddha preached against vanity:

If a man delights in quieting doubts, and, always reflecting, dwells on what is not delightful, he certainly will remove, nay, he will cut the fetter of Mara.

He who has reached the consummation, who does not tremble, who is without thirst and without sin, he has broken all the thorns of life: this will be his last body.

He who is without thirst and without affection, who understands the words and their interpretation, who knows the order of letters (those which are before and which are after), he has received his last body, he is called the great sage, the great man.

7. *Ibid.,* chap. II.

I have conquered all, I know all. In all conditions of life I am free from taint. I have left all, and through the destruction of thirst I am free. Having learnt myself, whom should I indicate as my teacher?

The gift of the law exceeds all gifts; the sweetness of the law exceeds all sweetness; the delight in the law exceeds all delights; the extinction of thirst overcomes all pain.

Riches destroy the foolish, if they look not for the other shore; the foolish, by this thirst for riches, destroys himself, as if he were destroying others.

The fields are damaged by weeds, mankind is damaged by passion: therefore a gift bestowed on the passionless brings great reward.

The fields are damaged by weeds, mankind is damaged by hatred: therefore a gift bestowed on those who do not hate brings great reward.

The fields are damaged by weeds, mankind is damaged by vanity: therefore a gift bestowed on those who are free from vanity brings great reward.[8]

Indian Religion and Education

Prayers, Buddha taught, are entirely in vain, for happiness or unhappiness is not caused by divine forces. As for a future life, Buddha denied the existence of a heaven, hell, or purgatory.

Buddha rejected both the cosmological and teleological proofs for the existence of God. There is no first cause. Just as a seed develops into a full-grown plant, just as man develops naturally, so the universe exists as an autonomous unit. The world is not caused by an outside force. In fact, according to Buddha, we do not need ultimate explanations—it is enough if we can describe the relations of phenomena. Even if we accept a first cause, our mind demands that the first cause itself be originated, which creates an insoluble paradox.

8. *Ibid.,* chap. XIV.

As for the teleological proof for the existence of God, Buddha felt that the universe is too imperfect to allow for a creator; nature itself does not reveal the providence of God, for every event is determined by laws. When we speak of evil we are only using human biases; for nature is beyond good and evil and is in every way the expression of the law of cause and effect.

Will the saint survive after death? Buddha denies personal immortality. Man is not characterized by a conscious personal ego; the self, like nature, is in a perpetual state of change. Still, Buddha accepts the concept of reincarnation; hence, *there is not continuity of personality but continuity of action.* Man's character thus transcends the limitations of space and time.

The ultimate goal of Buddha was to find Nirvana. It is difficult to describe this ultimate state since it transcends verbal predications. In the Buddhist teachings it is used in the following ways:

1. As a release from rebirth.

2. As the overcoming of all individuality and all consciousness.

3. As the extinction of selfhood.

4. As the merging of the individual with the principles of reality.

5. As a state of heaven that man experiences after death.[9]

We may now ask what differences existed between the teachings of Buddha and the beliefs of the authors of the *Upanishads.* We find that Buddha did not accept revelation; he recognized no sacred scriptures; no infallible word that man had to accept. Also, Buddha was more positivistic than were the teachers of the *Upanishads;* for him, the problems of metaphysics were secondary, and what mattered, above all, was man's moral life. As to the problems of infinity and free will, they could not be solved by man's finite intellect. Unlike the authors of the *Upanishads,* Buddha rejected asceticism. The way to education is not reserved

9. See T. Stcherbatsky, *The Conception of Buddhist Nirvana.*

to the priests or to one group of people but can be found by all.

Likewise, in his attitude regarding the caste system, Buddha revealed his unusual independence. The real struggle in life is between those who accept the dictates of morality and those who are guided by selfish desires. Although he was not primarily a social reformer, Buddha made it clear that ultimate religion is a matter of individual responsibility, not of social organization and ecclesiastical ritual.

Buddha stressed with eloquence the positive aspects of the moral life.[10] The enlightened man is not bound by fear or by attachment to transitory goals; he is guided by a deep sense of compassion that includes all parts of creation.

Hinayana, Mahayana, and Zen Buddhism

HINAYANA BUDDHISM   The philosophy of Hinayana Buddhism is a rather austere form of Buddhism. To the Hinayana Buddhists, Buddha is primarily a teacher, not a god. They maintain that enlightenment may be achieved without the aid of any deity; thus Buddha is to be worshipped mainly, because he gave us the supreme example of the religious life. Prominent in Hinayana Buddhism is the ideal of asceticism. The educated man will live a celibate life apart from society; if he engages in social intercourse he cannot realize true tranquillity.

What is the goal of man? What is the aim of his existence? According to Hinanyana Buddhism, the goal of man is the extinction of consciousness—a state identified with Nirvana. This can be achieved through concentrated meditation on the Four Truths. We note again that this emancipation can be accomplished through one's *own power,* not through external aid.

Important in Hinayana Buddhism is the emphasis on the change that governs the universe; there are no permanent en-

10. For a critical survey of Buddhist ethical teachings, consult L. de la Vallée Poussin, *La Morale Bouddhique.*

tities or permanent substances. Whatever we perceive is in a state of flux. Frequently, Hinayana Buddhism made a concession to popular beliefs and thus developed polytheistic ideals. The gods, however, are not eternal or immortal, and they are subordinated to Buddha himself. In Hinayana Buddhism, the gods mediate between Buddha and the worshipper. This is quite different from the Christian concept of one God who is all-powerful.

MAHAYANA BUDDHISM The philosophy of Mahayana Buddhism, unlike Hinayana Buddhism, is extremely colorful. Mahayana Buddhism regards Buddha as a savior, and speaks of saints who could have attained Nirvana but who have chosen instead to aid human beings. These saints have such compassion that they rescue even the worst sinner and make salvation possible for all. As in Catholicism, the saints mediate between man and God, and their spiritual achievements compensate for the limitations of the common man.

Theistic features dominate Mahayana Buddhism. There is a heaven and a hell, and a paradise that is a form of personal existence. Survival after death is not a delusion, but a definite fact.

Education in Mahayana Buddhism represents an attempt to achieve sainthood. The wise man combines knowledge and moral fervor. He fights a perpetual war against the forces of ignorance.

In Mahayana Buddhism we find a great deal of metaphysical speculation, usually in the direction of idealism: *to be is to be perceived*. A distinction is made between absolute truth, which can be known only by the enlightened saints, and relative truth, which is all the common man can know.

ZEN BUDDHISM The teachings of Zen Buddhism stress above all the independence of the individual. Devoted to nature, Zen Buddhists protest against the artificiality of city life; no wonder that most Buddhist temples are established on isolated mountains. Detachment is the keynote to Zen Buddhism. We are not to be moved by selfish desires or by the love of possessions. The Zen ideal is spiritual poverty, which is a state of mind rather than a matter of physical possession.[11]

In many ways, Zen Buddhism reminds us of the conclusions of Socrates. It holds that the individual contains within himself the seeds of truth. Education thus implies the clearing away of all biases and prejudices—a process that necessitates a return to nature. We learn more from the contemplation of majestic mountains than from the lectures of learned scholars. Real knowledge is based on intuition and unites an understanding of nature with a comprehension of the self.

To be more concrete: in Zen education a disciple may ask his master a question and receive what appears to be a nonsensical answer. According to Zen principles, plain answers are to be avoided. Rather, the disciple may be asked to study under various teachers; thus his vision will expand and his intellectual horizon will broaden. Travel will bring him into contact with eminent masters and he will learn new ways of living. At the same time he will learn to appreciate the simplicity of nature. One day as he contemplates nature his question may be answered and he may achieve an insight into the nature of life. All this will happen spontaneously, for the Zen teacher believes that the student has to achieve his own conclusions and find his own path to truth.

In the end, the disciple returns to his first master, convinced that education has a symbolic meaning and that truth transcends verbal statements. He is grateful to the master; he has found his own way to wisdom and he has not been indoctrinated with a preconceived viewpoint.

The Zen concept of education reminds us of progressive education. Both viewpoints stress the importance of the pupil—the learner; both believe that our nature is creative and that interest

11. See A. Watts, *The Spirit of the Zen*, pp. 57-60. Zen Buddhism became especially popular in China.

should guide our intellectual development. However, Zen Buddhism emphasizes the importance of intuition, while leaders in progressive education, like William H. Kilpatrick, believe in the supremacy of the scientific method.

Buddhist Educational Ideals

Buddhist students are not selected on the basis of caste; rather, the ideal of equality is cherished. The Buddhist child starts his studies at the age of six and completes them at about the age of twenty. Then he begins advanced studies in literature, philosophy, metaphysics, science, and other courses. If he wants to enter a university, he has to pass rigorous tests.

Among the famous Buddhist universities is Nalanda, which developed around A.D. 425. It is said to have attracted over 10,000 students, and to have had a teaching staff of 1,500. Students did not have to pay for tuition and lodging. There were several gates through which applicants had to pass, at which they were subjected to a difficult test by a dean of admissions. More than 70 per cent failed the examination.

Nalanda attracted not only students but scholars, who came to dispute ideas or who wanted a center for quiet study. Both the sciences and philosophy were cultivated; law received only a secondary emphasis.

Buddhism also developed monasteries in which education flourished. Monasteries were open both to those who desired to lead an ascetic life and to students who wished to pursue knowledge.

The aim of Buddhist education was to produce a compassionate individual, emancipated from egocentricity. The scholar had to be an example in virtue and in loving-kindness. His main interest was to be in morality rather than in metaphysics.

3. Confucius

Through the ages, unity of the family provided the foundation for Chinese education. The Chinese were taught to respect age and superior achievement. As Confucius pointed out, states could prosper only when filial piety prevailed and when a system of etiquette governed social life. Chinese education emphasized the past rather than the present.

Whereas the Indian ideal of scholarship taught the virtues of nonattachment and the subjugation of desire, the Chinese scholars believed in the enjoyment of life in this world. This did not imply enjoyment to an extreme, but rather the sense of moderation and balance.

What is the difference between the educated and the uneducated individual? According to the Chinese view, the educated man has respect for knowledge, whereas the ignorant man follows irrational passions. Knowledge, however, is not to be worshipped for its own sake; it is important as the prelude to correct ethical action.

China did not develop a national system of education. Private schools were created to prepare students to pass state examinations. The main types of educational centers were elementary schools and academies for advanced instruction. Elementary classes were usually conducted in the teacher's house.

The educational training of the Chinese was divided into three periods. The first period stressed the art of writing and literature. In the second period the nine sacred books were studied, and in the third the student advanced in his skills and concentrated upon philosophical and moral ideals.

The discipline in Chinese schools, as in Indian schools, was firm, and corporal punishment was frequently used. Teachers stressed repetition, and students were instructed and encouraged to imitate the teacher. Since the past was the model, originality and inventiveness were discouraged.

The Spirit of Chinese Philosophy and Religion

Chinese philosophy is characterized by its tolerant and eclectic spirit. Chinese scholars respect a variety of opinions, for they feel that truth cannot be monopolized by one nation or one religious group. Consequently, there is little dogmatism in Chinese thought. Philosophical and religious controversies are not fought with the sword; there is no persecution of heretics.

The tolerance of the Chinese is based to a great extent on educational training. Confucianism teaches that the superior man is eager to learn and that he is moderate in his behavior. The gentleman in China has a sense of propriety and does not try to impose his opinion on others. He sees the grayness of most issues and consequently avoids extreme partisanship.

Religious worship in China is founded on individual rather than on congregational factors; the church is not an absolute institution. Basically, a strain of individualism dominates Chinese social relationships, and this individualism extends to man's relationship with God. The family is a cornerstone of Chinese religion, and the purpose of the family is to insure the continuity of ancestral relationships rather than the welfare of the individual. Respect for ancestors can influence man's life on earth. Furthermore, ancestor worship adds stability to man's social life. The family is often responsible for the conduct of its members, and when family relations rest upon a sound basis, Confucius teaches, the state can prosper.

Whereas Indian philosophy rests upon a metaphysical basis, the Chinese are primarily concerned with moral problems.[1] Ethics replaces theology; in vain do we look for an Aquinas or a Shankara in China. The Chinese educator feels that it is useless to discuss the attributes of God and that it is impossible to rely upon revelation. He identifies morality and faith; thus, the educated man would be religious and the religious man would be truly educated.

To the Chinese, religion is not a separate subject; it includes *all aspects of life.* The belief in God is strong, although God is frequently regarded as an impersonal force, as "Heaven" or "Providence." Belief in God implies faith in the validity of moral laws. Thus the Chinese feel that those who follow the dictates of heaven will be rewarded and will prosper, while those who violate the laws of morality will inevitably be failures.

Confucius and Education

Chinese philosophy has been championed most effectively by Confucius (c. 551–478 B.C.), whose life was dedicated to the search for a perfect government.[2] His father, a member of a distinguished family that was related to Emperor Huang-ti, passed away while Confucius was still in his infancy. Confucius helped to support his mother by working after school; still, he took his education seriously and became especially proficient in archery and music. When his mother died, he showed his feelings for her

1. For a survey of Chinese moral ideals see Fung Yu-Lan, *A Comparative Study of Life Ideals.*
2. *See* G. Gabelentz, *Confucius und seine Lehre;* W. E. Soothill, *The Three Religions of China;* J. Legge, *The Life and Teachings of Confucius,* Vol. I of *The Chinese Classics,* 3 vols.

by mourning for twenty-seven months. Thus, in his personal life he did not always practice his teachings. He married at the age of seventeen; apparently, it was an unhappy marriage; he was divorced four years later.

At the early age of twenty Confucius became an overseer of the fields of the kingdom of Lu and the authorities became aware of his talents. He started his career as a teacher two years later, teaching mainly three subjects: history, etiquette, and poetry. He did not charge a stipulated fee, but demanded from every student whatever he could pay without hardship.

When Confusius visited Lao-tse, the famed old philosopher apparently tried to discourage him from reforming the existing governmental system. The Duke of Tsi considered the possibility of employing Confucius until one of his advisors told him that Confucius was too pedantic and too intent on ceremony.

Later, Confucius had more luck in the state of Lu. He was made chief magistrate of an important town; then he became superintendent of public works; finally, he became minister of crime. He was so efficient that criminal activities were curtailed in Lu and honesty governed the state. Strangers came from all over China in search of the perfect government that at last had been established.

However, two neighboring princes conspired against the Duke of Lu. To tempt him, they sent him a number of sing-song girls as well as a collection of splendid horses, after which the Duke of Lu showed little interest in the governmental affairs of his perfectly governed town. Confucius gave him an ultimatum: Either the sing-song girls would leave or Confucius would resign. The ruler did not hesitate in his choice and Confucius left his governmental position.

From 496 to 483 B.C., Confucius traveled from one principality to another, always in search of a perfect government. He was offered a tempting position by the Duke of Wu, but he did not approve of the Duke's moral standards, and so refused the position. He returned to the state of Lu when he was sixty-eight years old and lived there in semiretirement until he died in 478 B.C.

Among his contributions to mankind are the five classics: the *Book of Songs,* the *Book of History,* the *Book of Changes,* the *Book of Spring and Autumn,* and the *Book of Rites.* With the exception of the *Book of Spring and Autumn,* these works were mostly written by his disciples.

Traditionally, we think of Confucius as a formalist who followed the ways of the past. However, this viewpoint is not justified for, above all, Confucius believed in sincerity. Manners and morals were to be united; reform was to come through the efforts of the superior man. Opposed to all types of dogmatism and narrow-mindedness, he believed in the constant cultivation of the *self.* Thus there is a strong *personal* element in the system of Confucius.

He describes his own educational development in the following passages:

> The Master said, "At fifteen, I had my mind bent on learning.
> At thirty, I stood firm.
> At forty, I had no doubts.
> At fifty, I knew the decrees of Heaven.
> At sixty, my ear was an obedient organ for the reception of truth.
> At seventy, I could follow what my heart desired, without transgressing what was right."[3]
> "If a man keeps cherishing his old knowledge, so as continually to be acquiring new, he may be a teacher of others."[4]

What is knowledge? Confucius says:

> When you know a thing, to hold that you know it; and when you do not know a thing, to allow that you do not know it:—this is knowledge.[5]

3. *Analects,* Book II. iv, I.
4. *Ibid.,* Book II, xi.
5. *Ibid.,* Book II, xvii.

The leaving virtue without proper cultivation: the not thoroughly discussing what is learned; not being able to move toward righteousness of which a knowledge is gained; and not being able to change what is not good:—these are the things which occasion my solicitude.[6]

Education, Confucius taught, demands an inquiring mind:

I do not open up the truth to one who is not eager to get knowledge, nor help out anyone who is not anxious to explain himself. When I have presented one corner of a subject to anyone, and he cannot from it learn the other three, I do not repeat my lesson.[7]

An important concept in Confucianism is filial piety, which requires an attitude of obedience on the part of the son. However, the father is not to exercise his rule dictatorially. Filial piety demands self-restraint on the part of the individual; thus, he has to subordinate himself to the welfare of the family.

In his religious philosophy, Confucius, like Buddha, had no patience with metaphysical disputes. He felt that no absolute answers could be obtained on the question of the existence of God. He counseled his followers to adhere to the traditional ritual and to act as if the ancestors were present. When someone asked him how the spirits were to be served, he replied that this was a useless question, for "we are to serve men first." We are to concentrate upon the facts of this life, not upon supernatural beings.

Still, this does not mean that Confucius was a nihilist. On the contrary, he saw a fundamental unity in the universe; hence he felt that the laws of morality and the laws of nature were one. Hence, the thief cannot escape the consequences of his evil actions, just as no one can deny and so nullify the law of gravity.

What, then, is wisdom according to Confucianism? The answer is quite definite. Wisdom consists in realizing our limitations and

6. *Ibid.*, Book VII, iii.
7. *Ibid.*, Book VII, viii.

in the acceptance of man's fundamental ignorance. Being a humanist, Confucius maintained that we must *first* serve man rather than supernatural beings. We should respect the laws of Heaven, although the mind of man can never understand them completely.

Education, according to Confucius, is founded upon morality. We must try to conquer ourselves, investigate our thoughts, and be perfectly sincere in our quest for truth. When the individual achieves peace, then he can order his family life. If the family life is harmonious, then the states can experience prosperity. If the states are at peace, then the empire can achieve tranquillity.

The moral method of Confucius is opposed to the ethics of the commissar. Reform does not come about through social legislation or through revolution; rather, it depends on the efforts of the individual. We must improve ourselves first—only then can we try to reform society.

In educational, as well as in spiritual matters, the Golden Mean is all important. This implies a careful regard for the laws of propriety. The gentleman avoids all excesses and all extreme passions.

The educational system of Confucius is based on his doctrine of the superior man. The ideal man does not live in an ivory tower, but he tries to reform society. He is respectful, righteous, and always sincere in his thoughts. Confucius contrasts the superior man and the common man:

> What the gentleman seeks is in himself. What the mean man seeks is in others. The gentleman is dignified, but does not wrangle. He is sociable but not a partisan.
>
> The gentleman does not promote a man simply on account of his words, nor does he put aside good words because of the man.[8]
>
> The master said, "The object of the superior man is truth. Food is not his object. There is plowing:—even in that there is sometimes want. So with learning:—emolument may be found in it. The supe-

8. *Ibid.,* Book XV, xx, xxi, xxii.

rior man is anxious lest he should not get truth; he is not anxious lest poverty should come upon him."[9]

Notice that Confucius did not believe in asceticism. Salvation is not to be gained through mortification of the flesh or through renunciation of material goods. Thus the scholar replaces the ascetic, or yogi, and etiquette replaces the striving for metaphysical knowledge.

The superior man, who represents the best of education, tries to perfect both his mind and his character:

> The superior man has nine things which are subjects with him of thoughtful consideration. In regard to the use of his eyes, he is anxious to see clearly. In regard to the use of his ears, he is anxious to hear distinctly. In regard to his countenance, he is anxious that it should be benign. In regard to his demeanor, he is anxious that it should be respectful. In regard to his speech, he is anxious that it should be sincere. In regard to his doing of business, he is anxious that it should be reverently careful. In regard to what he doubts about, he is anxious to question others. When he is angry, he thinks of the difficulties [his anger may involve him in]. When he sees gain to be got, he thinks of righteousness.[10]

The superior man is in awe before three things: First, he has a sense of awe when he deals with the ordinances of Heaven. Secondly, the superior man is in awe when confronted by great men. Thirdly, the superior man stands in awe when he encounters words of wisdom.

Confucius felt great disdain in regard to the controversies of philosophy. Having no use for obscure passages and foggy thinking, he demanded a rectification of names; thus a father who neglected his duties should not be called a father; a prince who abdicated his power should not be called a prince. In short, verbal meaning ought to correspond to actual function. As for

9. *Ibid.*, Book XV, xxxi.
10. *Ibid.*, Book XVI, x.

theological controversies, Confucius thought they were too un-important and their subject matter too obscure. He was concerned mainly with social relationships and not with man's understanding of the beyond.

His moral ideals were reflected in his concept of government. He maintained that rulers should be exemplary in their conduct, and that the princes should employ only the most efficient and scrupulous ministers. He looked forward to an educational utopia in which there would be eternal peace and in which no poverty would exist. In this state no man would be oppressed and the rights of all would be safeguarded. The community would rank above the demands of the individual, each of whom would realize his essential identity and act for the welfare of the group. This concept of a utopia is based on secular foundations; unlike the utopia of the Hebrew prophets it is dominated by humanistic rather than supernatural foundations.

4. Socrates

The life span of Socrates (470?–399 B.C.) embraces the rise and fall of the Athenian empire. His last years were marred by the fall of Athens and by the ravages of the oligarchic and democratic factions. Around him old foundations were crumbling, with naked power replacing justice, and the political rulers becoming more arrogant than ever.

Athenian youth, in this period, was guided by the doctrines of moral relativism. This skepticism made it distrust tradition and any faith in absolutes. Socrates, however, believed in definite and categorical moral standards and thought that it was the task of philosophy to resurrect a stable social order, based on rational ideals and expert knowledge. Living in dark times, he experienced (in 429) the plague of Athens, during which thousands died. The disease, which was explained as an act of divine vengeance, caused the death of Pericles, the leading light of the Athenian state.

Between 421 and 416 B.C. an uneasy truce governed the relations of Athens and Sparta. This period witnessed the rise of Alcibiades, one of the disciples of Socrates. Shiftless, unscrupulous, interested only in his own welfare, Alcibiades was one of the main factors in the downfall of Athens. He was responsible for the Sicilian expedition that failed in 413 B.C., when the Athenians were defeated at Syracuse.

Several of the city-states rebelled against the Athenian overlordship. This revolt marked the beginning of the end for Athens. Eight years later the Spartans, under their great commander Lysander, destroyed the Athenian fleet. In 404 B.C. the Peloponnesian War ended, with Athens becoming subject to Sparta. Between 404 and 403 B.C. the oligarchic party was supreme in Athens; the Thirty Tyrants ruled with an iron hand, using terroristic methods. In 403 B.C. democracy was finally restored, but it was not a government by the wisest and most excellent citizens. Under its jurisdiction, in 399 B.C., Socrates was charged with two crimes: corrupting the youth of Athens and denying the official gods of the state.

Various Interpretations of Socrates

Socrates remains one of the most controversial figures in education. We do not know his exact teachings, since he did not leave any writings at his death. We must rely mainly on the accounts of Plato and Xenophon. To Plato, Socrates was the ideal philosopher, engaged in a tireless quest for wisdom and able to inspire his disciples with a lofty view of human life. Idealizing Socrates, Plato used him as the narrator for his most profound ethical and metaphysical teachings.

Xenophon, on the other hand, gave very religious interpretations of Socrates:

> What evidence did they produce that Socrates refused to recognize the gods acknowledged by the state? Was it that he did not sacrifice? or that he dispensed with divination? On the contrary, he was often to be seen engaged in sacrifice, at home or at the common altars of the state.[1]

Aristophanes has given us still another picture of Socrates, in

1. Xenophon, *Recollections of Socrates* i, I.

The Clouds. To be sure, it is a caricature, since it pictures him as one of the Sophists. We find Socrates in a dialogue with Strepsiades, a peasant married to an aristocratic lady, who wants to send his son to Socrates' school. He is admitted to the house and finds Socrates suspended in a basket:

STREP. Oh, first of all, please tell me what you are doing.

SOC.   I walk on air, and contemplate the sun.

STREP. Oh, then from a basket you contemplate the gods,
      and not from the earth, at any rate?

SOC.   Most true.
    I could not have searched out celestial matters
    Without suspending judgment, and infusing
    My subtle spirit with the kindred air.
    If from the ground I were to seek these things,
    I could not find: so surely does the earth
    Draw to herself the essence of our thought.
    The same too is the case with water-cress.

STREP. Hello! what's that?
    Thought draws the essence into water-cress?
    Come down, sweet Socrates, more near my level,
    And teach the lessons which I come to learn.

SOC.   And wherefore art thou come?

STREP.   To learn to speak.
    For owing to my horrid debts and duns,
    My goods are seized, I'm robbed and mobbed, and
      plundered.

SOC.   How did you get involved with your eyes open?

STREP. A galloping consumption seized my money.
    Come now; do let me learn the unjust logic
    That can shirk debts; now do just let me learn it.
    Name your own price, by all the gods I'll pay it.

SOC.   The gods! Why, you must know the gods with us
    Don't pass for current coin.[2]

2. Aristophanes, *The Clouds.*

All in all, Socrates cuts a rather ridiculous figure in *The Clouds*. He is pictured as a radical moralist who denies the traditional religious truths and as a corrupter of Athenian youth.

The Humanists in the Renaissance, however, had the opposite view of this philosopher. To them, Socrates was a saint, a veritable Christian in his faith and virtue. They thought the ideal scholar must inevitably be Socratic.

Kierkegaard, the father of modern Existentialism, likewise greatly admired Socrates, whom he used as his model philosopher. He wrote his doctoral dissertation on the philosophy of Socrates. To Kierkegaard, Socrates' constant fight against the Sophists of all time had profound meaning. He stressed the fact that most of the nineteenth-century philosophers, especially Hegel, were essentially Sophists in their beliefs. Kierkegaard appreciated Socrates' method of teaching through questioning, and from him adopted the motto "Know thyself" as the starting point of philosophy.

Nietzsche likewise had much to say about Socrates, but he was less complimentary than Kierkegaard. He favored the pre-Socratics, who, he thought, exhibited real strength and real impartiality and were the supermen of philosophy. In attacking Socrates, Nietzsche felt that he was fighting against impulses in his own nature. Decadence, to Nietzsche, meant faith in morality and in absolute standards instead of guidance by natural instincts.

Bertrand Russell, in his *History of Western Philosophy*, pictures Socrates almost as a Victorian with a definite faith in immortality. He points to the puritanism of Socrates' beliefs and his preoccupation with the *demon,* the religious voice inside.

John Burnet stressed the fact that Socrates had many metaphysical interests and was responsible for the doctrine of the Ideas as taught by Plato. Socrates, Burnet claimed, was not primarily a moralist but had cosmological interests, and hence his philosophy cannot be understood without this metaphysical background.

Character and Life

We find Socrates as a loyal citizen of Athens, taking part in several military campaigns and distinguishing himself by his courage. He was given, occasionally, to Spartan sacrifices. We are told that he went barefoot and was also subject to mystical trances. Never cowardly, he was ready to defy the democratic faction as well as the Thirty Tyrants. He risked his life when, as a responsible officer, he refused to agree to the trial of the Athenian generals after the battle of Arginusae. Although he had many friends among the Thirty Tyrants, he believed in the supremacy of the law; and when they issued an illegal order, he refused to carry it out.

Socrates was intensely human; perhaps his marriage contributed to this attitude. Certainly he was not a scholar who preferred isolation, for we find him disputing in the market place and attending many banquets. His conversation was always sparkling and witty. There was a certain strain of stoicism in his character, too, for he never lost his dignity, not even during the last dreadful days of his life. During his entire trial he retained his composure. Unlike others who had been accused, he did not ask favors.

Excepting his trial, there are not many climactic events in the life of Socrates. His father was a sculptor, his mother a midwife; at first he thought he would follow in the footsteps of his father, but he changed his mind and turned to philosophy, which he regarded as the most important subject of education.

To some extent he was connected with the Orphic Mysteries, traces of which appear in his religious teachings. When he was thirty-five, the oracle at Delphi declared him to be the wisest man of Athens. In the *Apology* there is an explanation of what the oracle meant. Socrates was perplexed:

> Why do I mention this? Because I am going to explain to you why I have such an evil name. When I heard the answer, I said to myself, What can the god mean? and what is the interpretation of

his riddle? for I know that I have no wisdom, small or great. What then can he mean when he says that I am the wisest of men? And yet he is a god, and cannot lie; that would be against his nature. After long consideration, I thought of a method of trying the question. I reflected that if I could only find a man wiser than myself then I might go to the god with a refutation in my hand. I should say to him, "Here is a man who is wiser than I am; but you said that I was the wisest." Accordingly I went to one who had the reputation of wisdom, and observed him—his name I need not mention; he was a politician whom I selected for examination—and the result was as follows: When I began to talk with him, I could not help thinking that he was not really wise, although he was thought wise by many, and still wiser by himself; and thereupon I tried to explain to him that he thought himself wise, but was not really wise; and the consequence was that he hated me, and his enmity was shared by several who were present and heard me. So I left him, saying to myself as I went away: Well, although I do not suppose that either of us knows anything really beautiful and good I am better off than he is,—for he knows nothing, and thinks that he knows; I neither know nor think that I know. In this latter particular, then, I seem to have slightly the advantage of him. Then I went to another who had still higher pretensions to wisdom and my conclusion was exactly the same. Whereupon I made another enemy of him, and of many others besides him.[3]

Socrates explained what real wisdom means; it is a mission to spread real knowledge and real enlightenment:

This inquisition has led to my having many enemies of the worst and most dangerous kind, and has given occasion also to many calumnies. And I am called wise, for my hearers always imagine that I myself possess the wisdom which I find wanting in others: but the truth is, O men of Athens, that God only is wise; and by his answer he intends to show that the wisdom of men is worth little or nothing; he is not speaking of Socrates, he is only using my name by way of illustration, as if he said, He O men, is the wisest, who,

3. Plato, *Apology* (Jowett translation).

like Socrates, knows that his wisdom is in truth worth nothing. And so I go on about the world obedient to the god, and search and make enquiry into the wisdom of any one, whether citizen or stranger, who appears to be wise; and if he is not wise, then in vindication of the oracle I show him that he is not wise; and my occupation quite absorbs me, and I have no time to give either to any public matter of interest or to any concern of my own, but I am in utter poverty by reason of my devotion to the god.[4]

The Death of Socrates

The execution of Socrates was delayed for a month. Throughout this period he remained faithful to philosophy, and in his cell in the final hours of his life held a discourse on immortality:

Now the hour of sunset was near, for a good deal of time had passed while he was within. When he came out, he sat down with us again after his bath, but not much was said. Soon the jailer, who was the servant of the Eleven, entered and stood by him, saying— To you, Socrates, whom I know to be the noblest and gentlest and best of all who ever came to this place, I will not impute the angry feeling of other men, who rage and swear at me, when, in obedience to the authorities, I bid them drink the poison—indeed, I am sure that you will not be angry with me; for others, as you are aware, and not I, are to blame. And so fare you well, and try to bear lightly what must needs be—you know my errand. Then bursting into tears he turned away and went out.

Socrates looked at him and said: I return your good wishes, and will do as you bid. Then, turning to us, he said, How charming the man is; since I have been in prison he has always been coming to see me, and at times he would talk to me, and was as good to me as could be, and see how generously he sorrows on my account. We must do as he says, Crito; and therefore let the cup be brought if the poison is prepared; if not, let the attendant prepare some.[5]

Crito, a disciple of Socrates, wanted him to wait a while. Why

4. *Ibid.*
5. Plato, *Phaedo.*

should he not take the hemlock later? Why should he not enjoy himself before passing on to another world? Socrates replied that he did not want to wait, and he drank the poison.

The disciples fell into a state of complete dejection:

> And hitherto most of us had been able to control our sorrow; but now when we saw him drinking, and saw too that he had finished the draught, we could no longer forbear, and in spite of myself my own tears were flowing fast; so that I covered my face and wept, not for him, but at the thought of my own calamity in having to part from such a friend. Nor was I the first; for Crito, when he found himself unable to restrain his tears, had got up, and I followed; and at that moment, Apollodorus, who had been weeping all the time, broke out in a loud and passionate cry which made cowards of us all. Socrates alone retained his calmness: What is this strange outcry? he said. I sent away the women mainly in order that they might not misbehave in this way, for I have been told that a man should die in peace. Be quiet, then, and have patience. When we heard his words we were ashamed, and refrained our tears; and he walked about until, as he said, his legs began to fail, and then he lay on his back, according to directions, and the man who gave him the poison now and then looked at his feet and legs; and after a while he pressed his foot hard and asked him if he could feel, and he said, No; and then his leg, and so upwards and upwards, and showed us that he was cold and stiff. And he felt them himself, and said: When the poison reaches the heart, that will be the end. He was beginning to grow cold about the groin, when he uncovered his face, for he had covered himself up, and said—they were his last words—he said, Crito, I owe a cock to Asclepius; will you remember to pay the debt? The debt shall be paid, said Crito; is there anything else? There was no answer to this question: but in a minute or two a movement was heard, and the attendants uncovered him; his eyes were set, and Crito closed his eyes and mouth.

> Such was the end, Echecrates, of our friend; concerning whom I may truly say, that of all men of his time whom I have known, he was the wisest and justest and best.[6]

6. *Ibid.*

The Teacher

In his teachings, Socrates used the dialectical method. This method brings out truth through a process of intellectual definition and finally achieves an absolute definition. The dialectic method was used by medieval educators who believe in logic rather than in the experimental method.

Why did Socrates become the supreme model for later educators? Why was his influence so pronounced? Why was he so greatly admired by Plato and Aristotle? It appears that Socrates was not merely a theorist, but he lived according to his educational ideals. He believed that the rich and the poor, the wise and the ignorant, the young and the old, all need real education. To Socrates, education was a spontaneous process; it required neither a formal school nor an organized student body. Plato tells us that Socrates taught most effectively when he attended banquets and when he would discuss such abstract concepts as virtue, truth, and immortality.

Socrates became important as an educational critic. He made it clear that many of Athens' leaders were ignorant and guided by irrational idols. He opposed the government of the people, for he noted that they were inclined to be swayed by emotions. He found that the professional philosophers were too arrogant about their beliefs and that they would readily accept the expediency of the moment.

Socrates was more concerned about the problem of man than about the nature of the universe; if man does not find himself, of what value is cosmological knowledge? Socrates' interest in teaching and education caused him to neglect practical matters. All his life he was a poor man—a fact that greatly distressed his wife. But he considered intellectual growth to be more important than external riches. Knowledge, to Socrates, was a good in itself. It banished anxiety. It created true serenity. It brought about emotional balance. Thus he was unafraid to die: death, he believed, would be either an eternal sleep, undisturbed by dreams, or a journey to a better world.

What strikes the modern observer is the dignity of Socrates. No reverse could change his basic attitude. When he was tried by the Athenians he did not appeal to emotion and prejudice; he remained objective and without fear. To Socrates, morality was not an abstract ideal, but a pattern to be realized in daily living.

The function of the teacher, according to Socrates, is to awaken the average man. The majority, he felt, are guided by irrational thoughts and lethargy, and live in a cave of half-truths and illusions. Once the student is stirred, once he becomes aware, he perceives a new meaning in life. He probes and he questions. He is guided by curiosity and takes pleasure in intellectual inquiry. Yet education, Socrates maintained, has ultimately a social function. What matters is not our own brilliance, but how we radiate our ideas and how we change society so that morality and intelligence are combined.

To Socrates, the teacher is anything but a specialist. Education, philosophy, ethics, and religion, all are basically one and they aim at the creation of a rational society.

5. Plato

In his lifetime, Plato (427?–347 B.C.) was witness to an unending change in political and social affairs. He was still quite young when the Peloponnesian War ended, with Athens humiliated by the victories of the Spartans. Ironically enough, a few years later, the Persians and the Athenians, aided by Corinth, Thebes, and Argos, joined forces against Sparta and defeated the Spartan fleet in the battle of Cnidus in 394 B.C. The Athenians, aided by the generous support of the Persians, rebuilt the long walls.

The noble spirit of Salamis and Marathon had long been forgotten. The Athenians, determined to restore their empire, were willing to make an alliance with anyone who would promote their military strength. In the wars between Thebes and Sparta, lasting from 379 to 362 B.C., Athens joined Thebes and defeated the Spartans in various sea battles. Gradually the Athenian empire was extended to include over seventy communities. In 371 B.C., at the battle of Leuctra, the Spartans were defeated by the brilliant Theban general Epaminondas. This victory established the supremacy of Thebes in Greece, and from 371 to 362 B.C. Thebes remained in power. Meanwhile, Athens switched sides and aided Sparta to establish the balance of power. It can be seen that there was little loyalty in Athenian politics.

This balance of power continued until Macedonia became supreme. In 359 B.C., Philip the Second started his rule of Macedonia and almost immediately began the process of expansion. By 352 he had advanced as far as Thermopylae, where he was temporarily halted by the Athenians. A year later, Demosthenes warned the Athenians of the great danger facing them from the Macedonians. In 348 B.C. various subject-states of Athens were conquered by Philip; and by 347, when Plato died, it already appeared certain that Philip would become the master of all Greece.

The Life of Plato

Whereas Socrates came from middle-class parents, Plato had a distinguished aristocratic background. His father was a descendant of one of the kings of Athens; his mother came from the family of Solon. He had many relatives who were active in political affairs, the majority on the side of the aristocracy. His education was supervised very carefully. There was the conventional curriculum—music, gymnastics, and instruction in the old poets, especially in Homer.

We must not think of Plato as a bookish thinker. We are told that he distinguished himself on the battlefield. Besides being an excellent athlete, he was interested in art; and there are accounts that tell us he wanted to be a dramatist. From the very beginning he showed exceptional intellectual promise and all-round excellence.

Plato's conversion to the philosophic life took several years. His first teacher was Cratylus, who taught the Heraclitean doctrines, refusing to make any positive intellectual assertations. Plato then came under the influence of Socrates, and his life was changed completely. Previously he had been politically ambitious; everyone knowing him thought he would be prominent in Athenian affairs of state, for he was handsome, talented, and possessed of both family background and ability. But the death of Socrates changed Plato's outlook. He began to realize that the Athenians were unstable, and he developed an intense contempt for the form of democracy that had killed their wisest citizen.

After the death of Socrates, Plato undertook various trips out of the country, perhaps because of the violent feeling of the Athenians against all the followers of Socrates. He went to Megara and later to Italy, where he visited the Pythagoreans, becoming especially friendly with Archytas, the chieftain of Tarentum.

Plato then made a visit to the city of Syracuse—indeed a fateful step. He was invited there through Dion, who was related to the reigning king, Dionysius the First, tyrant of Syracuse for more than thirty-eight years. As a ruthless conqueror, Dionysius usually sold his victims into slavery, and even robbed temples of their treasures. It was reported that he sold the robe of the goddess Hera to the Carthaginians for 120 talents. But he expanded the realm of Syracuse, and he loved the arts. Consequently, in beautifying Syracuse, he made it one of the most magnificent cities of the Hellenic world. He had pretensions in literature; one of his plays, *Ransom of Hector,* won a prize in Athens.

The relationship between the tyrant and the philosopher was strained, since they had divergent views on politics and art. Dionysius eventually caused Plato to be sold as a slave. This was a simple matter, for he merely handed Plato over to the Spartans, who were then at war with the Athenians. But Plato was fortunate; for one of his friends, recognizing him at a slave market, caused him to be freed and sent home.

At Athens, Plato devoted himself to philosophic instruction, mainly at the Academy, where he taught political science, mathematics, and dialectic. Many of the ruling princes of the Greek world sent their sons to him for study and enlightenment. The instruction he provided was quite informal; it consisted mainly of a personal interchange of views between teachers and students.

When Dionysius died, in 367 B.C., he was succeeded by his son, who, lacking the ability of his father, turned for advice to his uncle, Dion. Plato was again invited to Syracuse. He accepted the invitation and was well received. For a time he was extremely popular with the new king, and the court studied his theories of politics and education. But the army was opposed to Plato, and there were rumors that linked him to the enemies of the king. Although Dion himself showed great affection for him, Plato wanted to return to Athens. When a war broke out, he used the opportunity to leave Syracuse.

Meanwhile, Dion had been exiled, and he and his nephews had become bitter enemies. Still, Dion was intent upon reconciliation, and when the war was over he urged Plato to return to Syracuse. Both Dion and Plato had hopes that the king might become the model ruler. The short return visit proved to be a complete failure. Unable to reform the king, Plato was made a prisoner; he was released only through the vigorous efforts of Archytas, after which he returned to Athens, where he continued his teachings.

His old age was marred by various disappointments. He supported Dion in his attempt to seize the rule at Syracuse. At first Dion was successful, but then he was stabbed by Callippus, who was also a student at the Academy. Chaos resulted. Callippus could not maintain his power, and in 346 B.C. the king returned to Syracuse, again to become its ruler. But the citizens still disliked him; they were finally delivered from his tyranny by Timoleon, who ruled from 344 to 337 B.C. Under him Syracuse experienced a golden era. He was a philosopher-king of whom Plato would have approved, but unfortunately Plato did not witness his reign, for he died in 347 B.C., presumably while attending a banquet. Cicero maintained that to the end of his life Plato was busy working on another dialogue.

The Works of Plato

Scholars have tried to discover the order in which Plato's works were written. The most accurate account is given by L. Campbell and W. Lutoslawski, who divided his literary productions into four periods: the first, the Socratic group; the second, the first Platonic group; the third, the middle Platonic group; the fourth, the works of his later period.

In the Socratic series, we find such dialogues as the *Apology,* which contains an eloquent defense of Socrates; the *Crito,* which tells of the fidelity of Socrates to the laws of Athens; the *Euthyphro,* which contains an outline of the ideal of piety that Socrates cherished. There follow other dialogues, including the *Charmides,* which discusses among other things the concept of temperance; the *Laches,* which deals with moral ideals, especially courage; the *Lysis,* which has the theme of friendship and shows that friendship has a transcendental meaning. Then we have the *Protagoras,* which deals with the teachability of virtue and attacks the relativistic views of Protagoras. The *Meno* gives an intimation of Plato's own concept of knowledge and defines knowledge as recollection. The *Euthydemus* also is directed against the Sophists, especially against their logical fallacies. The *Gorgias* likewise inveighs against the superficiality of Sophist rhetoric. It offers an excellent contrast between the philosopher and the practical politician who used Sophist principles.

The first Platonic series includes the *Cratylus,* which has been neglected by the historians of philosophy; it is nevertheless quite significant, for it contains Plato's concept of language. He maintained that words do not arise purely from artificial convention, and showed that a knowledge of truth must come before a knowledge of words. In it he also gave a comprehensive account of verbal fallacies. There follows the *Symposium,* which deals with his concept of love; the *Phaedo,* which gives an impressive account of his doctrines of immortality; and the early books of the *Republic*.

The middle Platonic group comprises the later books of the *Republic*, outlining Plato's concept of the ideal state. The *Phaedrus* starts out with a speech of Lysis on love, followed by a full discussion of the nature of Eros; also, there are references to philosophical rhetoric. The dialogue combines the theory of Ideas with the Orphic belief in transmigration of souls. Then we have the *Theaetetus*, dealing with the problems of epistemology and directed against the Protagorean view that man is the measure of all things. There is the *Parmenides*, exposing the concept of the Ideas to criticism, and thus revealing that Plato was conscious of the paradoxes involved in his views of the Ideas.

Finally, we have the dialogues of Plato's later years. The *Sophist* is a continuation of the epistemological viewpoint of the *Theaetetus*. The *Politicus*, or the *Statesman*, is an attempt to depict an expert statesman who alone can rule the state. The *Philebus* contains a discussion of ethics, and shows how pleasure is related to the Good; likewise, it portrays the influence of Pythagoreanism. The *Timaeus*, which was to be extremely influential in the Middle Ages, contains many of Plato's most significant cosmological doctrines. The *Critias* pictures an agricultural utopia, which is compared with the imperialistic power of Atlantis.

The last work of Plato is the *Laws*. Containing his political and social ideals, it is a continuation of the *Republic*. In it there are also discussions of science, metaphysics, and religion. This last work is characterized by a dogmatic and austere spirit.

Plato's Theory of Knowledge and Education

In turning to Plato's epistemological theories, we find that he starts his examination of the process of knowledge by a discussion of *imagination, the first stage of opinion*. In this state, knowledge is very imperfect and can scarcely distinguish between illusion and fact; everything is hazy, indefinite, and vague. The difference between external and internal sensation is scarcely noticed, nor is there a clear distinction between subjective and objective viewpoints.

The second stage of opinion he calls *assurance,* or *confidence.* In this state we learn to describe objective *phenomena.* Thought becomes more distinct and more clearly defined. We realize that there is a difference between our own views and the external world. We note that phenomena exist outside ourselves and cannot be controlled by our wishes. All this brings about a feeling of confidence in our mental powers. But as yet our knowledge is not unified; we merely perceive an unending flux: a Heraclitean picture of the universe.

We then arrive at the third stage, which Plato calls *intelligent understanding.* We leave the realm of opinion behind and enter the province of *real knowledge.* Intelligent understanding makes it possible for us to describe phenomena. We establish a relationship between causes and effects. Briefly, we are using our scientific resources. Previously the universe appeared chaotic and disordered, but now we realize that it obeys definite laws, thereby making it possible for us to control the forces of nature.

Science, however, according to Plato, does not give us a concept of true reality. It is lacking in many respects. It accepts first principles and is still dependent upon sense knowledge, thereby giving us an incomplete view of nature. It deals too much with concrete objects and concrete phenomena, and Plato believed that knowledge in its highest aspects must transcend phenomena and concrete representations.

Plato's view has important consequences. It signifies that science is not the key to reality and that real knowledge must be *freed from bondage to the senses.* This freedom is attained by dialectic, or philosophy, which attempts a unification of knowledge. Leaving the realm of phenomena behind, philosophy is concerned with the realm of immaterial *Forms.* Reason, thus, gives complete order and unity. It synthesizes all the other aspects of knowledge and produces a splendid view of the interrelationship and interdependence of knowledge.

Ultimately, however, Plato maintained, not even reason is sufficient. The final stage of the mind involves *mystical intuition,* by which we obtain a vision of the intelligible realm of Ideas, or Forms.

The Forms are climaxed by the concept of the Idea of the Good. The Idea of the Good should not be conceived as a personal force; it can only be compared with the sun, which gives light to all parts of creation. Plato made it clear that the Idea of the Good is higher than existence and truth; in fact, it even surpasses the concept of God.

The Platonic view of knowledge turns away from mere opinion. When we use our senses we obtain only a fallible account of the universe; reliable knowledge depends on understanding, which provides for a scientific interpretation of reality. The highest type of knowledge is philosophy, which sees reality as a whole. Philosophy is concerned not with empirical facts but with a synthesis of reality. While the sciences analyze, philosophy tries to obtain a complete view of reality.

It must be pointed out that Plato was vigorously opposed to popular religion. He blamed Homer for picturing the gods in an unfavorable light. Other poets, like Hesiod, likewise show that frequently the wicked are rewarded while the virtuous suffer.

Plato reasoned that the popular religious teachings would lead to a disintegration of morality and would ultimately produce atheism. How do we know that God exists? Can we believe in God? Plato maintains that the universal acceptance of the existence of God indicates its definite empirical foundation. Another Platonic argument appeals to the existence of motion: bodies do not move themselves, they need a teleological principle that comes from the outside. Just as the soul is man's ruling principle, so God rules the universe. Furthermore, Plato points to the remarkable order displayed in the universe, which cannot be accidental and so implies the providence of a supreme force.

The philosophy of Plato rests upon his belief in the immortality of the soul. How do we know that the soul is immortal? How can we be certain that it will not perish through death? Plato argues that the soul is not dependent upon the body; rather, it is the dominant force in the body. The soul is unalterable and cannot be destroyed through successive reincarnations. The central idea of the soul is that of life, which excludes the idea of death. From a logical standpoint, Plato appeals to the identity of opposites. The existence of life demands the existence of death, whereas the existence of death demands the existence of life. Also, death can only touch those substances that are composite; it cannot touch a simple substance—the soul. The soul, imprisoned in the body, longs for eternal union; it naturally transcends the limitations of human existence.

Furthermore, Plato points out that while bodies are moved from the outside, the soul is completely autonomous and contains its own principle of motion. Not dependent on external forces, it can neither be created nor destroyed; it thus transcends the categories of space and time.

Plato definitely accepts the theory of reincarnation. The type of life we enter into after death is determined by the quality of our existence on earth. Our character produces a continuity throughout our pilgrimage in the universe. Hence, the evil man may become an animal in another existence, whereas the good man may become a philosopher. The fate of the soul on earth is essentially somber and melancholy; therefore, the aim of the soul is to regain its original purity. The world process ends with the absorption of the soul into the world stream, a condition that approximates the Buddhist Nirvana and which can scarcely be expressed in philosophical terms.

Plato, in his later philosophy, especially in the *Laws,* almost advocates a theocratic government. Heresy is to be strictly punished; religion is to be the center of the state. The rulers of the state are to be especially trained in theology. This parallels medieval beliefs, which usually upheld the supremacy of religion. The status of the priesthood in the Middle Ages reminds us of the role of the philosopher-kings in Plato's *Republic*.

Plato's educational philosophy rests upon his political ideals. In the *Republic* he describes three classes: the philosopher-kings, who rule; the guardians, who defend the state; and the common people, who do the menial work. Plato feels that education, ethics, politics, and economics form an indissoluble unit, for how could a utopia be established without a correspondence between theory and practice?

Many modern theorists of education show certain weaknesses in their isolation of education as a specialized study, and in their preoccupation with details of philosophy or curriculum construction. They overlook the fact that our actions are determined by social values and that society cannot be changed by intellectual ideas alone. In this way, Plato was far more realistic than many modern thinkers, for the author of the *Republic* stressed the interrelatedness of all aspects of life.

Plato believes in an integrative approach to life. Thus, knowledge rises from opinion, which is fallible, to reason, which generalizes and establishes laws, to intuition, which sees the universe in its totality. Is not our sense-perception a prelude to the nature of Ideas, which are eternal? Is not the specific the prelude to generalization? Is not human existence a yearning for spirituality?

To Plato, the state represented the highest interests of the individual. Hence, the state would establish educational standards and could use any means, even lies, to indoctrinate the citizens. This indicates certain Machiavellian undertones in Plato's philosophies.

In all his beliefs Plato was inspired by the educational standards of Sparta. In this city-state, simplicity was the keynote; individualism was outlawed; men and women received the same basic training. From birth, boys were taught how to endure hardship and how to be brave in battle. The arts, especially music, were used to inspire patriotism; music, however, was limited to strict Doric rhythms. This was indeed a paradise for those who believed in austerity as a way of life.

Plato believed that Athenian education contributed to anarchy. He especially opposed the conventional stress upon Homeric literature. In Homer, according to Plato, the just are frequently not rewarded, bravery is not always recognized, and the gods are portrayed in a very skeptical light. As a result, both young people and adults develop a false conception of man, society, and religion.

Traditionalism, thus, is a prominent feature of Plato's philosophy and is especially emphasized in the *Laws:*

> The argument says that to change from anything except the bad is the most dangerous of all things; this is true in the case of the seasons and of the winds, in the management of our bodies and the habits of our minds—true of all things except, as I said before, of the bad. He who looks at the constitution of individuals accustomed to eat any sort of meat, or drink any drink, or do any work which they could get, may see that they are at first disordered but afterwards, as time goes on, their bodies grow adapted to them, and they learn to know and like variety, and have good health and enjoyment of life; and if ever afterwards they are confined again to a superior diet, at first they are troubled with disorders, and with difficulty become habituated to their new food. A similar principle we may imagine to hold good about the minds of men and the nature of their souls. For when they have been brought up in certain laws, which by some Divine Providence have remained unchanged during long ages, so that no one has any memory or tradition of their ever having been otherwise than they are, then everyone is afraid and ashamed to change that which is established.[1]

1. Plato, *Laws.*

This conservatism even extends to music, as the following selection indicates:

> There are many ancient music compositions and dances which are excellent, and from these the government may freely select what is proper and suitable; and they shall choose judges of not less than fifty years of age, who shall make the selection, and any of the old poems which they deem sufficient they shall include; any that is deficient or altogether unsuitable, they shall either utterly throw aside, or examine and amend, taking into their counsel poets and musicians, and making use of their poetical genius; but explaining to them the wishes of the legislator in order that they may regulate dancing, music, and all choral strains, according to his mind; and not allowing them to indulge, except in some minor matter, their individual pleasures and fancies. Now, the irregular strain of music is always made ten thousand times better by attaining to law and order, and rejecting the honied Muse—not however that we mean wholly to exclude pleasure, which is the characteristic of all music. And if a man be brought up from childhood to the age of discretion and maturity in the use of the orderly and severe music, when he hears the opposite he detests it, and calls it illiberal; but if trained in the sweet and vulgar music, he deems the opposite cold and displeasing.[2]

While women played only a minor part in Athenian education, Plato recommended that, essentially, they should receive the same training as men. This was indeed a revolutionary suggestion, and it scandalized many of his contemporaries. He also recommended that infants who were unfit should not be allowed to live. His view of the family was extremely unorthodox. He considered the family an inferior institution, and he believed that marriage should be regulated by the state. Only slaves were to be permitted to lead an unrestricted family life. He also thought that nursing and bringing up of children were important enough not to be left to the discretion of private individuals.

2. *Ibid.*

Plato described exact levels of education. He emphasized the importance of infancy—education up to the age of three, during which time the child can already develop good habits and be taught by example; it is important to stress the ideal of bravery at this early age. From ages three to six, the child undergoes informal education; now, disciplinary measures should be used freely if the child misbehaves. At this stage the child is introduced to fairy tales, but care should be taken that only ennobling stories are told to him. From age six to thirteen, boys are separated from girls; from now on boys associate only with their own group. The curriculum is to expand and, besides morals, should include music, letters, mathematics, and religion. At the age of thirteen, boys receive more specialized instruction in mathematics, poetry, and instrumental music. Plato warns against the use of the enfeebling Lydian rhythms, since music should serve to strengthen the boy's character.

From age sixteen to twenty, boys should concentrate on military training and strenuous physical exercise. Plato felt that, compared with the Spartans, the Athenians were inadequately prepared for war.

After the age of twenty, only the superior students would continue their educational program. They would study the relationship between the various sciences in order to better understand the unitary aspects of life. At the age of thirty, the future philosopher-kings would study philosophy and dialectics, and, at the age of thirty-five, they would be equipped to lead the state. At fifty, they would retire to a life of contemplation.

There is a strain of mysticism in Plato's educational philosophy; it is not, however, of an emotional, ecstatic variety. This sense of mysticism does not imply that the senses are to be neglected, but rather that life is a spiral leading from the present to eternity, from the immediate to more distant perspectives.

Plato felt that peace, prosperity, and happiness could only be achieved under the rule of the "wisest." But intelligence is not the sole factor necessary for good government; even more important factors are morality and dedication to the welfare of others.

Many of Plato's concerns and beliefs are meaningful and applicable in our times. He believed that education was essentially the vision of man's greatness, and that there could be no progress in a mediocre environment. He wanted the state to expose children to the beautiful; thus, their lives would be ennobled.

To Plato, schooling has two parts: the training of the body and the training of the soul; both are equally important. The formal organization of education would be supervised by a superintendent who would hold office for five years; he would have two assistants: a director of music for supervision of the arts, and a director of gymnastics to supervise the physical development of the future citizens.

One strong point of Plato's scheme of education lies in his recognition of the importance of individual differences. There cannot be the same training for all. In the United States, on the other hand, we have given to all students essentially the same scholastic diet; we have neglected the superior student. We have not realized the importance of great teachers and we certainly have not recognized their worth. Only by understanding the importance of inspiration, living greatness, and an ennobling atmosphere can we build a truly significant system of education.

Plato's weakness lies in his totalitarian tendencies: He had contempt for the masses; his vision of art was limited; his educational utopia, like Sparta, would make only insignificant contributions to the progress of mankind. The negative inclinations of Plato have been eloquently described by Karl Popper in *The Open Society and Its Enemies.* Nevertheless, we must recognize the genius of Plato, who, in the *Republic,* developed a blueprint for modern times.

6. Aristotle

In turning to the philosophy of Aristotle (384–322 B.C.), we note a pronounced difference from the philosophy of Plato. What strikes us immediately is the more sober approach, for Aristotle wrote like a college professor—systematically, with a proclivity for definition and a love of order. Plato, on the other hand, best represents the poetic spirit. In him philosophy was truly literary; frequently he used mythology and allegory to illustrate his points. In Plato the religious spirit is quite evident, and his doctrine of reincarnation indicates his connection with the Orphic Mysteries. In Aristotle, however, religion is subordinated to science; and, unlike Plato, he was interested in biology rather than in mathematics.

Aristotle represents the climax of Greek education. Probably no one surpassed him in intellectual versatility and power of synthesis. We owe to him much of our knowledge of earlier Greek philosophy, for he was not merely a speculative thinker but also a compiler and historian. While he did not always state the opinions of his predecessors too objectively, it must be remembered that he was frequently carried away by the heat of the argument and his own philosophical convictions. In philosophical disputes objectivity very frequently is lacking. This is true not only in ancient times—for example, in the disputes between Plato and the Sophists and between Aristotle and Plato—but in modern times, as in the disputes between Descartes and Hobbes, Schopenhauer and Hegel, and James and Royce.

What is most admirable about Aristotle is his intellectual balance; there was little emotionalism in his character. He appears to us mainly as a bystander, immensely inquisitive, incessantly industrious, with interest in all the varied aspects of life.

Aristotle became a universal man. In the history of civilization his variety of interests has, perhaps, been equaled only by Francis Bacon, Leonardo, Goethe, and Spencer. But Aristotle surpassed almost all these later thinkers in the scope of his investigations, and in his influence on succeeding generations. His accomplishments in the field of science were as significant as his contributions to ethics, esthetics, and politics. As can readily be seen, he was interested both in an understanding of reality and in a description of the universe.

In his many-sided genius, Aristotle is an excellent representative of the Greek spirit. His stress on reason, his faith in moderation, his appreciation of external goods, his love for compromise—all these traits were part of the Greek ideal of life. Modern thinkers may have a more adequate scientific background than Aristotle, but they seldom achieve his objectivity and intellectual balance.

We may now ask why Aristotle has had such a firm hold on the human mind. First, his theories could be readily adapted by various ecclesiastical organizations; therefore his philosophy became the virtual foundation of philosophical Catholicism, philosophical Judaism, and medieval Mohammedanism. In his emphasis on cosmic purposes, he gave a spiritual interpretation of the universe, and in his attempt to picture the world as a hierarchy he almost anticipated medieval Scholasticism.

Second, Aristotle spoke with *authority*. His opinions were not expressed as hypotheses but as authoritative conclusions. It appears that mankind is inevitably impressed by definite, categorical affirmation. Aristotle gave a complete analysis of the various sciences, leaving almost no field untouched and very few questions unanswered.

Third, the Aristotelian philosophy is *geocentric*. It stresses the importance of man and the potentialities of man's reason. It flatters human pretensions and human ideals. Modern science, on the other hand, has dehumanized the universe and shown how infinitesimal man's status is. Naturally, such a view is distasteful to the average man; and it must struggle assiduously against the Aristotelian view, which is antimechanistic and teleological.

Life and Time of Aristotle

Aristotle's father was court physician to the Macedonian king Amyntas, the grandfather of Alexander. His family had long been interested in medicine, and this scientific leaning probably had a powerful influence on him.

Aristotle was born in Stagira, a town in Thrace. His parents died when he was young, and he was brought up by Proxenus, who provided him with an excellent education. When he was eighteen years old he was sent to Athens, where he entered Plato's Academy. It was the custom in those times for people, if they could afford it, to send their sons to distant centers of learning. The Platonic Academy had already achieved a wide reputation and was regarded as an excellent school, not only for preparation in politics but also for scientific studies.

This removal to Athens marked an important step for Aristotle. Macedonia, it must be remembered, was not as cultured as Athens, although its ruling class was of Hellenic stock and claimed to be related to the ruling house of Argos. The common people of Macedonia did not speak pure Greek. Generally unrefined, they lacked the advantages of city life. No wonder that the more sophisticated Athenians looked upon them as barbarians!

At the Academy, however, Aristotle did not lag behind, and he soon gained a reputation as a brilliant student. He studied there until he was thirty-five. When he finished, he had surpassed almost all the disciples of Plato.

It is quite certain that at the Academy Aristotle's interests were mainly along metaphysical lines. Scientific studies alone were inadequate for him; his early treatises, especially the *Protrepticus,* definitely exhibit the Platonic spirit. But later he transcended the Platonic influence and became independent in his speculations regarding the nature of reality.

In ancient times much gossip arose regarding the alleged estrangement between Plato and Aristotle. That there was such an estrangement, however, does not seem to be based upon factual evidence. Aristotle was conscious of the debt he owed his master. His attacks were rather directed against the shallow interpreters of Plato, especially Speusippus, whom he regarded as extremely mediocre. The followers of Plato adopted an ontological interpretation of the Ideas, a view that intensely displeased Aristotle.

We must not think of Aristotle as an isolated scholar, interested merely in research. We are told that he was extremely vain about his personal appearance and wore clothes of the latest fashion. As a sophisticated man of the world, he could converse on equal terms with the rulers of his time. After the death of Plato, Aristotle was invited to the court of Hermeias, ruler of Atarneus and Mytilene, who had studied at Plato's Academy, and was himself somewhat of a philosopher. The relationship between him and Aristotle was excellent, and Aristotle married one of his close relatives.

An important event took place in Aristotle's life in 343 B.C., when he was invited by Philip of Macedonia to become the tutor of his son Alexander. Philip, an excellent diplomat and an eminent general, laid the foundation for the rise of Macedonian power. A master in the art of strategy, he gradually consolidated his power until he gained dominance over all Greece. His work has been compared with that of Czar Peter of Russia; and, like the latter, Philip was determined to unify and civilize his state. He cherished the ideal of panhellenic unity; and in 338 B.C., at the congress of Corinth, he drafted a constitution that united the Greek states under Macedonian leadership. He was assassinated while planning an expedition against Persia and was succeeded by his son, Alexander.

As tutor of Alexander, Aristotle had great influence on the course of world history; not that Alexander accepted all the ideas and plans of his teacher, for he was self-willed and obstinate. Still, Alexander represented the ideals of high-mindedness and genuine statesmanship that Aristotle preached. But this fact must not be overlooked: there was a significant spiritual difference between the two. Aristotle felt only contempt for the barbarians —for those who did not share the blessings of Greek civilization. However, it was the ambition and aspiration of Alexander to unite the Hellenic and Oriental civilizations. If he had succeeded permanently, history might have taken a different turn, and the clashes between East and West might have been avoided. In this respect, at least, Alexander had a more penetrating vision than his teacher.

Between 340 and 335 B.C. Aristotle was mostly engaged in scientific research at Stagira, where he was aided by Theophrastus, who later succeeded him at his school in Athens. Constantly his research was aided by liberal grants from Alexander, who in this manner contributed to scientific and philosophic progress.

When Alexander embarked upon his conquest of Asia, in 334 B.C., Aristotle returned to Athens. This time he went as a teacher, however, not as a student, and he established a new school, the Lyceum, named after Apollo Lyceus. There was vigorous competition between the Lyceum and the Academy, and very soon Aristotle's school surpassed Plato's. This supremacy was due mainly to the comprehensive and stimulating lectures of Aristotle, who not only taught the principles of science but also gave instruction in politics, rhetoric, and dialectic.

Despite his success in the educational field, Aristotle's position in Athens was insecure, since he was a foreigner and Alexander's friend, and there was much resentment against the Macedonian ruler. The popular prejudice was intensified by the efforts of Demosthenes, Alexander's implacable opponent. At the same time, Aristotle was losing favor with Alexander, who in his last years was adopting Oriental customs and the Oriental way of life. All these, Aristotle thought, would only lead to decadence and to disintegration of the Greek spirit, and he protested openly to Alexander.

When Alexander died suddenly, in 323 B.C., there were rumors that Aristotle or Antipater had poisoned him. These rumors, however, were unfounded, for it appears certain that he died of natural causes. As soon as the news of his death spread, open rebellion broke out in many parts of Greece. The anti-Macedonian faction regarded Aristotle as a subversive influence. He was also accused of atheism; and since he did not wish to become a martyr, he thought it wise to leave Athens. He went to Chalcis, where he died in 322 B.C.

The Works of Aristotle

Unfortunately, many of the works of Aristotle have been lost. Still, what remains of his researches is quite bulky and gives evidence of his indefatigable labors. His logical treatises are called the *Organon*. They consist of the *Categories*, which are especially occupied with the discussion of substance and which name the eight categories of thought. Then there is his book *On Interpretation*, which discusses the various types of propositions. The *Prior Analytics* is occupied especially with the syllogism; in it we find the rules for the categorical syllogism and the concept of induction. The *Posterior Analytics* deals with scientific demonstrations and the nature of scientific knowledge. The *Topics* deals with dialectical reasoning, and a special section is devoted to ambiguous meanings. Another part of his logical work is *On Sophistical Refutations,* which exposes the verbal and logical fallacies of the Sophists and makes a distinction between genuine and apparent reasoning.

Aristotle's main work in the field of physical science is the *Physics.* It discusses such topics as the condition of change and the problem of teleology, and it examines such philosophical concepts as motion, time, space, the void, and the infinite. Another significant treatise in physical science is *On the Heavens.* It deals with the nature of heaven and compares it with the elements of the earth. Special sections in this treatise are devoted to a discussion of motion and the properties of the various elements.

We must not omit Aristotle's other contributions to physical science, especially his book *On Generation and Corruption,* which is concerned with the problem of alteration and the basic elements of the universe. In this work he is critical regarding the theory of Empedocles, who believed that the four elements could not be transformed into one another. Another treatise in physical science is entitled the *Meteorology;* it deals with the realm between heaven and earth, and also contains some elementary psychological theories. It discusses the nature of comets, planets, and meteors; and it had considerable influence on scientific developments in the Middle Ages.

Turning to the biological sciences, we find his treatise *On the Soul.* In this field we also find the *Short Physical Treatises,* which discusses such topics as memory, reminiscence, and the significance of dreams. More important is his discussion of animals in *On the Parts of Animals,* which, among other topics, contains Aristotle's observations on the methods of natural science, his theory of classification, and his views on animal structure. In still another treatise in biology, he deals with concepts of sexual generation. They are portrayed in *On the Generation of Animals,* in which the physiology of animals is discussed, as well as various views on generation. In all these treatises a great deal of repetition prevails. As a model teacher Aristotle realized that important points must be stressed repeatedly if they are to be understood.

The Division of Aristotle's Philosophy

Undoubtedly, Aristotle's most influential book is the *Metaphysics* (*Metaphysica*). Its title was probably derived from the fact that it follows the physical treatises in the collection of the Aristotelian works that were edited by Andronicus of Rhodes. Some of the problems of the *Metaphysics* deal with Aristotle's definitions of philosophical terms and his criticism of earlier philosophers, especially Plato. He made a distinction between actuality and potentiality, and in Book 12 of the *Metaphysics* he discusses the nature and function of the Prime Mover.

In the field of ethics, we have the *Nichomachean Ethics,* dealing with the various types of virtues, continence, pleasure, friendship, and happiness. The ethical views of Aristotle are distinguished by his concept of the golden mean and by his faith in the power of reason and the validity of intellectual virtues. The *Eudemian Ethics* also vividly portrays the spirit of Aristotelian moral ideals.

In the field of political science Aristotle's *Politics* is especially important. Under this heading he discusses not merely the problems of statesmanship but also the goals and function of education. The tenor of his political observations is extremely realistic, and to some extent there are in them Machiavellian strains.

In the field of rhetoric and literary criticism, Artistotle likewise made far-reaching contributions. In his *Rhetoric* he gives a systematic treatment of this subject. His observations regarding composition, style, and the forms of speech are as valid today as they were in his own time.

In the *Poetics* we have the Aristotelian views regarding tragedy, epic poetry, and comedy. Through these studies Aristotle became the founder of literary criticism; even today we hear much concerning his definition of tragedy, and his insistence on the three unities: place, time, and action.

In observing Aristotle's works from a broad perspective, we are awed by the breadth and scope of his researches. His power of unification, his ability to synthesize, his immense depth—all these traits have seldom been duplicated in philosophy. Thus we can understand why a modern thinker like Santayana believed that almost all subsequent thinking is a mere footnote to the system of Aristotle.

Aristotle's Methods

The development of philosophy was aided greatly by Aristotle's talent for classification. Unlike Plato, he was concerned with specific as well as universal facts. Indeed, Aristotle started with *particular phenomena* and then arrived at a universal conclusion. Induction arrives at a generalization through a methodical enumeration of particular facts, whereas deduction starts with a universal premise, from which it then derives a specific conclusion.

Unlike Plato, Aristotle devoted much attention to natural science in his philosophy. Yet he was not concerned exclusively with the observation and study of the phenomena of nature, for he believed that the highest and most important science is *metaphysics, the study of immaterial being.* This viewpoint is extremely significant. It established the tone of much of later philosophical speculation, for Aristotle emphasized his tenet that the practical sciences must be subordinated to the theoretical sciences. The material is to be followed by the immaterial. Thus, educators throughout medieval and early modern times were more concerned with theory than with practice, and frequently had a dislike for the realm of action and concrete fact.

In making metaphysics the climax of all knowledge, Aristotle gave emphasis to the importance of immaterial truths. This love for metaphysics has never disappeared in philosophy; and although various movements have arisen in modern times—such as positivism and dialectical materialism—which protest against metaphysics, it is still regarded with respect and admiration by most professional philosophers.

Returning to Aristotle's definition of philosophy, we find that he considered logic to be a preparatory science to philosophical thinking. Thus we have theoretical philosophy, which embraces three subjects: metaphysics, physics, and mathematics. Theoretical philosophy is followed by practical philosophy, which includes politics and ethics. Last, we find poetical philosophy, which contains his theory of art, especially poetry.

Ideals

Aristotle tells us that there are four types of causes: 1. material cause, 2. efficient cause, 3. formal cause, and 4. final cause. This doctrine can be clarified by a concrete example: Imagine an artist who is trying to erect a statue. The content of the statue is the material cause; the artist is the efficient cause; the form of the statue is the formal cause; the goal of the artist represents the final cause. Now, according to Aristotle, the most important cause is the *final cause*.

This doctrine has important consequences. It implies a rejection of a mechanistic philosophy. The universe cannot be interpreted according to absolute laws; rather, it exhibits definite levels. The highest levels determine the function of the lowest levels, and all levels are dominated by the climax of creation: *God*. The doctrine also implies that the actual is prior to the potential. The purpose of the artist determines the nature of the thing that he creates; the plan of the universe determines the content of the universe. According to Aristotle, God is completely *immutable*. He is not a personal deity in the Christian sense, nor does he possess a sense of morality. His main activity is a meditation upon his own perfection.

We must not omit Aristotle's adherence to the geocentric hypothesis. Aristotle firmly believed that the earth was the center of the universe; he was certain that there could be no more than one heaven and that outside that heaven there could be no place or void. His teleological interpretation of science had a significant impact upon many medieval thinkers, who likewise were mostly concerned with the religious purpose of science, rather than with the practical application of scientific knowledge.

From an educational standpoint, it is important to understand Aristotle's doctrine of immortality. Aristotle did not believe in personal survival after death. He considered the intellect to be composed of a potential or *passive reason.* The passive reason is determined by physical forces and, when the body disappears, the passive reason likewise suffers extinction.

The *active reason,* however, is truly immortal. Consequently, when we apprehend the truth we become timeless spectators of our existence. Whatever is personal, on the other hand, does not survive after death. Our sensations, our memories, and our consciousness are all destroyed when we pass away. The active reason, according to Aristotle, is not dependent on any outside force. It transcends time and space. In using the active reason, man becomes like God and absorbs part of God's majesty.

The Aristotelian ideal of education is based upon a definite view of man. Aristotle maintains that man's most important attribute is his rational capacity; hence, he believed in the cultivation of the intellect. The emotional life is only the prelude to our rational development. Man is endowed with three souls: a vegetative soul, an animal soul, and a rational soul. The rational soul, most important of the three, has two parts: one is practical, the other is theorectical. The rational soul is the faculty that allows man to make judgments and evaluations.

Aristotle considers leisure the most important element in education. Only in times of leisure can man contemplate and speculate and become conscious of his higher powers. Labor is a secondary activity; in this respect, Aristotle represents the Athenian view of life.

According to Aristotle, the state is the fulfillment of our social drives. Hence, the state is to be in charge of education, and it should prohibit all vulgar activities.

> That education should be regulated by law and should be an affair of state is not to be denied, but what should be the character of this public education, and how young persons should be educated, are questions which remain to be considered. For mankind are by no means agreed about the things to be taught, whether we look to virtue or the best life.
>
> Neither is it clear whether education is more concerned with intellectual or with moral virtue. The existing practice is perplexing; no one knows on what principle we should proceed—should the useful in life, or should virtue, or should the higher knowledge be the aim of our training; all three opinions have been entertained. Again, about the means there is no agreement; for different persons, starting with different ideas about the nature of virtue, naturally disagree about the practice of it.
>
> There can be no doubt that children should be taught those useful things which are really necessary, but not all things; for occupations are divided into liberal and illiberal; and to young children should be imparted only such kinds of knowledge as will be useful to them without vulgarizing them. And any occupation, art, or science which makes the body or soul or mind of the freeman less fit for the practice or exercise of virtue is vulgar; wherefore we call those arts vulgar which tend to deform the body, and likewise all paid employments, for they absorb and degrade the mind.[1]

Youth is to be protected from all debasing influences:

> A freeman who is fond of saying or doing what is forbidden, if he be too young as yet to have the privilege of a place at the public

---

1. *Politics.*

tables, should be disgraced and beaten, and an elder person degraded as his slavish conduct deserves. And since we do not allow improper language, clearly we should also banish pictures or tales which are indecent. Let the rulers take care that there be no image or picture representing unseemly actions, except in the temples of those Gods at whose festivals the law permits even ribaldry, and whom the law also permits to be worshiped by persons of mature age on behalf of themselves, their children, and their wives. But the legislator should not allow youth to be hearers of satirical iambic verses or spectators of comedy until they are of an age to sit at the public tables and to drink strong wine; by that time education will have armed them against the evil influences of such representations.[2]

To Aristotle, the best government is government of the middle class. The most moral way of life is life according to the golden mean, a life of moderation. Aristotle is less opposed than is Plato to a more sophisticated type of music because he realized it could play an important role in the curriculum.

The question what is or is not suitable for different ages may be easily answered; nor is there any difficulty in meeting the objection of those who say that the study of music is vulgar. We reply (1) in the first place, that they who are to be judges must also be performers, and that they should begin to practice early, although, when they are older, they may be spared the execution; they must have learned to appreciate what is good and to delight in it, thanks to the knowledge which they acquired in their youth. As to (2) the vulgarizing effect which music is supposed to exercise, this is a question (of degree), which we shall have no difficulty in determining, when we have considered to what extent freemen who are being trained to political virtue should pursue the art, what melodies and what rhythms they should be allowed to use, and what instruments should be employed in teaching them to play, for even the instrument makes a difference. The answer to the objection turns upon

2. *Ibid.*

these distinctions; for it is quite possible that certain methods of teaching and learning music do really have a degrading effect. . . .

The right measure will be attained if students of music stop short of the arts which are practiced in professional contests, and do not seek to acquire those fantastic marvels of execution which are now the fashion in such contests, and from these have passed into education. Let the young pursue their studies until they are able to feel delight in noble melodies and rhythms, and not merely in that common part of music in which every slave or child and even some animals find pleasure.[3]

How do we learn? Aristotle, interested in a systematic presentation of knowledge, shows that our mind rises from the specific to the universal, from the particular to the general. Experience is to be our guide and induction is to guide our reasoning. He emphasizes the point that without a correct method education and philosophy cannot progress.

In education, according to Aristotle, three principles are to be kept in mind. The first is *nature,* which is the foundation of our biological activities and which gives us our emotional drives. The second is *habit,* which implies a control of our irrational activities. Children tend to act instinctively, as do animals; only by instilling good habits in their lives can they progress in a creative manner.

In this respect, Aristotle had a far more realistic perspective than some contemporary twentieth-century educators. Interest alone is not an adequate motive in the education of children. For real knowledge and real creativity, discipline is also essential. We learn from the Aristotelian concept of education how character is built through right associations and how reason can be established through self-control.

But the important part of education, according to Aristotle, is the third principle: *the cultivation of the intellect.* Reason can understand the totality of life; it can give order to chaos. When

3. *Ibid.*

we use our reason we virtually achieve a divine status; we rise above the trivialities of the present.

Education, Aristotle maintains, can be divided into several phases. At first, from birth to age seven, the child should be brought up in a healthy manner. Special attention should be paid to his physical development; he should be taught how to endure hardship. Association with slaves should be avoided.

A break takes place when the child reaches the age of five, as Aristotle explains in the *Politics:*

> The next period lasts to the age of five; during this no demand should be made upon the child for study or labor, lest its growth be impeded; and there should be sufficient motion to prevent the limbs from being inactive. This can be secured, among other ways, by amusement, but the amusement should not be vulgar or tiring or riotous. The Directors of Education, as they are termed, should be careful what tales or stories the children hear, for the sports of children are designed to prepare the way for the business of later life, and should be for the most part imitations of the occupations which they will hereafter pursue in earnest. Those are wrong who (like Plato) in the *Laws* attempt to check the loud crying and screaming of children, for these contribute towards their growth, and, in a manner, exercise their bodies. Straining the voice has an effect similar to that produced by the retention of the breath in violent exertions. Besides other duties, the Directors of Education should have an eye to their bringing up, and should take care that they are left as little as possible with slaves. For until they are seven years old they must live at home; and therefore, even at this early age, all that is mean and low should be banished from their sight and hearing.[4]

From the age of seven to puberty, the child is exposed to an extensive curriculum, which includes the study of the fundamentals of music and gymnastics as well as reading, writing, and arithmetic. During the next phase, from puberty to age seven-

4. *Ibid.*

teen, the boy would study rhetoric, grammar, literature, and geography, as well as instrumental music and mathematics. Now the stress would be upon exact knowledge. The climax of education comes after the boy reaches the age of twenty-one; only the really superior students may continue with their studies. Now the young man would develop truly encyclopedic interests since he would study the biological and physical sciences, psychology and ethics, and rhetoric as well as philosophy. Knowledge of these subjects would give him a complete concept of man and the universe. The school founded by Aristotle (the Lyceum) stressed the knowledge of science and had a more empirical foundation than Plato's Academy.

The aim of education, in Aristotle's view, is to guide youngsters so that they "love which they ought to love and hate which they ought to hate." Education is concerned not merely with a fragmentary concept of man, but with the development of all his capacities—physical, moral, and intellectual. The wise man, according to Aristotle, would combine theory and practice, intuition and scientific knowledge. Thus, Aristotle's view of man and knowledge is similar to the Renaissance conception, which stressed the development of all our capacities.

The Aristotelian view of education may be compared to that of Confucius. Both believed in the golden mean; both were concerned with right habits; both had confidence in the powers of reason. However, they differed greatly in one respect: Aristotle was less concerned with tradition and with the past, but more interested in religion and metaphysics, than the great Chinese thinker.

It has often been stated that a fundamental gulf exists between the world view and the educational ideals of Plato and those of Aristotle. Plato maintained that art has a secondary reality; it is to be strictly regulated. Aristotle believed that art is an incentive to creative living; in watching dramas or listening to music our emotions are stirred; a catharsis takes place, and we expand our vision and see life on a cosmic plane. Aristotle also opposes professionalism in art, since art is to be the sport of the gentleman.

While Plato is essentially concerned with the realm of forms, Aristotle stresses specific experience. According to Aristotle, life is development, from lower forms to higher forms, from inorganic existence to man. Of utmost significance is man's *purpose*, for it defines his function in the universe.

Aristotle considers the ideal of justice as a basic concept of education and politics. The aim of the legislator is to produce good men, which implies that education is tested by *actual results,* not by theories.

The basic weakness of Aristotle's educational ideal is its antidemocratic tendencies: He had a low opinion of women; he defended slavery; and he had contempt for the culture of other nations. Furthermore, he neglected the importance of vocational training, a necessary supplement to any liberal education.

The greatness of Aristotle lay in his emphasis upon reason. By the use of reason man surpasses his animal nature; through rational insight emotional impulses can be controlled. Reason, used pragmatically, can remold the conditions of existence. Even Freud, who glorified man's animal impulses, stated in a letter that "there is no control of our passions except through intelligence."

In his educational ideals, Aristotle symbolized the Athenian view of life, which stressed moderation and a balanced concept of man and his intellectual powers. In Athens, there was no infallible theology. There was not one standard of morals and religion. The Athenians believed in free inquiry, and thus they laid the seeds for our own intellectual development.

Man's most formidable asset is curiosity, which is a truly explosive force. It makes us eternally restless, so that we seek and yearn and never stand still. To cultivate curiosity in education is to cultivate a power that surges beyond life and death and that gives meaning to the uncertainty of human existence.

Santayana one time remarked that the life of reason was most perfectly embodied by the Greeks, even though it was limited by political insecurity and by the struggle between totalitarianism and democracy. But the Greeks, especially thinkers like Aristotle, were more creative than perhaps any other civilization; to them, education became a way of life; unending curiosity became man's most important trait in his quest for the good life.

7. Epicurus

We have few facts regarding the career of Epicurus (342?–270
B.C.). He was born on the island of Samos, where his father had
settled as an Athenian colonist. His father was a schoolteacher,
and from him Epicurus learned the rudiments of education. We
are told that his mother was a seller of charms and holy relics and
that Epicurus helped her in her profession. We do not know if
the story is true, but if it is, it explains why Epicurus felt such
hatred for popular religion.

In 323 B.C. we find Epicurus in Athens, where he obtained
military training and took part in the political affairs of the
community. In this period he met the poet Menander. This was
probably a very formative stage in his philosophical development. Athenian philosophy was already experiencing a twilight,
and only second-rate figures were teaching in the Lyceum. No
wonder that Epicurus had contempt for many of the philosophers! He satirized both Plato and Aristotle, and he called
Heraclitus a "confusion-maker."

Shortly after 323 B.C. Epicurus left Athens and traveled widely.
He became a teacher of philosophy and in 310 established a
school of philosophy at Mitylene. Yet he was homesick for

Athens; hence, four years later, he moved back to that city, which then became the center of his activity.

In Athens Epicurus explained his philosophy in a garden that has become extremely famous in the history of philosophy. His teaching was informal; not only free men but also women and slaves were allowed to attend. Epicurus must have made an unusual impression on his listeners, for they all testify to his intellectual strength, sharp wit, and convincing arguments. He never married, since he believed that a wife would interfere with his philosophic studies. Besides, he had too much faith in friendship and too little faith in love. But he was a man with tender human feelings. The letters that have been preserved show his unflagging interest in the affairs of his students. When one of his disciples died, leaving a son and daughter, Epicurus took care of their education and in his will provided for them.

Throughout his life he was an industrious writer. Over three hundred treatises are ascribed to him. His great book *On Nature* was written in thirty-seven volumes. Unfortunately we have only a few fragments of his work. In his style Epicurus was less elegant than Plato, but he expressed himself in a comprehensive and succinct manner. While he lacked poetic imagination, his clarity is admirable.

In his later years Epicurus suffered greatly from ill-health. He had never been strong; even as a young boy he had endured a variety of diseases. As he grew older, gout and indigestion plagued him, but he never lost his cheerfulness. On the last day of his life he wrote a letter to one of his disciples, in which he described his pain and the weariness of his tortured body but his spirit was still the same as he recalled a past conversation they had enjoyed.

Thus it can be seen that Epicurus was sincere in his beliefs, and that his philosophy was not merely a theory of life but a way of action. Living frugally, he despised luxuries. He had no desire to reform the world, and he was not interested in creating social utopias but was satisfied to search for the meaning of existence, in teaching real wisdom, and in living a tranquil life.

New Education

It is interesting to note that Epicurus rejected the training that was offered in the established schools of philosophy. The Platonic Academy recommended especially mathematics, but Epicurus had little use for this subject. He likewise disregarded logic which had been cherished by Aristotle. In fact, for deductive logic Epicurus had profound contempt. He thought that too much preoccupation with logic would lead to false pretensions and give the mind an exaggerated power of its own range. Thought, he asserted, should be applied; and its object must be the external world, not abstruse propositons.

The more we advance in education, Epicurus taught, the more we are able to confront life with tranquillity. True knowledge liberates, widens our perspective, and leads to a genuine appreciation of the universe. True knowledge, however, cannot be gained merely through quantitative studies and pedantic scholarship; rather, it depends on the cultivation of a serene attitude, through which the pains of life and the reverses of our existence can be overcome.

Foundations

The foundation of the metaphysical system of Epicurus was atomism, the pre-Socratic system taught by Democritus but, unlike the latter, Epicurus used the atomic theory to bolster his own system of ethics. His scientific proclivities were thus subordinated to his moral interests. The starting point of Epicurus is materialistic. Nothing is created out of the nonexistent; this theory denies spontaneous generation. He affirmed that matter always exists and that we can understand natural phenomena only by learning their natural causes.

Did Epicurus teach that matter can decrease? The answer is in the negative. We cannot speak of destruction in the universe, said he; elements merely change their composition. Thus the content of the world remains the same; it is a self-existent and autonomous whole. This view invalidates any belief in a spiritual creator. Epicurus thought that we need no external force to account for the structure of the universe, for it is not subject to generation or decay, and its processes can be understood through science, not through theological ideals.

The two basic realities of Epicurus' system are atoms and motion. Atoms he described as being indivisible, unchangeable, and completely compact. They have three qualities: size, shape, and weight.

The important feature of the metaphysical system of Epicurus is his belief that the atoms have free will. As they move around in the universe, they swerve from their paths. Their motion causes a collision. As a result of this collision compounds arise, and definite world systems are born. In holding this theory Epicurus differed markedly from Democritus, who believed everything to be governed by necessity. At first glance it makes the Epicurean system inconsistent. In fact, many ancient commentators, especially Cicero, thought it almost invalidated its basic presuppositions.

But it must be remembered that Epicurus did not believe in absolute necessity, for if we accept such determinism there can be no place for moral teachings. To make the matter clear let us imagine that a predetermined path governs all our actions. Would this not result in fatalism and in passive resignation to nature?

From a scientific standpoint, the theory of the swerving of the atoms proved to be useful to Epicurus. He reasoned that the heavier atoms would naturally fall at a more rapid rate than the lighter atoms. Now, if we accept absolute determinism there could be no contact between the two; therefore no world system could arise. However, the swerving of the atoms, undetermined by external necessity, shows why the planets arose in the universe.

This stress on indeterminism has important implications. It indicates that Epicurus refused to believe in an absolute system of science. Not being willing to be bound by religious orthodoxy, he likewise refused to accept a fatalistic physical science. To him freedom was real both in the cosmic structure and in the acts of the individual. This view, strangely enough, has been verified by modern science. Heisenberg's theory of indeterminacy has almost an Epicurean flavor, and it shows that mechanical causality is not valid in the study of nuclear physics.

Epicurus also suggested by his doctrine that an infinite number of worlds exist. In this view he was consistent, for it was based on his belief in the infinity of atoms and the infinity of space. Some of the worlds, he held, are unlike our own, while others resemble our universe rather closely.

Spiritual Education

It is a mistake to think of Epicurus as an atheist, for he maintained that the gods exist but live far away and are unconcerned with human destiny. In short, they are quite different from the orthodox concept, which pictured them as being in constant contact with man. He asserted that their form is everlasting but their material contents are transitory and composed of atoms that move in the void. These atoms unite for a moment and then enter into other combinations. They give off certain films, or "idols," which are perceived by human beings and which can be trusted when they tell us that gods exist.

Epicurus made it clear that the gods live a completely peaceful life. They have no desires that cannot be fulfilled; they are not exposed to the vicissitudes of life as mankind knows it.

How, then, are we to conceive of the gods? Epicurus believed that we must first of all get away from the human view that the gods know emotion. They are not touched by anger or wrath.

They are completely unlike Jehovah, for Epicurus thought emotion a sign of weakness that certainly would disturb the peace of mind of the gods. In his opinion, those who believe then that the gods will reward the virtuous and punish the wicked are mistaken, for gods are not concerned with human actions. They do not take part in human affairs; such activity would detract from their majesty and self-sufficiency. Hence it is useless to pray to the gods; they will not respond. In other words, they are complete isolationists; but their lack of response is not to be interpreted as a sign of weakness but rather as a sign of the perfection of the gods.

What happens, then, to orthodox religion? The answer of Epicurus is: It is usually based on fraud and deception, for it pictures a universe in which the gods intervene in human affairs, and men try to please the gods. The philosopher, however, will overcome this illusion and order his actions, not according to vain beliefs but according to the precepts of wisdom.

Epicurus felt that in replacing orthodoxy by this new concept of life he actually had achieved a more pious perspective. Was this not a faith based on freedom rather than on spiritual slavery? Was this not worthy of a rational human being rather than a savage?

He was so deeply convinced of the evils of conventional religion that he constantly dwelt on them. So, too, did Lucretius, his great Roman follower. If all prayers were answered, Epicurus noted, most of them would result in evil, for men constantly pray for their neighbors to be punished. He also pointed out that orthodox religion is frequently based on barbaric rites that are cruel and sadistic in their inhumanity.

What matters is not how long we live but how pleasant our existence is. If we keep this idea in mind, death has no terrors. Those who state that life has no value at all, that it is better not to be born, are hypocrites. If they truly believe this, why do they not commit suicide? If they say it without sincerity, their words are not to be taken seriously.

Morals and Reason

In Epicurus' system of ethics, as in his scientific concepts, naturalism prevails. Thus the basis of his ethical concept is not an absolute ideal but concrete observation. He called pleasure the beginning and end of life: it becomes the standard for the good and the criterion for men's actions. This concept, however, does not include bodily pleasures, for we should observe that frequently these cause only pain. For example, if we eat too much, indigestion results. If we experience too much sensual pleasure, we are left in a state of weakness and fatigue, and ultimately we arrive at satiation. Furthermore, if we seek bodily pleasures too intently, we will be constantly agitated; our minds will become restless, forever seeking more stimulations without being able to achieve contentment. But this is not the way of the wise man, who cherishes tranquillity, repose, and serenity—a condition that Epicurus called ataraxia, a state of imperturbability.

The end of our actions is freedom from pain and fear. Such freedom indicates the end of our moral search. No longer are we exposed to emotional tempests and to the changing moods of fortune.

It must be realized that Epicurus based his conclusions on his study of the psychology of desires. The more we multiply our desires, he thought, the less likely we are to find repose and tranquillity. We must concentrate on those desires that are necessary and essential for our well-being. As for those that are admired and sought for by the crowd, they are purely superfluous and we can neglect them. In other words, not all pleasures are to be chosen just as not all forms of pain are to be avoided.

Above all, Epicurus taught, we must not be guided by our fears; if we are, we will be completely unstable. We will forever worry and fret and wait for imaginary disasters. We must neither be afraid of the gods nor worry about what happens to us when we die, for science teaches us that death is the extinction of consciousness and that the gods do not concern themselves with human destiny.

In his view that anxiety is the cause of most of our troubles, Epicurus sounds strikingly modern. To overcome anxiety, he believed, education is necessary. Hence it is the task of philosophy to counteract the ills of the mind and to give us a sense of intellectual stability. Such stability, Epicurus maintained, cannot be found in an active social life. Thus the wise man will not take part in political affairs; nor will he try to reform the existing government. Rather, he will cultivate his own capacities and cherish his own happiness.

To achieve this painless existence, Epicurus advocated, above all, friendship. Marriage, he thought, involves too many tempests, too many storms, and too many uncertainties; it creates ties and leads to emotional serfdom. Friendship, on the other hand, being less possessive and less intimate, leads to true tranquillity. Evidently Epicurus followed his own precepts for the good life, for he never married.

His discussion of the various virtues is extremely realistic. He did not idealize justice; rather, he found its source in expediency. The state, he held, is the result of a compact between subjects and rulers whereby both profit. Right and wrong are determined by laws, not by ideal standards, as Plato had imagined. Accordingly, we cannot speak of an ideal utopia or of ideal beauty or ideal justice or ideal truth. Rather, in evaluating moral acts we must look at the consequences.

Why does the wise man obey the laws? Why does he subordinate himself to political authority? The Epicureans believed that he does so because of self-interest, for he will then have more intellectual tranquillity. He will sleep well at night, while those who evade the laws and commit acts of injustice will suffer from their fear of being detected.

It is true that this is not an idealistic view when measured by Platonic standards, but it must be remembered that the Epicureans were interested in describing society as they saw it, not in picturing ideal standards. Like the Sophists, they noted that there are no absolute institutions—all are relative. They applied this concept to international law, in which field they showed that various types of justice prevail. For example, there is one type of justice that prevails between equally strong nations and another type that exists between a strong nation and a weak nation. This theory almost anticipates Hobbes, who likewise stressed realism in international politics.

The climax of the educational system of Epicurus is his belief that the most important pleasures are those of the mind. The mind has the power of reflection and can contemplate life as a whole. It can reflect upon the pleasant occurrences of the past as well as anticipate the happy things it may expect to happen in the future. Furthermore, it can triumph over bodily infirmity. Even when sick and plagued by disease, we can achieve a cheerful perspective on life through mental concentration.

At the same time, Epicurus taught, the mind can suffer more intense pain than can the body. Modern psychology with its concept of neuroses and psychoses verifies his viewpoint. We must cultivate the resources of our mind so that we will not suffer from pain but lead a tranquil existence.

Life, it may be said in objection, often presents us with situations in which the pleasure element is not dominant. Imagine that we are suffering from cancer and are in great pain. Can we still accept Epicurean standards? Epicurus would answer in the affirmative, for pain, he felt, cannot last very long and, at any rate, acute suffering persists for only a short period. We can always endure it by the thought of the happiness that is still obtainable. To revert to our case of cancer, even under the suffering it imposes we can use our intellectual resources. And if the pain lasts very long, we will be released by death, which should not be dreaded but regarded as a natural event.

The teaching of Epicurus may appear rather impractical, yet he lived up to his own ideals. Throughout his life he disregarded his frail condition and never let pain conquer him. It takes a vast amount of endurance and strength to cherish such a philosophy, and certainly Epicurus possessed these virtues.

Such a way of life is not out of our reach. Although occasionally we may be overcome by certain pains, we can still attain a tranquil existence. This is a philosophy not just for the professional thinker but for the multitude. It is not a utopia for the future but a theory that can be followed in the present.

Thus it can be understood why the Epicureans were so vigorous in their beliefs and why they had a strong sense of mission. They wanted to lighten the burden of humanity, to remove the evils of supernaturalism and blind faith, and to preach instead a way of life leading to true peace of mind and educational enlightenment.

Significance

In Epicureanism we find one of the perennial philosophies of education. It is a theory that does not depend on national or religious barriers. Thus we find Epicureanism in a Catholic like Gassendi, in a pantheist like Whitman, and in a mathematician like Bertrand Russell. In some ways the spirit of the famed Epicurean Lucretius as reflected in his great poem *De rerum natura*, reminds us of Russell's *A Free Man's Worship*.

It may be asked why this philosophy is so attractive and why it has a constant appeal. In the first place, it is based on individualism. Its starting point is not society but the individual. It is an acknowledged fact that most artists and thinkers are introspective, interested primarily in their own emotions, sensations, and needs rather than in the salvation of society. Thus, they are frequently attracted by Epicureanism.

In the second place, it is a philosophy that gives us hope in times of chaos and anarchy. While empires may collapse and wars ravish the earth, we can still cultivate our own garden and find peace of mind. It is not surprising that Jefferson regarded Epicurus as one of the great spiritual teachers of man.

8. Quintilian

Roman education was at first dominated by the family. In the Roman family the father was supreme and his word was like an edict of the state. The ideal of Roman education was to cultivate manliness and self-control. Individualism was not tolerated in the early Roman republic. As Rome expanded, the Greek influence became more significant. After 272 B.C. many Greek scholars came to Rome, among them Livius Andronicus, who translated many Greek writings into Latin and who popularized Greek literature, and Plautus, who specialized in the translation of Greek comedy scenes. Later, the Roman statesman Cato the Censor attempted to arrest the Greek influence, but he was unsuccessful.

There are important parallels in the development of Roman and American educational systems. Both started in an atmosphere of puritanism. Both emphasized utilitarian endeavors. Both were rather uninterested in speculation; instead, they emphasized practical subjects. Both were faced by complex social problems, such as juvenile waywardness. Both made the most significant contributions in the field of technology.

In Rome three types of schools developed. On the elementary level the *litterator* taught the elements of reading and writing.

On the secondary level the *grammaticus* instructed students in the fundamentals of the liberal arts. In more advanced education, schools of rhetoric developed, which often were liberally endowed by Roman emperors.

Roman professional education was extensive: In legal education the natural rights of all human beings and equality before the law became important legal concepts. At Constantinople, Theodosius established a professorship of law. Justinian continued this tradition, and his code of laws influenced medieval scholars, especially at the University of Bologna. In medical education, Galen stressed the empirical method, and his ideas influenced the scholars of the Middle Ages and of the Renaissance. Empirical instruction in medicine was on a high level at Rome; Roman physicians were highly skilled in pharmacology and surgery.

Compared with Greek education, the Roman schools were too practical and under too much state control, especially after the first century of the Christian Era. The most important subject in the curriculum was rhetoric, often taught in an uninspiring manner. Generally, teachers were paid low salaries. Juvenal, the great Roman satirist, complained that teachers in Rome received only a jockey's wage. To quote Juvenal directly:

> Do you teach? Bowels of iron is what a teacher needs when each pupil stands up in turn and recites the self-same things in the self-same way. The same daily fare again and again—it is death to the wretched master. "What would I not give," cries he, "that the boy's father might listen to him as often as I do." And you live in a hole no blacksmith would put up with. . . .[1]

Stoicism

Stoics, like Seneca, Marcus Aurelius, and Epictetus, influenced ancient education. They taught that evil has no metaphysical

1. *Satires.*

reality. In their arguments for the nonexistence of evil they showed that evil is educational and that the world is improved by apparent tragedies. Furthermore, they explained that evil and good are interdependent. The virtuous, according to the Stoics, will never be overcome by evil but will triumph in spite of misfortune. Ethically, the Stoics believed in self-sufficiency and extolled the virtue of apathy. According to their beliefs, the mind is to control all emotions. Thus the educated man will not yield to hope or regret, but will cultivate the independence of his own soul.

The Stoics extended their philosophy to social matters. They preached the brotherhood of man and accepted the concept of natural law that was extended to all human beings. They believed in following the dictates of duty, which they regarded as an aspect of man's divinity.

The piety of the Stoics is revealed in the following hymn by Aratus, which was dedicated to Zeus:

With Zeus let our song begin! Him never may we men leave
Unpraised! Full of Zeus are all the streets,
All the gathering-places of men; full is the sea,
Full the harbors. In all respects we have need of Zeus, all of us,
For we are also His offspring, and He, being gracious to men,
Signifieth what is favorable, and waketh up the peoples to work,
Reminding them of their livelihood. He telleth it, when the clod is best
For oxen and for mattocks; He telleth it, when the seasons are favorable.
Both for the planting of trees and for the strewing of seed of every kind.
For He Himself established the signs of these things in the heavens,
When He ordered the stars; and He took thought to provide for the
    year,
Stars, which most chiefly should signify things made,
As touching the seasons, unto men, in order that all things might grow
    soundly.
Wherefore Him always first and Him last they propitiate.[2]

2. Aratus, *Phaenomena.*

The Stoics had great respect for the popular gods, whom they explained in a symbolic fashion. Also, they worshipped the stars, and they peopled the universe with spirits who mediate between man and the deities. However, the Stoics did not have a definite doctrine of immortality. According to Zeno, the founder of Stoicism, the souls of the virtuous do not perish after death; Chrysippus, however, felt that only the Stoic philosophers would be immortal.

The lyrical spirit of Stoicism is perhaps best revealed in Epictetus, once a slave of one of Nero's followers. Although he was tortured by ill-health, Epictetus was certain that man should praise God. Indeed, man and God are comrades.

> If these statements of the philosophers are true, that God and man are akin, there is but one course open to men, to do as Socrates did: never to reply to one who asks his country, "I am an Athenian" or "I am a Corinthian," but "I am a citizen of the universe." . . . When a man has learnt to understand the government of the universe, and has realized that there is nothing so great or sovereign or all-inclusive as this frame of things wherein men and God are united, and that from it come the seeds from which are sprung, not only my own father or grandfather, but all things that are begotten and that grow upon earth, and rational creatures in particular—for these alone are by nature fitted to share in the society of God, being connected with Him by the bond of reason— why should he not call himself a citizen of the universe and a son of God?[3]

Stoicism influenced Christian thinking by developing a God-centered philosophy of life. Further, the Stoics anticipated the internationalism of the Christian church. The Stoic doctrine which states that all man are part of the natural law is comparable to the Christian doctrine that all men are children of God. Furthermore, the Stoics believed in resignation to the will of God—a view well adapted to the spread of Christianity.

In education, the Stoics preached the importance of dignity.

3. Epictetus, *Discourses* I. ix. 1-7.

Intellectuals ideals are secondary to right moral action. The educated man, in his self-control and poise, is to be an example to
the irrational masses.

Quintilian's Impact

The Roman ideal of character and education is best represented by Quintilian (A.D. c.35–A.D. c.95). His emphasis on self-
control, his dislike of speculation, his practical bent—all stamp
him as a Roman citizen. He was born in Spain at Calagurris; he
studied at Rome, where he later became a famous teacher of
oratory and rhetoric and was rewarded for his efforts by Emperor
Vespasian.

To Quintilian, the only worthwhile life is that of action; contemplation is for the scholar who wants to escape from reality.
The philosopher fails when he tries to reform society according
to his own dictates and ideals. Quintilian cites the example of
history, showing that philosophers had usually not won fame in
public assemblies.

Note the profound difference between Quintilian and Plato,
Plato considered education as the study of immaterial truth; society was to be governed by a philosopher king. To Quintilian,
the philosopher was at best inferior to the experienced statesman
and his role in life was a secondary one.

Quintilian divides philosophy into three fields, all three of
which are important for the orator. First, the study of dialectics
—the laws of reasoning; second, ethics—the laws of justice; and
third, physics. However, Quintilian did not think of physics as a
science; to him, it was rather a study of the ways of providence.
Quintilian thought that the universe had a moral purpose and
that it is man's duty to find the divinity that is within his soul.
Physics would inspire the orator, who thus would cherish a religious interpretation of life.

To become an orator, according to Quintilian, an individual
should seek virtue above all other considerations. He should de-

fend the interests of his client and he should never espouse false-hood. He should study the emotions of audiences and at the same time cultivate the techniques of public speaking. Mere special-ized knowledge of speech was not adequate, for Quintilian be-lieved that the orator should have a wide educational back-ground.

In the twentieth century, Winston Churchill was certainly one of the outstanding orators. The reasons for his success in public speaking are complex. He expressed himself in dramatic terms; he had the ability to coin fresh new terms; his eloquence was almost epic; we are reminded of Shakespeare and Milton. Quintilian was undoubtedly right when he designated public speaking as one of the foundations of education.

Quintilian also tells us that in a child's development the early training is especially important:

> Let a father, then, as soon as his son is born, conceive, first of all, the best possible hopes of him; for he will thus grow the more solicitous about his improvement from the very beginning; since it is a complaint without foundation that "to a very few people is granted the faculty of comprehending what is imparted to them, and that most, through dullness of understanding lose their labor and their time." For, on the contrary, you will find the greater number of men both ready in conceiving and quick in learning, since such quickness is natural to man; and as birds are born to fly, horses to run, and wild beasts to show fierceness, so to us peculiarly belong activity and sagacity of understanding; whence the origin of the mind is thought to be from heaven.
>
> But dull and unteachable persons are no more produced in the course of nature than are persons marked by monstrosity and de-formities; such are certainly but few. It will be a proof of this assertion that, among boys, good promise is shown in the far greater number; and, if it passes off in the progress of time, it is manifest that it was not natural ability, but care, that was want-ing.[4]

4. *Institutes of Oratory* (12 books), Book I.

The morals of children are easily corrupted. Our mistake, Quintilian maintains, is that we indulge them too much. We provide too many luxuries for them, and as a result they lack genuine appreciation. Like Socrates, Quintilian believed that simplicity is to be stressed on all levels of education.

Progressive for his time, Quintilian objected to corporal punishment, which, he believed, only created fear and an attitude of submission. The wise teacher would use a method of positive rewards and thus appeal to the idealism of the students. Corporal punishment of students meant failure on the part of teachers. Education was to be conducted in such a way that the student would develop a sense of honor and a sense of integrity.

Quintilian held that all parts of knowledge were interrelated; a boy should know not only the elements of reading, writing, and arithmetic; he should also be familiar with poetry and science.

In regard to the boy who has attained facility in reading and writing, the next object is instruction from the grammarians. Nor is it of importance whether I speak of the Greek or Latin grammarian, though I am inclined to think that the Greek should take the precedence.

Both have the same method. This profession, then, distinguished as it is, most compendiously, into two parts, the art of *speaking correctly* and the *illustration of the poets* carries more beneath the surface than it shows on its front.

For not only is the *art of writing* combined with that of speaking, but *correct reading* also precedes illustration, and with all these is joined the exercise of *judgment,* which the old grammarians, indeed, used with such severity, that they not only allowed themselves to distinguish certain verses with a particular mark of censure, and to remove, as spurious, certain books which had been inscribed with false titles from their sets, but even brought some authors within their canon, and excluded others altogether from classification. Nor is it sufficient to have read the poets only; every class of writers must be studied, not simply for matter, but for words, which often receive their authority from writers. Nor can the grammar be complete without a knowledge of music, since the grammarian has to speak of meter and rhythm; nor if he is ignorant of astronomy can he understand the poets.[5]

Quintilian's educational plan of instruction consists of three levels. The first level of instruction is composed of the three R's and Latin and Greek grammar; Quintilian placed special emphasis on the study of Greek at an early stage of a child's development.

> I prefer that a boy should begin with the Greek language, because he will acquire Latin, which is in general use, even though we tried to prevent him, and because, at the same time, he ought first to be instructed in Greek learning, from which ours is derived. Yet I should not wish this rule to be so superstitiously observed that he should for a long time speak or learn only Greek, as is the custom with most people; for hence arise many faults of pronunciation, which is viciously adapted to foreign sounds, and also of language, in which when Greek idioms have become inherent by constant usage, they keep their place most pertinaciously even when we speak a different tongue. The study of Latin ought therefore to follow at no long interval, and soon after to keep pace with the Greek; and thus it will happen, that, when we have begun to attend to both tongues with equal care, neither will impede the other.[6]

The second level of instruction includes oratory, literature, geometry, astronomy, music, and philosophy. The third level, for exceptional students only, is the school of rhetoric, which corresponds to a modern university. Here the curriculum includes logic, history, literary criticism, dialectic, and, above all, public speaking. These schools would aim to turn out a man who has the eloquence of the lawyer, and who uses theorectical knowledge for the advancement of his professional life.

The inadequacy of Quintilian's educational plan lies in his

5. *Ibid.*
6. *Ibid.*

disregard of speculation. Education thus becomes a pedestrian matter. Quintilian reminds us of many American educators who are so concerned with activities and practical matters that they lose sight of the real purposes and ideals of the educative process. Quintilian, seduced by immediacy, was a victim of limited vision.

His example should be a warning to us. Education should stress the art of communication, but, even more, it must emphasize intellectual and moral qualities. Education is basically a vision, not a methodology. It is a vision of man's awareness and potentialities; man can only find himself when he cultivates the inward spark. To be too practical in education, or in philosophy, is to be misled by the idols of the tribe; it is to lose direction and a sense of purpose.

9. Jesus

The Ideals of Jesus

The impact of Jesus of Nazareth (bet. 8 and 4 B.C.–c. A.D. 29) upon educational history in the West is enormous. The teachings of Jesus have influenced groups as diverse as the Quakers and the Jesuits; His impact was strong upon the deists, who believed in reason, as well as upon the pietists, who favored emotion as the keynote of religion. Orthodox believers, like Loyola, felt His power, and liberals, like Schweitzer, regarded Jesus as the inspiration for their philosophical and humanitarian labors.

Jesus was bound to be misunderstood. He lived in a period of profound social upheaval. The Jews were oppressed by the Romans, and they looked for a leader to free them from the foreign yoke. The Hebrew religion at the time of Jesus was intensely legalistic: to know the Law was to be saved. Many of the most pious individuals were Pharisees—spiritual exhibitionists who proclaimed their virtue, their righteousness, and their superiority. In reality, they lacked the most important virtue: inwardness.

We must not forget the gulf between the ideals of the inhabitants of a city like Jerusalem and the concepts of life cherished by the people of a rural community like Nazareth. The city inhabitants, more sophisticated than their country neighbors, often imitated Roman manners and Roman behavior. The rural inhabitants, on the other hand, were simple in their lives and faith.

The keynote of the character of Jesus is His sincerity. He appeals to the heart. He shows that what matters is not our material possessions; it is our spirit that counts. He is an idealist because He believes that man is the child of God, and that within himself man holds a kingdom of unlimited possibilities.

Jesus believed that all people are teachable: the rich and the poor, the scholars and the ignorant. Yet real education and real religion—and to Jesus the two activities were identical—required the openness of a child. How often does the scholar lose his enthusiasm and his capacity for awareness; how often does he debate endlessly about minor points.

Jesus was bound to be misunderstood. He wanted a faith based upon unqualified love, a love that respected no barriers of race, religion, and nationality, a love that included all in the common bonds of fellowship. The test of this love was action: how would it change the ideals and patterns of the individual? Yet many of His followers were particularistic in their allegiance. They stressed that they alone, the elect, could find salvation and that anyone who disagreed with them was bound for hell-fire.

Educational Impact

Why was Jesus so successful as a teacher? He used a simple method; He told innumerable parables; He appealed to the moral idealism of His audience. The universe was His textbook, and every day afforded a new lesson. His schoolroom was the open field and the market place.

Like Socrates, Jesus believed in the identity of virtue and knowledge. The moral man would know the essence of the universe and the man who understood nature would love God. Was not life itself a miracle? Were not human beings expressions of divine creativity?

Pascal, the French philosopher, wrote: "The heart has reasons that reason does not know." Jesus was guided by intuition, not by analytical knowledge. He felt the needs of His disciples and they experienced His dedication and sincerity.

Education can be advanced in two ways. The first way is through science and analytical knowledge, whereby real progress can be made. But we all know that analysis and intellectual knowledge may be empty and lead to conceit. We realize, as we become philosophically aware, that intellect and knowledge may not create happiness; for the more we ponder, the more we may experience a Faustian sense of dissatisfaction. Our analysis may lead to constant neuroses and to a feeling of complete disenchantment.

The second way in which education may be advanced is through wisdom of the heart. This is the road of Buddha and of Jesus. Such wisdom goes to the center of things; it establishes harmony and a sense of serenity. It creats balance and perspective. It leads away from the knowledge of facts to understanding and compassion. Education thus becomes a way of living rather than an empty theory.

Modern psychology teaches us the importance of warmth and love. If we read books like Fromm's *The Art of Loving,* Frankl's *Doctor and the Soul,* Menninger's *Love Against Hate,* we find a common emphasis upon the importance of warmth, understanding, and kindness. The child who is unloved, the student who is not encouraged, the teacher who finds no emotional meaning in his work—all are bound for serious emotional maladjustment. To learn how to love, as Jesus teaches, is to become truly educated.

The educational ideals of Jesus rest upon His moral insights. The essential factor in our relationship with our neighbors is our motive: our hearts must be pure. Hatred can never be conquered by hatred, but only through love. Suspicion would create more suspicion, envy would only lead to more unhappiness. We must love our neighbor the way God loves us. Even when we err, even when we are wayward, even when we stray from the path of righteousness, God will treat us with mercy.

Man, according to Jesus, needs few goods to be happy and to find meaning in life. Attachment to material goods is only a hindrance. It is difficult for the rich man to find the path to salvation. Honor and fame only create illusory goals. We should not worry about tomorrow, for today is important; today is the time for decision and creative action.

All this is extremely important in education. We preach spirituality and respect for the individual; yet most of the time we are so concerned about buildings, equipment, and other material considerations that we neglect the teacher and the student. We provide for the comforts of the body, but we neglect the welfare of the soul. We look upon laboratories and stadiums as signs of progress, when they may only hide an empty spirit. We do not know the core of education; thus, many of our institutions of higher learning are centers of organized confusion.

The educational lesson of Jesus is that we must cultivate the individual. This demands more than lip service. We must be conscious of the individual not only as an intellectual being but also as an emotional being desiring something more than knowledge.

Real education is existential: it demands a living encounter between teacher and student, just as Jesus pictured the encounter between man and God.

Contemporaries of Jesus believed God to be a force of fear who punished human beings for their transgressions. They thought that He was localistic and that He had His favorites among nations. Jesus taught that God is everywhere and that He can be worshipped everywhere; He demands not sacrifice and slavish obedience but an upright heart. We honor God by loving our neighbor; God is not confined to one nation or to one civilizatian; He controls the universe.

Some thinkers might say that the knowledge of God is unessential in our concept of education. But if we translate the ideals of Jesus in a broader way and in a more profound manner, knowledge and understanding of God becomes one of the central problems of education. The question is: Does education give us the perspective of universality? Are we worshipping false idols, like mere utilitarian pursuits, or are we conscious of the centrality of human personality? Is our philosophy of education based upon materialism or on the love of God? This does not imply endorsement of one concept of religion or theology, for man must always be open to new experiences and must be a constant explorer. However, this does imply that education must be concerned with the present as well as with the future. Education must be concerned with man's total personality and his total adjustment.

Jesus was educated at home and in the synagogue. He was in intimate contact with His teachers. To Jesus, the teacher was the representative of God, for he brought forth what is best in man. Jesus converted others by using informal conversation. In simple statements—as, for instance, "Man does not live by bread alone" —Jesus could express in a few words what philosophers would state in volumes. Thus Jesus, rather than formalizing the educational process as we know it today, made it part of our entire life, of all our concerns and all our ideals.

The great teachers of mankind, like Buddha, Confucius, and Jesus, were all *personalistic* in their approach: they taught by example. They appealed to the many, not just to the élite. They believed in democracy, for they had faith that all could learn and that wisdom was universal. They spoke with firmness and not merely as debaters. They were inspired by an inner vision which they communicated to their audience.

Most teachers have little vision; they are mainly technicians. They are guided by routine and dominated by intellectual slumber. Thoreau once said that he had met few individuals who were awake; this remark he applied to teachers. But how can we teach when we ourselves live an isolated life? Our words are empty, our formulas are meaningless, if they are not exemplified by action.

Jesus reminds us of the importance of sympathy in education. He never talked down to His audience; He always respected their ability; He saw life through their perspective. Sympathy is the prelude to wisdom, and understanding is the basis of progress.

One may object that modern man can only advance through technical training, since knowledge is becoming more complicated all the time. Thus it will be impossible to be guided by the simple educational philosophy of Jesus. The answer is: We still are confused about the nature and destiny of man. We still want inner security; we still need warmth and love; we still yearn for permanent satisfactions; we still have not conquered the conflicts within and the conflicts without that threaten the very existence of our society. Like Jesus, a teacher must have a vision of his importance; he must see beyond technical details. His task is not merely to impart knowledge, but to develop patterns for behavior. He must stir his students, and this can only be achieved when he really understands them and becomes a part of their lives.

Influence

The stamp of Jesus upon educational history in the West can never be erased. To the medieval educators, like St. Augustine, He was the great disciplinarian who taught men how to avoid evil and how to find the path to God. To mystics, like Eckhart, He taught the importance of self-sacrifice and abandonment to utter poverty; that the acknowledgment of ignorance is the beginning of wisdom.

To Renaissance scholars, like Erasmus, Jesus was a more religious version of Socrates who demonstrated how the scholar must avoid folly and hypocrisy. To the leaders of the Reformation, Jesus became the symbol of a living faith who demanded education of the poor and the rich. To Comenius, Jesus was the symbol of mysticism; He showed that universal understanding was possible. To the Jesuits, Jesus indicated the importance of discipline so that spiritual damnation can be avoided. To Quakers, like George Fox and William Penn, Jesus was the symbol of love; all men are educable.

Pietists, like Philipp Jakob Spener and August Hermann Francke, were encouraged in their educational reforms, especially in their regard for the common people, by the example of Jesus, Pestalozzi was inspired by His example as he cared for the children of the poor and for orphans. Froebel looked upon Jesus as the ideal educator who had demonstrated the unity of man and God, and who had shown that life has unlimited possibilities.

The example of Jesus indicates the importance of creativity exemplified in action. Beyond methodology, beyond formal knowledge, is the living vision of greatness. We move forward in educational history when we stress essentials, when we feel the inspiration of great ideas and great ideals, and when we overcome all forms of lethargy and indifference.

10. Augustine

St. Augustine and the Search for Religious Education

St. Augustine (A.D 354–430) ranks among the most profound and influential of all the Christian philosophers.[1] However, his acceptance of Christianity did not come at once: a Christian mother and pagan father were among many factors that caused his long hesitation before joining Catholicism.

His religious pilgrimage reflected a wide variety of intellectual currents. As a student, he believed in the pleasures of the world with an essentially hedonistic outlook. Then, through reading one of the treatises of Cicero, he became interested in philosophy. Later, he joined the Manicheans, for he could not accept the Old Testament view of morality. Conscious of the great dualism between good and evil, he thought that the Manichean faith offered the best explanation for the existence of evil. After his disillusionment with the Manicheans, he became a skeptic. He doubted man's ability to find an absolute standard of truth, although he still accepted the existence of God. From skepticism, he turned to Neo-Platonism with its view of God's transcendence and its concept of emanation. This movement proved to be his

1. *See* J. McCabe, *St. Augustine and His Age;* A. Narille, *Saint Augustine;* A. J. Dorner, *Augustinus, sein theologisches System.*

bridge to Christianity. After his conversion, he became a fanatical enemy of all heresies and all attempts to subvert Catholic dogma.

The educational record of the experiences of St. Augustine can be found in the *Confessions,* one of the masterpieces of religious autobiography. In it, Augustine describes with eloquence the harsh educational system that prevailed in his childhood:

> If I proved idle in learning, I was soundly beaten. For this procedure seemed wise to our ancestors: and many, passing the same way in days past, had built a sorrowful road by which we too must go, with multiplication of grief and toil upon the sons of Adam.
>
> As a boy I fell into the way of calling upon You, my Help and my Refuge; and in those prayers I broke the strings of my tongue—praying to You, small as I was but with no small energy, that I might not be beaten at school. And when You did not hear me (*not as giving me over to folly*), my elders and even my parents, who certainly wished me no harm, treated my stripes as a huge joke, which they were very far from being to me. Surely, Lord, there is no one so steeled in mind or cleaving to You so close—or even so insensitive, for that might have the same effect—as to make light of the racks and hooks and other torture instruments (from which in all lands men pray so fervently to be saved) while truly loving those who are in such bitter fear of them. Yet my parents seemed to be amused at the torments inflicted upon me as a boy by my masters, though I was no less afraid of my punishments or zealous in my prayers to You for deliverance. But in spite of my terrors I still did wrong, by writing or reading or studying less than my set tasks. It was not, Lord, that I lacked mind or memory, for You had given me as much of these as my age required; but the one thing I revelled in was play; and for this I was punished by men who after all were doing exactly the same things themselves. But the idling of men is called business; the idling of boys, though exactly like, is punished by those same men.[2]

2. From *The Confessions of Saint Augustine,* translated by F. J. Sheed, copyright, 1943, Sheed & Ward, Inc., New York.

He shows how he was motivated by vanity:

> Yet in acting against the commands of my parents and school-masters, I did wrong, O Lord my God, Creator and Ruler of all things, but of sin not Creator but Ruler only: for I might later have made good use of those lessons that they wanted me to learn, whatever may have been their motive in wanting it. I disobeyed, not because I had chosen better, but through sheer love of play: I loved the vanity of victory, and I loved too to have my ears tickled with the fictions of the theatre which set them to itching ever more burningly; and in my eyes a similar curiosity burned increasingly for games and shows of my elders. Yet those who put on such shows are held in high esteem. And most people would be delighted to have their sons grow up to give similar shows in their turn—and meanwhile fully concur in the beatings those same sons get if these shows hinder study: for study is the way to prosperity necessary for giving them. Look down in mercy, Lord, upon such things; and set us free who now beseech Thee: and not only us, but those also who have never besought Thee—that they may turn to Thee and be made free.[3]

He tells how he hated Greek but enjoyed Latin. He favored strict discipline in learning:

> The drudgery of learning a foreign language sprinkled bitterness over all the sweetness of the Greek tales. I did not know a word of the language: and I was driven with threats and savage punishments to learn. There had been a time of infancy when I knew no Latin either. Yet I learnt it without threat or punishment merely by keeping my eyes and ears open, amidst the flatterings of nurses and the jesting and pleased laughter of elders leading me on. I learned it without the painful pressure of compulsion, by the sole pressure of my own desire to express what was in my mind, which would have been impossible unless I had learnt words: and I learnt them not through people teaching me but simply through people speaking: to whom I was striving to utter my own feelings. All this goes to prove that free curiosity is of more value in learning than harsh disci-

3. *Ibid.*, I, x.

pline. But by Your ordinance, O God, discipline must control the free play of curiosity—for Your ordinance ranges from the master's cane to the torments suffered by the martyrs, and works that mingling of bitter with sweet which brings us back to You from the poison of pleasure that first drew us away from You.[4]

Classical learning, Augustine stated, may corrupt morals:

In this matter of classical studies how woeful are you, O torrent of established custom. Who can resist you or when will you run dry? How long will you continue to roll the sons of Eve into that vast and terrible sea in which even those who mount the cross scarcely escape drowning? In you I read of Jove, both as the God of thunder and as an adulterer. How could he be both? But so the story goes: and so sham thunder is made to legitimize and play pander to real adultery: yet these robed and gowned masters are furious when Cicero, a man trained in their own school, protests: "Homer invented these stories, ascribing things human to the Gods: would that he had brought down things divine to us." It would have been even truer to say that Homer invented them, attributing divinity to the vilest of men, with the result that crimes are held not to be crimes, and those who do commit them are regarded as acting not like abandoned men but like Gods from Olympus.

And still, O torrent from hell, the sons of men pay fees to be hurled into you in order that they may learn such things. And there is great interest when this sort of teaching is carried on publicly in the forum under the very eyes of laws allotting salaries to the masters over and above the fees paid by the pupils.[5]

He tells about his wrongdoings and how they symbolize man's proclivity for evil:

These were the ways of the world upon whose threshold I stood as a boy, and such was the arena for which I was training—more concerned to avoid committing a grammatical error than to be void of envy in case I did commit one and another did not. This I say

4. *Ibid.,* I, xiv.
5. *Ibid.,* I, xvi.

and confess to Thee, O my God: and in this I was praised by those whom my one idea of success was to please. I did not see the whirl of vileness into which I had been cast away from Thy eyes: for what was more unclean than I, seeing that I did not win the approval even of my own kind: I told endless lies to my tutors, my masters, and my parents: all for the love of games, the craving for stage shows, and a restlessness to do what I saw done in these shows.

I stole from my parents' cellar and table, sometimes because I was gluttonous myself, sometimes to have something to give other boys in exchange for implements of play which they were prepared to sell although they loved them as much as I.

Is this boyhood innocence? It is not, Lord. I cry Thy mercy, O my God. Yet as we leave behind tutors and masters and nuts and balls and birds and come to deal with prefects and kings and the getting of gold and estates and slaves, these are the qualities which pass on with us, one stage of life taking the place of another as the greater punishments of the law take the place of the schoolmaster's cane.[6]

Basic Ideas

EXISTENCE OF GOD Augustine built his philosophy upon the intellectually provable existence of God. For the order of the universe indicates a creator; our conscience leads us to believe in a divine moral force. Creation itself indicates contingency and demands a necessary cause. Furthermore, Augustine maintained, our knowledge is relative and finite; we cannot be certain of anything unless we have an absolute standard of truth: God. The skeptics only have to open their eyes and see the order of nature, to listen to the voice of mankind, which universally and eloquently proclaims that God exists.

How can we find God? Is knowledge sufficient? Is the road of philosophy the only true road? Augustine answers that knowledge itself is not adequate. Above all, we must *love* God. The

6. *Ibid.*, I, xix.

search for the supreme principle is profoundly emotional and transcends intellectual desires and interests. In the highest stage of knowledge, we have a mystical experience; we feel the presence of a divine light that reveals the splendor and majesty of God.

The man who experiences this illumination realizes that scientific knowledge is secondary. He can only feel the presence of God; he cannot describe it in intellectual terms. He sees life from a new viewpoint, not from the standpoint of fragmentary and partial truth but from the perspective of an all-embracing principle of reality.

IMMORTALITY OF THE SOUL   Together with the existence of God, the spirituality of the soul was vigorously affirmed by Augustine. He denied that the soul is material and that it existed in another form before man was born. The soul itself is a copy of the Divine Trinity. Its three manifestations, memory, understanding, and will, mirror the three aspects of the Trinity. Through self-examination and contemplation, we can substantiate the truths that authority has transmitted to us.

Augustine believed that the immortality of the soul could be established by reason. He claimed that the soul is the principle of life and is superior to the body; hence, when the body dies, the soul continues. Identifying soul and reason, he maintained that reason transcends the limitations of matter. Since reason is eternal, the soul likewise must be eternal. The soul, furthermore, is part of eternal truths, which are not bound by spatial and temporal limitations. Just as certain laws of the universe always prevail, so the soul will be everlasting.

The philosophy of Augustine depends on the authority of the Church. We are frail and insecure as long as we are outside of it; within, we find comfort, grace and salvation. The Church, as a distributor of the sacraments, has a unique function in life, for the sacraments mediate between man and God. It does not matter whether the priests lead blameless lives or lives of immorality, for the sacraments are valid regardless of the moral standards of the administrators.

With all his power, Augustine led the fight against individualism. The edicts of the Church are not to be disobeyed, its fundamental doctrines are not to be questioned, and its basic tenets are not to be challenged. As the link between Christ and man, the Church stands throughout the centuries as a visible expression of God's purpose in the universe.

The question now arises whether or not the Church has national limits. Should its work be confined only to Europe? Augustine answers in the negative: he was certain that the function of the Church was universal, and he looked forward to the day when there would be only one Church, one sacramental system, and one system of philosophy.

The political ideals of Augustine are best represented by *The City of God*. This work was written under the impact of the invasion of Rome by the Vandals, which caused immense suffering to the Romans and which shook their faith in the Christian religion. To Augustine, the sacking of Rome was only an incident in a vast world drama. For life on earth is essentially a prelude to life in the beyond. This is merely a journey, infinite from the standpoint of the present but infinitesimal from the viewpoint of God. The power of kings and emperors, which most men admire and worship, is shattered by the providence of God, who has no respect for earthly fortunes.

In Augustine's view of history, there is a perpetual opposition between the *city of God* and the *city of the devil*. Outwardly, the city of God appears to be defeated, for the world is frequently dominated by the wicked, but in reality the city of God will triumph and the sinners will be punished through God's justice.

God, according to Augustine, is not a transcendent force; rather, He takes part in shaping history. He sees to it that the arrogance of earthly rulers is punished. This explains the disintegration of the Roman Empire, for it had defied the laws of morality and now was reaping the results of its crimes. History ends with the dwellers in the city of the devil being punished, while those who belong to the city of God enjoy infinite bliss.

In this dualistic concept of history there can be no neutrality. Every man had to make up his mind and join either the forces of righteousness or the legions of doom. This was not a solitary struggle; the good were aided by angels, the saints, and by the power of the Church; the evil forces were supported by the devil and were under the influence of the most corrupt and treacherous men of all ages.

In Augustine's moral ideals the puritanical strain is only too evident. Thus, he inveighed against the temptations of the flesh, identifying original sin with Adam's temptation by Eve. What is to be preferred—the life of the hermit or the life of family relations? Augustine had no doubts in regard to this problem: Any relationship with a woman undermines a man's love of God; it is impossible to love the flesh and the spirit at the same time. Hence, asceticism is the only road for those who really want to dedicate themselves to the service of God.

Few thinkers have been more aware than St. Augustine of the ever-present reality of sin. Sin represents a rebellion against the majesty of God; thus, it comes in a thousand different forms, subjectively and objectively. As slaves of desire, we frequently crave that which is incompatible with our salvation.

Augustine was deeply pessimistic regarding human merit. In fact, since the fall of Adam all of us have deserved damnation. He made it clear that God, from the beginning, had elected most men for damnation, while only the minority were destined for heaven. This doctrine of predestination at once caused much controversy, for it made God's will arbitrary and detracted from the freedom of the will. The Pelagians took the opposite viewpoint and insisted that man's free will can attain salvation. However, the Church maintained a middle road between the

Pelagians and Augustine, and tried to give hope to the individual that through faith in the sacraments, Christ, and good works, salvation could be achieved.

Educational Principles

Augustine, influenced by Plato, believed that truth can be grasped only by the few. Truth is not relative but absolute, and it is taught through the Church. The task of education is to avoid independent judgment and to subordinate private ideas to ecclesiastical organization.

Real truth can be found through mystical knowledge when the mind has been purified by prayer and contemplation. Most individuals are guided by their senses, and thus they become the victims of illusion and falsehood.

The Christian scholar should be acquainted with literature, rhetoric, logic, arithmetic, ethics, and natural philosophy; these subjects are not to be studied as ends in themselves, and care should be taken that they do not corrupt the scholar's faith. They are, however, only preludes to the study of Church doctrines.

Even the study of mathematics may be helpful. Augustine felt that the Bible was full of number symbolism, and that mathematics was a tool of clear thinking. Science, in general, could be a method of combating superstitition.

He warns the Christian again and again not to be seduced by classical learning. Classical studies are full of error and falsehood and overemphasize man's rational powers.

Learning cannot be promoted without discipline. The teacher has to control the child, and if necessary has to use the cane and the strap. Thus the pupil learns to control his evil impulses and becomes conscious of the importance of obedience. Augustine, constantly aware of original sin, believed that children are naturally evil; therefore, their nature has to be changed by the schoolmaster.

Augustine's Influence

The influence of Augustine can scarcely be overestimated. His ideas inspired many great medieval thinkers, especially Anselm. St. Thomas Aquinas rejected the Platonism of the Bishop, but he shared with him a basic faith in the authority of the Church and a strong hatred of all forms of heresy. Duns Scotus, theologist of the fourteenth century, followed St. Augustine in his belief about the separation of faith and reason, as well as in his insistence that man is nothing, while God is all-powerful.

The impact of St. Augustine on Calvin produced a system of thought that stressed the sovereignty of God, the depravity of man, and the idea that man is predestined to either heaven or hell. Like St. Augustine, Calvin emphasized the importance of puritanism. Was not the flesh an obstacle in man's search for salvation? Did not earthly pleasures alienate man from God?

In the United States Jonathan Edwards absorbed the spirit of Augustinianism. With eloquence Edwards pictured the tortures of damnation. Like the Bishop of Hippo, Edwards believed that hell-fire was an actual reality and that most individuals would land in hell rather than in heaven.

In a more sophisticated vein, Reinhold Niebuhr, in *The Nature and Destiny of Man,* represents an Augustinian version of history. Niebuhr pictures man as a rebel against God, and he is certain that, without faith, man is doomed and civilization will perish.

Many religious existentialists have claimed Augustine as one of their foremost saints. Augustine indicated that man's personal awareness of God is most significant, and that life demands a religion of the heart rather than of the intellect. We are still wrestling with the problem that agitated the Bishop of Hippo: How can man find security in a world governed by flux and rebellion?

Augustine as an educator influenced both Catholic and Protestant ideas. By pointing out the need for discipline and puritanism he made education a rigorous process. By subordinating free inquiry to orthodoxy he made education a form of indoctrination. This view is still cherished by many religious teachers in the twentieth century.

St. Augustine and the scholars that followed in his footsteps were not interested in new ideas. They wanted to preserve the orthodoxy of the past. Living in a period of turmoil, they were conservators rather than creators. Still, the West owes them a debt, for they laid the foundations of both Protestant and Catholic education.

PART II

11. Abelard

The conflict between Peter Abelard (1079–1142) and Bernard of Clairvaux was more than a battle of clashing personalities. They typified the two conflicting viewpoints of the twelfth century: the desire for reason versus the unquestioning acceptance of dogmatic truths. But it was mainly Abelard's work that lent such historic interest to the struggle, for Bernard represented simply the traditional ascetic spirit and the reformist tendencies in the Church. Although he was one of the outstanding saints of the Middle Ages, he did not contribute anything original to either the emotional or the intellectual development of the period.

Abelard, on the other hand, is part of the educational renaissance that enlightened the twelfth century. His accomplishments tended to give greater prominence to logical thinking and rational investigation of Church dogmas.[1]

It is interesting and instructive to follow his career. He was born near Nantes of noble parents. His father, Berengar, although a feudal lord, exhibited none of the then prevalent uncivilized habits and coarse manners of his class. He had his son

----

1. For a survey of Abelard's achievement, see J. McCabe, *Peter Abelard;* C. de Rémusat, *Abélard,* H. Rashdall, *Universities of Europe in the Middle Ages.*

instructed in letters, and encouraged him to pursue a scholarly career. Very early in his life Abelard made up his mind to relinquish his inheritance, since he possessed little proclivity for fighting. In his own words, he "gave up the lure of Mars to be educated in the lap of Minerva."

Abelard was a boy of no more than fifteen or sixteen years when he left his home to obtain a higher education. As a wandering scholar he availed himself of the best teachers in the various educational centers of the day, and is reported to have been a student of Roscellinus, canon at Tours and one of the most famous dialecticians of his time. This teacher leaned in the direction of nominalism and maintained that universals have no reality apart from particulars. Roscellinus had freely employed reason in the explanation of the Trinity; and this application of reason in addition to his nominalism had led him to statements that deviated from the official church dogma; he was therefore strictly condemned by a council. From Roscellinus, Abelard learned the fundamentals of logic, but he later showed so little respect for Roscellinus' knowledge that he did not even mention his studies under him in his autobiography, *Historia calamitatum.*

Arriving in Paris in the full vigor and enthusiasm of his youth, Abelard became a student of the most formidable philosopher of the day, William of Champeaux. The latter enjoyed the reputation of being a veritable pillar of orthodoxy and was considered so brilliant and stimulating a teacher that students from nearly every country flocked to Paris to hear him. As an orthodox churchman, William held, contrary to Roscellinus, that universals exist independently from any material substance, and that the group has a real existence outside of the mind conceiving it and apart from the individuals making it up.

The controversy between the realists, William's followers, and the nominalists, Roscellinus' scholars, aroused considerable attention in intellectual circles. Wherever students gathered, the

question was assiduously debated; in fact, it became the outstanding intellectual problem of the century.

Abelard plunged into the conflict with all the arrogance of his
youth and the brilliance of his debating abilities. Strictly speaking, he was neither a realist nor a nominalist; for him, universals
were neither things nor names but *concepts,* predicated upon particulars. Although his viewpoint was neither original nor new,
it still constituted a formidable weapon in his hands against the
realism of William. Abelard lost no time in attacking the famous
teacher. One can imagine the delight of his fellow students and the
chagrin of the teacher at hearing day after day his pupil's caustic
jibes.

Soon William of Champeaux was forced to retreat from his
extreme realism. Students began to lose faith in him. At last,
after taking monastic vows, he retired to the bishopric of Châlons-
sur-Marne, where he became friendly with Bernard of Clairvaux.
He could never forgive Abelard for the humiliation suffered at
his hands.[2]

In the meantime, before this triumph, Abelard had retired
from Paris and established himself as a professor at Melun, near
Paris, where he taught his subtle philosophy to a large crowd of
admirers. So successful was he that in 1115, after he had been
denied the right to teach in the cathedral school of Notre Dame
at Paris, he taught at St. Geneviève, and students left his rivals to
listen to his stimulating lectures.

His health was poor, however, and this condition, together
with his filial duty, took him back to Brittany, where he stayed
for several years. Later, when he looked back more impartially
upon his first academic triumphs, he repented of having incurred
the antagonism of William of Champeaux, whom he regarded as
one source of his afflictions.

2. Later he championed the theory of *indifferentism,* which tries to mediate
between extreme realism and extreme nominalism. It holds that while substance
is individual, it possesses at the same time universal properties.

After his return to Paris and St. Geneviève, Abelard found that his scholarly fame had not been eclipsed during his absence. Notwithstanding promising opportunities, he decided to study theology at Laon in order to gain acquaintance with the "queen of sciences." Possibly his mother, who had become very religious, influenced him. He chose to be instructed by one of the outstanding theologians of his age, Anselm of Laon, who had made Laon a center of theology. But again Abelard appeared little impressed by the authority of the master; he exhibited the same contumacy as he had against Roscellinus and William of Champeaux. In taking up theology, Abelard did not discard his logical and progressive mind, so he could scarcely be expected to agree with the conservative Anselm. He ridiculed the master as one who "filled his house with smoke rather than lighting it with the blaze" and compared him in his empty eloquence and distrust of reason to a barren tree that is like the "shadow of a mighty name."

Abelard's character is illustrated by an incident that took place at Anselm's school. With his usual tactlessness, he missed classes and thought it unnecessary to attend Anselm's lectures. In addition, he referred to Anselm in uncomplimentary terms. During a dispute with his fellow students, he stoutly maintained that it was superfluous for scholars to have instruction in the Scriptures, and boasted that he, the beginner, could lecture upon the most difficult prophets on but a day's notice. He selected Ezekiel as the topic of his lecture and impressed his audience to such an extent by his learning and eloquence that more students were eager to hear him. Anselm's feelings at the phenomenal success of the new student have not been recorded, but he certainly was not willing to tolerate his competition. Abelard voluntarily departed for Paris to resume his teaching, regarding himself as entirely justified in his arrogant behavior.

In Paris, he was offered the chair at Notre Dame. There he reached the zenith of his career. From all over Europe students thronged to Paris to hear Master Abelard. They admired him for his extraordinary mind and subtle reasoning, his clear and intriguing lectures, which were enlivened by disputes, his use of imagery and frequent quotations from classical authors. Besides these scholarly gifts, he was quite handsome and expressed his ideas in a rich, well-modulated voice.

The disputes of his scholars awakened the mental slumber of medieval Europe. Abelard, by his unique gifts, had challenged the imagination of his eager students. They learned from him that scholarship can be a way of life, not reserved for the monk in his solitary cell but open to all who possess inquiring minds. This movement took place at the time when belief in the existence of an *absolute* truth was universal. The young students could be as fanatical and singleminded in their quest for enlightenment as the monk who consecrated his life to the service of God or as the knight who went to conquer Jerusalem.

Then Abelard made an unfortunate step. He fell in love with Héloïse, the niece of the canon Fulbert. The canon had placed her under the tutorship of Abelard—a fateful event for both master and student. Abelard described Héloïse as a girl of remarkable beauty and supreme intelligence. No wonder that they became thoroughly enamored of one another! Later they were married secretly. Consequently, Abelard put his wife into a convent. This step would, she thought, for all practical purposes undo the marriage and also save the career of her husband. But her uncle who felt betrayed by Abelard, took a terrible revenge by hiring ruffians to inflict upon Abelard the most terrible of all mutilations: they deprived him of his manhood.

This event proved to be the turning point of Abelard's career. Not only the physical pain that he suffered, but the shame that he felt influenced his decision. According to the old Church laws, his chances for an ecclesiastical career were now lost. In his torment he decided to enter the monastery of Saint-Denis, and he persuaded Héloïse to take the veil at Argenteuil. Henceforth, until his death in 1142 his life was full of suffering, disappointments, and persecutions. Yet his scholarly influence did not wane; students deluged him with petitions to resume his teaching. He consented and instructed a huge gathering at a priory belonging to Saint-Denis. So great was the deluge of students that many could not be fed or housed, and the neighboring schools suffered a marked loss in attendance.

Abelard and the Church

By the publication of his *Introduction to Theology*,[3] written to bring the light of dialectic in the mystery of the Trinity, Abelard's enemies were given a chance to accuse him of heresy. At the Council of Soissons, in 1121, he was condemned, forced to burn the book with his own hands, and sentenced to do penance in a monastery. Soon thereafter, the papal legate reversed the judgment of the council and pronounced Abelard innocent; hence, he could return to Saint-Denis.

This time Abelard incurred the wrath of the monks by asserting that Dionysius could not have been the founder of their monastery. Regardless of the truth of his statements, the monks would not believe him, since a loss of revenue and reputation was involved. His life was in jeopardy, and so one night he fled from the monastery to the diocese of Troyes, where he built himself a hermitage and dedicated it to the Holy Ghost.

This action, again, constituted an insult to his enemies, who had taken a stand against his dialectical investigation of the Trinity. It is obvious that the sentence of the Council of Soissons had had no visible effect upon him; to the contrary, it had made him more critical and challenging.

Abelard seized the opportunity to leave the hermitage when he was called to become Abbot of St. Gildas in Brittany. Yet his troubles were not ended; St. Gildas needed reform, and Abelard sought to improve the moral condition of the monastery. The monks responded by making several attempts to kill him. In order to save his life, he finally left the monastery in 1136, and returned to Paris, where he resumed his teaching.

3. His other theological works were *De Trinitate* and *Theologia Christiana*.

At this time Bernard became interested in Abelard's writings, because of Abelard's association with Arnold of Brescia, who taught that the Church should go back to the apostolic ways of poverty. He was not the only ecclesiastic intent upon silencing Abelard, but he took the lead in opposing him. At the Council of Sens, in 1141, Bernard secured the condemnation of the master dialectician, who was charged by William of Saint Thierry with being "the abuser and not the disciple of the faith; the corrector and not the imitator of the authorized masters."

Abelard did not wait for his final sentence by the council, having decided to appeal to Rome. But he never arrived there; instead, he entered the monastery at Cluny. Here, Peter the Venerable, who disliked Bernard for his criticism of Cluny and for his excessive puritanism, was a more pleasant associate. Besides, Abelard was looked upon as a distinguished guest at Cluny, for he was still considered one of the ablest minds of Europe. In agreeable surroundings he spent his last months in calm meditation, officially reconciled to the Church. He died in 1142.

Abelard's Character

In a letter of condolence, which was as sincere as it was eloquent, Peter attempted to comfort Héloïse by reminding her that she and her husband would be reunited in Heaven. Probably Abelard's only happy experience, if one excepts his teachings at Paris after his entrance into Saint-Denis, arose out of his relationship with Héloïse. The hermitage at Troyes, which he left when he became the Abbot of St. Gildas, he gave to Héloïse, who was chosen abbess of a group of nuns.

To her, religion was less important than Abelard: a letter from him proved more valuable than any ecclesiastical office. Her love was self-sacrificing and strong, defying the caprices of fortune. In her letters to Abelard, Héloïse claimed that she would rather be his mistress than the wife of an emperor. How she sympathized with him in his many calamities. Seldom have letters unfolded more feeling and attachment. She confessed that she was constantly blaming God for the injustices inflicted upon Abelard, and that she was still reliving the days when they had been together.

Abelard's replies to her, however, represent a new facet of his character. He had absorbed a deeply religious feeling, and he now called her the "spouse of Christ." These letters disclose an Abelard who was not concerned with mundane pleasures but only with the salvation of his soul; who, furthermore, expressed himself as if he were insensible to human feelings: "In my fate I find the working of grace," he wrote to console her, yet probably thereby deepening her agonies. Toward the last, his letters turned to purely religious topics, to the history of the nuns, to hymns and prayers.

Nothing illustrates Abelard's character more vividly than his view of the persecutions he suffered. To him they were indeed tragic, and he lived in constant anticipation of a new disaster, like a hero in a Greek tragedy. His autobiography was written under the impact of misfortune while he occupied the abbotcy of St. Gildas. Of one thing he felt certain—that his enemies were all motivated by the basest of all motives. In his opinion they were either ignorant, immoral, or envious. Such are the impressions one obtains from his descriptions of William of Champeaux, Anselm of Laon, and Roscellinus. His only comfort lay in recalling the fate of Christ and the example of the Apostles. By opposing the errors of his time, he thought he might imitate the example of the saints, hoping finally that everything would work out to the "good of the just." Even in these thoughts, and though crushed by many misfortunes, Abelard was thoroughly convinced of his own brilliance.

Abelard's Beliefs

The strange feature of the story of Abelard is that he combated the official heretics of his day as violently as did Bernard. He wrote with vehemence against Tanchelm, who called himself the Son of God, and Peter of Bruys, who was forcing men to be rebaptized and telling them to remove crucifixes and to cease celebrating the mass. But with similar ardor Abelard turned his rebukes against those who thought ignorance in credal matters blessed, relying upon "Amens" as signs of religious devotion, believing the more readily dogmas which could neither be understood nor discussed.

It is not surprising to note that Abelard showed no respect for authority. He criticized, disrespectfully, misstatements in the Bible and questioned the infallibility of the Prophets and Apostles. He knew that the Church Fathers themselves did not agree upon many points of the faith. Therefore he wrote his famous *Sic et non,* containing one hundred and fifty-eight propositions upon which the Fathers disagreed. The purpose in his compilation was to incite a quest for truth among his young readers. "For by doubting we come to inquiry, by inquiry we discover the truth." Faith itself Abelard called judgment, or opinion, about things unseen, a definition that scandalized Bernard.

Abelard considered the dogmas of the faith reasonable and reasoning itself a noble activity. By reason, Abelard held, man becomes like God and most worthy of his creator; hence reason for the dialectician was the highest activity. Not only the faith, he said, but even the universe obeys the laws of rationality. Yet, there are limits to the application of dialectic in religious disputes. In an earlier theological work, Abelard attacked some Sophists who applied logic in religious disputes without any constructive purpose.

Abelard's religion was far removed from the practices current in the twelfth century. He was a bitter enemy of the growing materialism in the Church. As a scholar, he was too sophisticated to believe in crude miracles and to take a deep interest in the Crusades and other fanatical enterprises of his contemporaries. Yet even a man of his caliber could not escape some of the limitations of his time. He too talked occasionally about the devil and his magic powers.

Abelard's Moral Ideals

It would be a serious mistake to regard Abelard as merely a vain professor with a love for disputations and a desire for glory. All his life he cherished the ideal of living a philosopher's life. For him this involved very definitely the acceptance of poverty. Héloïse had told him that riches and philosophic detachment cannot be combined, and he himself had written about such philosophers as the Pythagoreans, who lived in the wilderness in order to escape the tempting luxuries of the city. How greatly Abelard admired and idealized the ancient philosophers can be seen in his frequent quotations from their books, even in his discussions of theological questions. He thought that they too were saved, and that in many ways they had foretold Christian truths.

In his work *Dialogue Between a Philosopher, a Jew and a Christian,* the philosopher seems to have the best of the argument. Philosophy, Abelard felt, is more in accord with Chrisianity than with Judaism, but his ideal type of Christianity was a positive moral law rather than a matter of prohibitions and ceremonies, a religion divested of a literal hell and heaven. He maintained that heaven constitutes communion with God, and hell a separation from God. The dialogue was not completed, but the philosopher finally agrees that the greatest good is not mere virtue but communion with God. Faith triumphs by this concession, although it is a very intellectual faith.

12. Luther and Loyola

Martin Luther (1483–1546) is one of the most impressive personalities in world history. The importance of his work equals that
of Augustine and Paul. He not only was the guiding spirit in the
rebellion against the Church, but he helped kindle the flame of
German nationalism, which reached a climax in the twentieth
century.

His parents belonged to the bourgeoisie; his father had advanced to membership in the town council; and both mother and
father were pious and strict with their children. Luther's youth,
like Augustine's, was blackened by terrible beatings administered
at home. At school, also, the teachers sought by flogging to drive
the devil out of their students, a superstition that has not yet
been completely overcome. Martin Luther, however, was a brilliant student. At twenty-two he was a master of arts; at twenty-
nine, a professor of theology; and at the age of thirty-two, vicar
of the Augustinian monks, in charge of eleven monasteries.

In spite of his intelligence, Luther was as blindly devout as his
parents and imbued with just as many fears. He was given to
black moods, during which life seemed to be utterly futile. He
always had a vivid awarness of the devil. His spiritual develop-

ment was strongly influenced too by the death of a close companion.

On October 31, 1517, Luther nailed his ninety-five theses on the church door at Wittenberg. They were directed against the efforts of a shrewd Dominican monk, Johann Tetzel, who was trying to aid not only Pope Leo X but also the Archbishop of Magdeburg and Mainz, who was heavily indebted to the Fuggers (a family of bankers) and was trying to get out of their clutches. Tetzel, a brilliant salesman, made supreme efforts to achieve his goal for money was urgently needed. He preached powerful sermons about the torments of purgatory, and he showed how effective papal indulgences would be. His methods outraged Martin Luther, whose ninety-five theses challenged Tetzel's interpretation of the indulgences.

How did Luther succeed in his struggle against the Church? He was aided by the then prevalent nationalistic fervor in Germany, by the support of the middle class, and by the disunity of his enemies. Martyrs like John Huss had paved the way for his victory. He had an excellent strategist, Melanchthon, and some of the ablest theologians were on his side. His own personality aided in the victory, and his speeches were powerful and overwhelming. His use of invective was unexcelled; not for a moment did he doubt the righteousness of his cause.

Martin Luther was a strange mixture of disparate traits. Reading the records of his dinner conversations, one sees him as a typical member of the German middle class. He married, not for love but to "please his father, vex the Pope, and spite the devil." There was little of the romantic strain in Luther, so earnest and so persistent was he in his search for God. He was superstitious and is said to have thrown an inkwell at the devil.

Luther represented the dualism of the German soul. On the one hand, there was an adherence to law and order; on the other, the kind of fanaticism that makes its possessor oblivious to humanity and solely concerned with the cause he champions.

Luther was a strong hater. Although Ulrich Zwingli, the Swiss reformer, had similar goals, a controversy between the two over the Lord's Supper caused a decisive split. To Luther, Zwingli was "mad and blasphemous"; Erasmus also was "bad through and through," and the papacy was positively a "den of thieves." The spirit of love and charity did not predominate in Martin Luther. Essentially, he was a fighter, an uncompromising warrior of God, spurred on in his crusade by the belief that he was speaking for a sacred cause.

In his religious doctrines he attacked with vigor the tenets of Romanism: first, that the Pope is superior to all temporal authorities; second, that only the Pope may interpret the Scriptures; and third, that only the Pope may call Church councils. Against these claims Luther insisted upon a universal priesthood of believers. There can be no distinction between bishops and priests, he declared, and between princes and popes, for all share alike in the heritage of Christ. Why should only the Pope interpret the Scriptures when many Christians have genuine faith? Luther could find no evidence in the Scriptures for this ecclesiastical claim, and he rejected it with contempt. As for the Church councils, he pointed out that they had been called together in antiquity by all the Apostles and elders, not by St. Peter alone. Was not the Council of Nicaea called by an emperor and not by the Bishop of Rome?

The implications of Luther's teachings were far-reaching, for they aided in the development of religious democracy. Again and again Luther spoke of Christian freedom. The seat of faith, he maintained, is not in the Pope or in the Church organization but in the individual worshipper, each of whom has a direct personal relationship with God.

At the same time Luther's faith had several negative aspects. It substituted the authority of the Bible for the domination of the Church. According to Luther, each Christian is able to interpret the Bible for himself, but the application of his theory led to endless intellectual confusion. His own colleague, Carlstadt, came to the conclusion, on the authority of the Old Testament, that polygamy was ordained by God; others believed they had been inspired with the prophetic spirit and, without any religious training, were ready to convert their contemporaries.

Luther's most fateful action came with the Peasants' War. Upheavals such as this had taken place in 1476, 1491, 1493, 1502, 1512, 1517, but the rebellion of 1524-26 was the most momentous, for it included not only the peasants but also city workers and even some of the lower aristocracy. At first Luther supported the peasants, since he sympathized with their cause and knew their grievances. He thought a new order would arise to curtail the privileges of the aristocracy. For the merchant class he had even less love, and often denounced their insatiable greed. Yet there were great doubts in Luther's mind. He knew his movement could not succeed without the support of the princes and the aristocracy. He also knew that the middle class was a powerful factor in the spread of Protestantism, for although the peasants had faith they had little money. Thus, the best attitude for him was to remain neutral and counsel a course of moderation.

In 1525 Luther wrote a pamphlet called *An Admonition to Peace*. He used numerous arguments to convince the peasants of their duty to submit to the established order. Christian liberty is not something derived from one's occupation, he wrote, but from one's spiritual state. Consequently, a serf could be just as free as his master. Follow your vocation, he counseled the serfs; submit to the laws of the land, just as Christ submitted to Caesar. He quoted the Old Testament to show that the patriarchs had slaves. Why should the serfs rebel against the Old Testament? The peasants did not listen to him but followed their revolt against the privileged class with wholesale looting, and the aristocracy called upon Luther to show his opposition to such activities. He obliged them and wrote against the "murderous and thieving" peasant bands. They should be treated as outlaws, he declared.

The peasants retorted by referring to Bible verses suggesting that man is created free and equal. Luther cited the New Testament and the action of Jesus in dealing with the Romans. When the peasants were subdued, he justified the harsh reprisals of the aristocracy and vehemently attacked his critics, who had urged mercy for the peasants.

In reality, the demands of the peasants were rather moderate. Their Twelve Articles demanded such things as the right to elect and discharge their own pastors and to determine the amount of taxes they were to pay. They also asked for the abolition of serfdom.

When the revolt of the peasants was crushed, the backbone of a truly democratic Germany was broken. Another formidable rebellion broke out in 1848, which was again crushed by the forces of conservatism. The Weimar Republic likewise was sabotaged by rightist forces after World War I.

Luther reinforced the ideal of obedience for the common people. Again and again he counseled them to follow the laws of the land. He taught that to break the civil law is almost as evil as to violate the commandments of God. With his help the forces of reaction in Germany used the mantle of legality to maintain the subservience of the common man.

In his formal theology Luther went back to St. Paul and stressed the primacy of faith as symbolized by Jesus Christ. Acts of charity were insignificant, he taught, compared to the overpowering faith in God's concern for all men and His desire to rescue lost sinners. In the Middle Ages it had been the Virgin rather than Jesus who was asked to intercede for the frailties of man; in Lutheranism, however, Jesus became the living symbol of Christian experience.

Regarding moral failings, Luther was far more strict than the medieval Church and far less cosmopolitan than the Italian Humanists. It would seem that moral rigorism is strongly imbedded in the middle-class character. German philosophers from

Leibniz to Fichte have emphasized the importance of morality. Italian thinkers, like Petrarch and Croce, on the other hand, had more respect for intelligence than for virtue and were more inclined to look upon the weaknesses of the flesh with a tolerant eye. To Luther, morality meant respectability. His ideal man is extremely devout, but at the same time narrow-minded, literalistic, and self-righteous.

Luther transformed the church service and made the sermon its most outstanding feature. This action aided in the development of Christian oratory. The effectiveness of a minister came to depend upon his eloquence; if he had little to say or was full of platitudes, he bored his congregation and possibly alienated them from religion. In the early days of Protestantism the sermons were very long and inattention was penalized.

One advantage was afforded, however, by the action of Luther and other reformers, for they substituted the vernacular language for the traditional Latin; hence the people could follow the church service more easily. Moreover, Luther's translation of the Bible was a landmark in the development of the German language. His style is powerful, moving, and almost epic in quality.

Education

Luther regarded the existing educational institutions as extremely inadequate. In the first place, they overemphasized scholasticism, which to Luther was a decadent method of philosophy. In the second place, they overrated rhetoric; this gave man an exaggerated pride in his accomplishments. In the third place, they endangered the moral development of young people. The universities especially, according to Luther, were "dens of iniquity."

Education, according to Luther, rested upon the instruction a child received at home. The first commandment was to honor our parents. The debt owed to them by their children had to be clearly recognized. A wayward child had to be disciplined;

otherwise, Satanic impulses would find expression and complete delinquency would result. This did not imply that the rod should be constantly used by the teacher; on the contrary, Luther urged a more humane form of discipline. All in all, he taught, inspiration was the best method of education.

In discussing the curriculums of the various schools Luther maintained that the elementary schools should stress religion as well as Latin, history, and music. Luther especially favored music in the curriculum, because it could inspire moral sentiments in children. The catechism, which he translated into the vernacular, was to be taught to children. Even girls were to receive some form of education, with particular emphasis on the instruction in religion.

Luther also urged a thorough reform of universities. The study of the Holy Bible was to become the core of the university curriculum. Opposed to scientific investigation, he followed the geocentric emphasis of Ptolemy. Among the subjects of study that he recommended were Latin, Greek, Hebrew, rhetoric, logic, and poetry. The main aim of university education was spiritual: It was to prepare candidates for the clergy.

The educational chasm between Luther and Erasmus was deep. Erasmus was a strong believer in the classics and independent thinking; Luther favored the role of faith; to him the Bible was the textbook for man. Unlike Erasmus, Luther had little sympathy for the learning of the ancients who, he thought, had a rather inferior system of morality.

In a letter to the mayors and aldermen of Germany he reminded them of the importance of education:

It is indeed a sin and shame that we must be aroused and incited to the duty of educating our children and of considering their highest interests, whereas nature itself should move us thereto, and the example of the heathen affords us varied instruction. There is no irrational animal that does not care for and instruct its young in what they should know, except the ostrich, of which God says, She leaveth her eggs in the earth, and warmeth them in the dust; and is hardened against her young ones, as though they were not hers. And what would it avail if we possessed and performed all else, and became perfect saints, if we neglect that for which we chiefly live, namely, to care for the young? In my judgment there is no other outward offense that in the sight of God so heavily burdens the world, and deserves such heavy chastisement, as the neglect to educate children.

Parents neglect this duty from various causes. In the first place, there are some who are so lacking in piety and uprightness that they would not do it if they could, but, like the ostrich, harden themselves against their own offspring, and do nothing for them. In the second place, the great majority of parents are unqualified for it, and do not understand how children should be brought up and taught. In the third place, even if parents were qualified and willing to do it themselves, yet on account of the other employments and household duties, they have no time for it, so that necessity requires us to have teachers for public schools, unless each parent employ a private instructor.

Therefore it will be the duty of the mayors and councils to exercise the greatest care over the young. For since the happiness, honor, and life of the city are committed to their hands, they would be held recreant before God and the world, if they did not day and night, with all their power, seek its welfare and improvement.[1]

Languages are to be studied to frustrate the designs of the devil:

But you say again, if we shall and must have schools, what is the use to teach Latin, Greek, Hebrew, and other liberal arts? Is it not enough to teach the Scriptures, which are necessary to salvation, in the mother tongue? To which I answer: I know, alas! that we Germans must always remain irrational brutes, as we are deservedly called by surrounding nations. But I wonder why we do not also say: of what use to us are silk, wine, spices, and other foreign articles, since we ourselves have an abundance of wine, corn, wool, flax, wood, and stone in the German states, not only

1. Martin Luther, *Letter to the Mayors and Aldermen of All the Cities of German in Behalf of Christian Schools.* . . .

for our necessities, but also for embellishment and ornament? The languages and other liberal arts, which are not only harmless, but even a greater ornament, benefit, and honor than these things, both for understanding the Holy Scriptures and carrying on the civil government, we are disposed to despise; and the foreign articles which are neither necessary nor useful, and which besides greatly impoverish us, we are willing to dispense with. Are we not rightly called German dunces and brutes?

Indeed, if the languages were of no practical benefit, we ought still to feel an interest in them as a wonderful gift of God, with which he has now blessed Germany almost beyond all other lands. We do not find many instances in which Satan has fostered them through the universities and cloisters; on the contrary, these institutions have fiercely inveighed and continue to inveigh against them. For the devil scented the danger that would threaten his kingdom, if the languages should be generally studied. But since he could not wholly prevent their cultivation, he aims at least to confine them within such narrow limits that they will of themselves decline and fall into disuse.[2]

The study of the gospel and of languages must be joined together:

Therefore, my beloved countrymen, let us open our eyes, thank God for his precious treasure, and take pains to preserve it and to frustrate the design of Satan. For we can not deny that, although the Gospel has come and daily comes through the Holy Spirit, it has come by means of the languages, and through them must increase and be preserved. For when God wished through the apostles to spread the Gospel abroad in all the world, he gave the languages for that purpose; and by means of the Roman empire he made Latin and Greek the language of many lands, that his Gospel might speedily bear fruit far and wide. He has done the same now. For a time no one understood why God had revived the study of the languages; but now we see that it was for the sake of the Gospel, which he wished to bring to light, and thereby expose and destroy the reign of Antichrist. For the same reason he gave Greece

2. *Ibid.*

a prey to the Turks, in order that Greek scholars, driven from home and scattered abroad, might bear the Greek tongue to other countries, and thereby excite an interest in the study of languages.

And let this be kept in mind, that we shall not preserve the Gospel without the languages. The languages are the scabbard in which the word of God is sheathed. They are the casket in which this jewel is enshrined; the cask in which this wine is kept; the chamber in which this food is stored. And, to borrow a figure from the Gospel itself, they are the baskets in which this bread and fish and fragments are preserved. If through neglect we lose the languages (which may God forbid), we shall not only lose the Gospel, but it will finally come to pass that we shall lose also the ability to speak and write either Latin or German.[3]

Finally, Luther urged the establishment of educational libraries:

This must be taken into consideration by all who earnestly desire to see such schools established and the languages preserved in the German states; that no cost nor pains should be spared to procure good libraries in suitable buildings, especially in the large cities that are able to afford it. For if the knowledge of the Gospel and of every kind of learning is to be preserved, it must be embodied in books, as the prophets and apostles did, as I have already shown. This should be done, not only that our spiritual and civil leaders may have something to read and study, but also that good books may not be lost, and that the arts and languages may be preserved, with which God has graciously favored us.

All the kingdoms that have been distinguished in the world have bestowed care upon this matter, and particularly the Israelites, among whom Moses was the first to begin the work, who commanded them to preserve the book of the law in the ark of God, and put it under the care of the Levites, that anyone might procure copies from them. He even commanded the king to make a copy of this book in the hands of the Levites. Among other duties God directed the Levitical priesthood to preserve and attend to the books. Afterwards Joshua increased and improved this library, as

3. *Ibid.*

did Samuel subsequently, and David, Solomon, Isaiah, and many kings and prophets. Hence have come to us the Holy Scriptures of the Old Testament, which would not otherwise have been collected and preserved, if God had not required such diligence in regard to it.[4]

Loyola's Impact

The guiding spirit of the Church's Counter Reformation was Ignatius of Loyola (1491–1556), a young nobleman. He started out to be a soldier, but turned to religion during his convalescence from a wound. At Manresa he went through a spiritual crisis and practiced the most severe types of asceticism; his feelings were like those of Luther at Erfurt. He tried all the accepted religious means of absolution and consulted various spiritual leaders, but in vain. He then began to keep a record of his sins so that he might become even more conscious of them. Seven times a day he prayed; three times daily he burned himself with fire. In addition, he fasted and his body became so frail that he almost died. He cried out: "Show me, O Lord, where I can find Thee; I will follow like a dog, if I can only learn the way of salvation." Still his spirit was not calmed. Frequently he thought of committing suicide, but at last he found the mercy of God.

As can be readily understood, Loyola was an uncomprising warrior. He followed his religious feelings wherever they led him. Obedience was the keynote of his life. He sacrificed everything to follow the dictates of the Church. The Jesuit order (Society of Jesus) that he founded was as compact and impersonal as a military organization. Its power was increased by an exact guide of meditation which he outlined. Meditation was conceived of as similar to a military drill. Five objects were stressed: sin and conscience, the earthly kingdom of Jesus, the Passion of Jesus, and the love for God and the glorious atonement of Jesus. It was explained that the pupil must live in complete solitude, that he

4. *Ibid.*

must empty his mind of all secular concerns, and that he must concentrate solely upon the objects of his meditation. No privacy was to be left to the disciple. He must reveal everything to his confessor, even his most trivial thoughts.

Loyola drafted an exact outline of the stages of meditation leading from prayer to personal contact with God. He laid emphasis upon visual experiences. The student was to see the torments of hell, actually smell the sulphur, and hear the shrieks of the sinners. The meditation did not admit anything from the Old Testament or allow any theological controversies.

To increase the power of the confessor, the disciple was ordered to make a complete self-examination in the afternoon and in the evening. His sins were to be entered in a book and shown to the confessor. His physical environment was also meticulously regulated. Certain exercises were designed for the morning and others for the evening. Loyola's exercises remind us somewhat of the techniques of psychoanalysis. The insight of the founder of the Jesuits was extremely penetrating. He utilized autosuggestion and hypnosis, and took advantage of all the subconscious fears of humanity. After such a course of training a disciple would lose his identity and subordinate himself to the teachings of the order. The same technique is often used by political parties in modern times, for they likewise stress confession, self-examination, and complete adherence to the party program.

It was the Jesuit spirit that was most responsible for recapturing many parts of Europe for the mother church. The Council of Trent was much influenced by Lainez, second head of the Jesuits and an uncompromising advocate of papal supremacy.

The Council of Trent reaffirmed the medievalism of the faith. The basis of Christianity, it claimed, is not the Bible alone but also the unwritten tradition of Christ's teachings as preserved by the Church. To be saved, faith alone is inadequate; a man must abide by the laws of God and those of Catholicism. As for the sacraments, the Council declared, they are all needed and they are holy, regardless of the moral life of the priests. The Council of Trent again confirmed the validity of the Vulgate, a Latin translation of the Bible, and made it clear that outside the Church no real Christianity can be found.

Educational Ideals

The most dynamic impact of Loyola came through the educational work of the Jesuits. In American civilization Jesuit institutions of higher education, like Loyola, Georgetown, and Notre Dame have made distinguished contributions to the cultural life of the nation. These universities emphasize both the humanities and the sciences; the classics are cultivated in a diligent way and the goal is to develop both the intellectual and the spiritual ideals of the students. Nor are the demands of the body slighted. Jesuit institutions believe that physical education contributes to the total development of the individual.

The Jesuit teachers were distinguished by thoroughness of preparation. Usually they had to study for sixteen to nineteen years before they could become instructors. Furthermore, they had to keep up with the research and developments in their particular fields. Scholarship was regarded as an aid to religion.

In Jesuit education, theology occupies the central place. All of knowledge, all of the arts and sciences, are mere preludes to the understanding of God and to the realization of the role of the Church in human affairs. Thus the task of the Jesuit teacher is to be an example in virtue and piety. His aim is not merely to describe and to analyze but also to create individuals who are imbued with religious concern and who dedicate themselves to the spiritual life.

Jesuit educators did not stress harshness, however. The teacher was not to be a drill sergeant; rather, his role was one of interpretation and inspiration. He interpreted the ideals of the Church to a vast audience and he inspired by his knowledge and by fearless self-examination. Occasionally, Jesuit education led to heresy, as in the case of Voltaire, who later became the foe of all forms of ecclesiasticism.

Students in Jesuit schools were taught in a systematic way. Fundamentals were mastered thoroughly. No superficiality was allowed. Ancient languages, especially Latin and Greek, were taught vigorously. It was thought that no one could be educated without a knowledge of Greek and Latin. Reviews were frequently given, and thus the student moved from simple to complex subject matter.

In Jesuit education truth is regarded as being absolute. Thus it fought an intellectual war against all forms of relativism. The Christian doctrine was to be taught in all classes, not just in philosophy and in theology. In this way, Jesuit education opposed heresy and strengthened the power of the Church.

13. Comenius

Among the educational reformers through the ages, John Amos Comenius (1592–1670) deserves a high place. His life history was marred by persecution and he lived admist the agonizing impact of the Thirty Years War. He was born in Nivnitz and was a member of the Moravian Brethren. His early education was extremely inadequate. At the age of twenty he entered a seminary at Herborn, Nassau, to study for the ministry. A tireless traveler, he visited England and Sweden. Several years he spent in Poland, where he was rector of a gymnasium. The later years of his life were spent in Amsterdam, where he was active in the work of his denomination.

Among his works we find *The Great Didactic, The School of Infancy, The Gates of Tongues Unlocked, The Palace of Authors, The World of Sensible Things Pictured,* and *The Vestibule.* In all of them we find a close connection between his religious views and his educational ideals.

Among the influences that conditioned Comenius' life was his deep mystical faith. As a member of a minority group that was inspired by the ideals of Huss he felt a deep personal relationship with God. His mysticism demanded absolute dedication to religious goals. He was certain that, basically, education should have a Christian orientation; otherwise, it would be a journey in vanity.

He had utopian tendencies that were representative of the view of his times. Sir Thomas More, in *Utopia,* had pictured an ideal society in which education was cherished and in which there was no division of property. Campanella, in *The City of the Sun,* had urged a more humane and progressive system of instruction. Johann Valentin Andrea, in *The Christian City,* had spoken of an ideal commonwealth in which love was cherished and education was for all. Sir Francis Bacon, in *The New Atlantis,* had portrayed a utopian commonwealth, founded on scientific principles.

Bacon's influence on Comenius was especially strong. Like Bacon, Comenius believed that knowledge was power, and he stressed the study of useful subjects. Like Bacon, Comenius believed in progress through science rather than through the humanities. An avid reader, Comenius enjoyed especially the writings of Plato, Cicero, Plutarch, and Quintilian. He praised the advanced ideas of the Catholic humanist Vives, and found much stimulation in them. He was not a classicist; this was perhaps fortunate for the advancement of education, for he was conscious of the limitations of language training and literary studies. His guide was the empiricism of Bacon rather than the humanism of Erasmus.

RATKE   Comenius was most directly influenced by Wolfgang Ratke (1571–1635), who believed in the use of the vernacular and disliked compulsion in education. Ratke, who favored a system of experimental learning, was opposed to the empty memorization that prevailed in the schools of his time. Ratke stressed the importance of student interest and his belief was that without correct methodology no real progress could be achieved in education.

Essentially, Comenius was an optimist. While most theologians of his time stressed man's evil and waywardness, Comenius emphasized man's greatness. To be sure, life was a battleground for good and evil, but he was certain that the good would prevail. Perhaps he was too optimistic about the capacities of people to learn, for he suggested a system of pansophic education, which implied that everyone should learn everything. He looked forward to universal learning, symbolized by a projected encyclopedia of knowledge to which major scholars would contribute. He even wanted to found a college that would be a world scientific center and a beacon of enlightenment. He not only had an abstract faith in education but also throughout his life he wanted to actualize his ideals and further the progress of civilization through practical action.

With his faith in the innate equality of all, Comenius tolerated no class distinctions in education. Christianity was not an abstract ideal or a mere system of theology; it demanded action based on the faith that all human beings can participate in education. As a liberal, he did not recognize the claims of the aristocracy; class privileges, he held, had no place in a sound educational scheme. He dreamed of a Christian Republic in which all men would be united through knowledge and faith.

Some critics have seen a Platonic strain in the teachings of Comenius, for, like Plato, Comenius believed in an ideal state. Unlike Plato, however, Comenius believed in equality; humanity could only progress where genuine democracy prevailed. Morality and wisdom were not the monopoly of any group; they belonged to all.

GOALS The goal and aim of education, according to Comenius, is to make human beings Christlike. This means training for life, not merely for a profession. This also implies a correspondence of action and ideals; virtue is the heart of the educative process. Comenius can be called a God-intoxicated thinker, for to him God was the beginning and the end of education.

With fervor, Comenius opposed the learning of his time. It caused snobbishness, it was impractical, and it alienated man from God. Education is mankind's hope; if rightly interpreted, it could establish a heaven on earth.

How can this goal be accomplished? How can these high ideals be put into practice? Comenius answers that education should shift from the home to the school. Students should be educated in groups. In this way, the teacher would become more influential. Exact organization and scheduling were to guide school life. Teachers were to be chosen who loved scholarship and who had real regard for children. Most schoolmasters of his time were strict disciplinarians. This attitude was deplorable, according to Comenius, who compared the child to a growing plant, whose progress had to be carefully and lovingly guided.

He proposed four types of educational institutions. The first was the *School of the Mother's Knee*, which represented the training of a child received at home. It was important that parents be constructive examples to their children and that religious and moral ideals be emphasized in the home. The second institution that he proposed was the *Vernacular School*, which would stress the study of the mother tongue rather than the classical languages. At the same time, the arts and sciences were not to be neglected. The third type of school, the *Latin School*, was for the better students; it would stress Greek, Latin, and Hebrew, as well as the fundamentals of science, literature, and the arts. The fourth school, *University and Travel*, would create the leaders of society; this school would be for the best students, who were to be encouraged to make original investigations and to explore the ideals and morals of various nations.

While Comenius believed, like his contemporaries, that the mind consists of faculties, he emphasized that knowledge is not innate but is derived from our sense experience. This means that the student can be guided by experience and that his mind is a tablet on which the teacher sets his mark, thus exerting a powerful influence. Mere information was not enough; what was important in the educative process was to stir the imagination of youngsters; here he anticipated the conclusion of Alfred North Whitehead in *The Aims of Education*.

EDUCATION Comenius was influenced by Juan Luis Vives in his stress upon memory. He felt that practice would strengthen the child's memory, and that if we established correct intellectual habits in childhood they would be of inestimable benefit in adult life. As a believer in visual impressions, he reasoned that object lessons would strengthen the child's intellectual life.

Like modern pragmatic educators, he stressed the importance of action. *Learn by doing* was the key to his system. We learn to write by writing, and we learn to reason by reasoning. But action alone is not enough; the critical and speculative capacities of students must be cultivated. This is the function of reason that provides the basis for sound judgment.

More than any other thinker of his time, Comenius stressed the interrelatedness of rational and emotional factors. The scholar who only treasured intellect would have only a minor impact upon life. On the other hand, the practical man too would fail because he overlooked the importance of reason. To Comenius, learning was an unending process, one that demanded interest and curiosity on the part of the student.

PRINCIPLES Comenius' educational method is summarized in nine principles, all of which follow the order of nature. The first principle is:

> *Nature observes a suitable time.* For example: a bird that wishes to multiply its species, does not set about it in winter, when everything is stiff with cold, nor in summer when everything is parched and withered by the heat; nor in autumn, when the vital force of all

creatures declines with the sun's declining rays, and a new winter with hostile mien is approaching; but in spring, when the sun brings back life and strength to all. Again, the process consists of several steps. While it is yet cold the bird conceives the eggs and warms them inside its body, where they are protected from the cold; when the air grows warmer it lays them in its nest, but does not hatch them out until the warm season comes, that the tender chicks may grow accustomed to light and warmth by degrees.[1]

The schools did not follow this principle, Comenius pointed out:

> In direct opposition to this principle, a twofold error is committed in schools:
> 1. The right time for mental exercises is not chosen.
> 2. The exercises are not properly divided so that all advance may be made through the several stages needful without any omission. As long as the boy is still a child he cannot be taught, because the roots of his understanding are still too deep below the surface. As soon as he becomes old, it is too late to teach him, because the intellect and the memory are then failing. . . .

We conclude, therefore, that

> 1. The education of men should be commenced in the springtime of life; that is to say, in boyhood (for boyhood is the equivalent of spring, youth of summer, manhood of autumn, and old age of winter).
> 2. The morning hours are the most suitable for study (for here again the morning is the equivalent of spring, midday of summer, the evening of autumn, and the night of winter).
> 3. All the subjects that are to be learned should be arranged so as to suit the age of the students, that nothing which is beyond their comprehension should be given them to learn.[2]

The second principle is:

> *Nature prepares the material before she begins to give it form.*

1. *The Great Didactic.*
2. *Ibid.*

For example: the bird that wishes to produce a creature similar to itself first conceives the embryo from a drop of its blood; it then prepares the nest in which it is to lay the eggs.[3]

He emphasized that to change prevalent attitudes these rules should be followed:

1. Books and materials necessary for teaching should be held in readiness.
2. The understanding should first be instructed in things, and then taught to express them in language.
3. No language should be learned from a grammar, but from suitable authors.
4. The knowledge of things should precede the knowledge of their combinations.
5. Examples should come before rules.[4]

The third principle is:

Nature chooses a fit subject to act upon, or first submits one to a suitable treatment in order to make it fit. For example: a bird does not place any object in the nest in which it sits but an object of such a kind that a chicken can be hatched from it; that is to say, an egg. If a small stone or anything else falls into the nest, it throws it out as useless. But when the process of hatching takes place, it warms the material contained in the egg, and looks after it until the chicken makes its way out.[5]

The schools violate this principle, wrote Comenius,

not because they include the weak of intellect (for in our opinion all the young should be admitted into the schools), but far more because:
1. These tender plants are not transplanted into the garden; that is to say, are not entirely entrusted to the schools, so that none who are to be trained as men shall be allowed to leave the workshop before their training is complete.

3. *Ibid.*
4. *Ibid.*
5. *Ibid.*

2. The attempt is generally made to engraft that noblest graft of knowledge, virtue and piety, too early, before the desire to learn has been excited in those who have no natural bent in that direction.

3. The side-shoots or root-suckers are not removed before the grafting takes place; that is to say, the minds are not freed from all idle tendencies by being habituated to discipline and order.

Rectification. It is therefore desirable:

1. That all who enter schools persevere in their studies.
2. That before any special study is introduced the mind of the student be prepared and made receptive of it.
3. That all obstacles be removed out of the way of the schools.

"For it is of no use to give precepts," says Seneca, "unless the obstacles that stand in the way be removed."[6]

The fourth principle is:

Nature is not confused in its operations, but in its forward progress advances distinctly from one point to another. [This means that] we should put off the study of Greek until Latin is mastered, since it is impossible to concentrate the mind on any one thing, when it has to busy itself with several things at once.

That great man Joseph Scaliger was well aware of this. It is related of him that (perhaps on the advice of his father) he never occupied himself with more than one branch of knowledge at once, and concentrated all his energies on that one. It was owing to this that he was able to master not only fourteen languages, but also all the arts and sciences that lie within the province of man. He devoted himself to these one after the other with such success that in each subject his learning excelled that of men who had given their lives to it. And those who have tried to follow in his footsteps and imitate his method, have done so with considerable success.

Schools, therefore, should be organized in such a manner that the scholar shall be occupied with only one object of study at any given time.[7]

6. *Ibid.*
7. *Ibid.*

The fifth principle is:

In all the operations of nature development is from within. For example: in the case of the bird it is not the claws, or the feathers, or the skin that is first formed, but the inner parts; the outer parts are formed later at the proper season.

In the same way the gardener does not insert his graft into the outer bark nor into the outside layer of wood, but making an incision right into the pith, places the graft as far in as it will go. . . .

[This means that the scholar] should first understand things and then remember them and that the teacher should be conscious of all methods of knowledge.[8]

The sixth principle is:

Nature, in its formative processes, begins with the universal and ends with the particular. For example: a bird is to be produced from an egg. It is not the head, an eye, a feather, or a claw that is first formed, but the following process takes place: the whole egg is warmed, the warmth produces movement, and this movement brings into existence a system of veins, which mark in outline the shape of the whole bird (defining the parts that are to become the head, the wings, the feet, etc.). It is not until this outline is complete that the individual parts are brought to perfection. . . .

An artist proceeds in the same way. He does not begin by drawing an ear, an eye, a nose, or a mouth, but first makes a charcoal sketch of the face or of the whole body. If he be satisfied that this sketch resembles the original he paints it with light strokes of the brush, still omitting all detail. Then, finally, he puts in the light and shade, and, using a variety of colors, finishes the several parts in detail. . . . [This means] (i) Each language, science, or art must be first taught in its most simple elements that the student may obtain a general idea of it. (ii) His knowledge may next be developed further by placing rules and examples before him. (iii) Then he may be allowed to learn the subject systematically with the

8. *Ibid.*

exceptions and irregularities; and (iv), last of all, may be given a commentary, though only where it is absolutely necessary. For he who has throughly mastered a subject from beginning will have little need of a commentary, but will soon be in a position to write one himself.[9]

The seventh principle is:

Nature makes no leaps, but proceeds step by step. It follows therefore: (i) That all studies should be carefully graded throughout the various classes in such a way that those that come first may prepare the way for and throw light on those that come after. (ii) That the time should be carefully divided, so that each year, each month, each day, and each hour may have its appointed task. (iii) That the division of the time and of the subjects of study should be rigidly adhered to, that nothing may be omitted or perverted.[10]

The eighth principle is:

If nature commences anything it does not leave off until the operation is completed. It follows therefore:
1. That he who is sent to school must be kept there until he becomes well informed, virtuous, and pious.
2. That the school must be situated in a quiet spot, far from noise and distractions.
3. That whatever has to be done in accordance with the theme of study must be done without any shirking.
4. That no boys, under any pretext whatever, should be allowed to stay away or to play truant.[11]

The ninth principle states:

Nature carefully avoids obstacles and things likely to cause hurt. For example, when a bird is hatching eggs it does not allow a cold wind, much less rain or hail to reach them. It also drives away snakes, birds of prey, etc.

In the same way the builder, so far as possible, keeps dry his

9. *Ibid.*
10. *Ibid.*
11. *Ibid.*

wood, bricks, and lime, and does not allow what he has built to be destroyed or to fall down.

So, too, the painter protects a newly painted picture from wind, from violent heat, and from dust, and allows no hand but his own to touch it.

The gardener also protects a young plant by a railing or by hurdles that hares or goats may not gnaw it or root it up.

It is therefore folly to introduce a student to controversial points when he is just beginning a subject; that is to say, to allow a mind that is mastering something new to assume an attitude of doubt. What is this but to tear up a plant that is just beginning to strike root? (Rightly does Hugo say: 'He who starts by investigating doubtful points will never enter into the temple of wisdom.') But this is exactly what takes place if the young are not protected from incorrect, intricate, and badly written books as well as from evil companions. . . . [Schools should be careful:] (i) That the scholars receive no books but those suitable for their classes. (ii) That neither in the school nor in its vicinity the scholars be allowed to mix with bad companions.

If all these recommendations are observed, it is scarcely possible that schools should fail to attain their object.[12]

SOCIAL FUNCTION   To Comenius, education has a social function. Love of fellow man is in direct proportion to knowledge. As he states in *The Great Didactic:* "The seeds of knowledge, of virtue, and of piety are naturally implanted in us."[13] He defined man as a teachable animal. According to Comenius, education was not the acceptance of the past but the anticipation of the future. As a utopian thinker he urged reform in government and in economics. As long as nations made war upon each other there could be little progress. He looked forward to universal books, a universal college, universal language, and universal schools.

We have today the United Nations as a structure for international peace. But we are still far removed from the dream of

12. *Ibid.*
13. *Ibid.*

Comenius, who urged real world unity. He realized that education is always threatened by provincialism and bigotry, and that violence and ignorance anywhere threaten the advancement of humanity.

We can be molded by violence or by peace. Violence usually creates further conflicts, as Comenius experienced in his own lifetime. For real education, peace is not a luxury but a dire necessity. Only in an atmosphere of peace can knowledge triumph; only in times of peace can reason be truly cultivated. The objection may be made that war aids technology, but ususally only weapons of destruction are furthered; the final result may be the extinction of humanity.

Comenius urged men of good will to unite; teachers, ministers, statesmen, and merchants were to create a society based upon love and charity. The human race was to be invigorated; a truly creative concept of life was to be established. Comenius urged that more money be spent for schools, that the best investment of society lay in great teachers, and that aids for instruction, especially textbooks, should be liberally provided. Religion should govern the school system; it is to follow the teachings of Jesus, not the dictates of orthodoxy.

This was the dream of Comenius; it was ambitious and profound. He was a mystic with a vivid sense of actuality, a teacher who wanted to reform society. He realized that creative education is man's highest good.

14. Locke

John Locke (1632–1704) was among the most influential of modern thinkers. Although his system lacks the depth and the speculative boldness of the Continental rationalists, and although he depended more on psychological analysis than on metaphysical constructions, his impact was felt not merely in the circles of technical philosophy but also in politics, education, and religion. It has been pointed out that Locke in his common-sense method reflects the English character. He was moderate and never went to extremes. He avoided any type of dogmatism and was not a blind partisan to any cause. Basically his temperament was skeptical, yet he never abandoned a rational religious faith. Moderation was the keynote to Locke's character and intellectual interests.

During his lifetime Locke witnessed some of the stormiest events in English history. Before he was born, the struggle between Parliament and the king, Charles I, had erupted; it led to many tyrannical acts on the part of the king, who had violated the constitutional rights of the English people. Charles used arbitrary imprisonment, tried to silence the opposition, and in every way caused dissatisfaction among the democratic forces in England. The Civil war between the Cavaliers, the followers of the king, and the Roundheads, the forces of Parliament, produced bloody battles and in 1649, when Locke was seventeen, Charles I was executed. Yet the roundheads did not win a lasting victory; internal dissension plagued their ranks. Two religious factions were especially at odds with each other—the Presbyterians and the Independents. The Presbyterians belonged to a higher social class and were in favor of a state church. The Independents, on the other hand, more radical both religiously and politically, wanted to extend political freedom to the common man. They regarded the state church as an organ of tyranny.

Under Cromwell the Independents won a resounding victory. Cromwell ruled as a virtual dictator and in every way tried to eliminate the influence of the Presbyterian faction. The protectorate under Cromwell consequently was almost as oppressive as the tyranny of Charles I. And when Cromwell died, England was ready for a new government.

The year 1660 marks the date of the Restoration, when Charles II returned to England. He had been strongly influenced by the French ideas of government, but was forced to be very careful in respecting the dearly won liberties of the English people. Parliament asserted its independence from the king and saw to it that the constitutional liberties were more than a scrap of paper. Charles II would have liked to impose autocratic principles on England, but he could not easily do so, for the English people were vigilant in protecting their rights and privileges.

Charles II was succeeded by James II, whose Catholicism infuriated the Protestant leanings of the English people. James II lacked both wisdom and tact, and his pro-French policy caused consternation among his subjects. England felt the same way about France as later on she was to feel about Nazi Germany. The massacre of the Huguenots in France was regarded as an act of barbarism and was condemned most strongly by the English people.

The year 1688 signalized the downfall of James II; business and the aristocracy combined to institute a new monarchy dominated by William and Mary. This was the beginning of a secure financial system, with the Bank of England becoming the cornerstone of English fiscal policy. The liberties of the English people were respected, religious tolerance was expanded, and Parliament became the supreme agency of English politics.

The "Glorious Revolution" formed the background of Locke's political thinking. Just as Hobbes had apologized for the arbitrary power of Charles I, so Locke became a fervent defender of the rebellion of the middle class against arbitrary government. Hobbes and Locke, consequently, represent two divergent trends of English political thinking. Hobbes was a totalitarian and a defender of state power. No wonder his influence has been more far-reaching on the Continent than in the British Isles. Locke, on the other hand, became the spokesman for liberalism, and his influence was great in the development of British and American democracy.

The Life of Locke

Locke's father, a man of Puritan leanings, fought on the side of Parliament and probably imbued his son with a dislike for all aristocratic pretensions. Both parents were severe in their piety and instilled in their son definite moral principles. However, these rigorous ideals were tempered when he traveled abroad and came into contact with other parts of the world.

At Oxford, Locke majored in physics. He had a dislike for scholasticism, which was still prevalent in the university. Moreover, he cared very little for the classics, which were taught in a most uninspiring manner by the Oxford professors. He was especially influenced by John Owen, vice-chancellor of the University, who was a liberal and believed in the principle of toleration. Owen's attitude made for a variety of opinions and for freedom of thought at the University, and aided in introducing new political and religious ideals. Locke became especially proficient in medicine; in fact, his interest in science never waned.

It is interesting to note that William James, who in many ways resembled John Locke, likewise started with the study of physiology. The pragmatic thinkers, it appears, are most readily influenced by physical science and have less understanding of mathematics than the rationalistic philosophers.

Locke was closely associated with the Shaftesbury family, which produced notable scholars and statesmen. The first earl of Shaftesbury distinguished himself in politics, while the third earl of Shaftesbury made a notable contribution to the field of esthetics. Locke's fortunes paralleled those of Lord Ashley (Earl of Shaftesbury). When the earl fled to Holland in 1683, Locke followed; and there he spent some of the most fruitful years of his life. He wrote *An Essay Concerning Human Understanding* while he was an exile in Holland. It was published in 1690 and remains one of the landmarks of modern philosophy. The English Government looked upon Locke's activities in Holland with deep suspicion. James II thought he was plotting against the security of England and therefore demanded his extradiction. But the Dutch Government refused to comply.

When James II was deposed, Locke's political fortunes improved considerably. He returned to England and occupied posts of political importance, becoming commissioner of trade and plantations in 1696. Most of his last years were spent in the country, where he was befriended by the Masham family, who did everything in their power to make him comfortable and to conserve his strength.

Locke's most important treatise, his *Essay Concerning Human Understanding,* is divided into four books. The first is an attack on the doctrine of innate ideas. The second holds that all ideas are dependent on experience and indicates how ideas are formed in the mind. The third deals with confusion in words and is one of the significant contributions to the science of semantics. The fourth makes a careful analysis of the types of knowledge, and sets forth the limits of human understanding.

In political theory, Locke's *Two Treatises on Government* have become classics; they were welcomed by the English liberals as an eloquent definition of their own position. As a political theorist, Locke exhibited skill and common sense, and, just as in his technical philosophy, he showed moderation and a spirit of reasonableness. In his other writings he displayed the same enlightenment, especially in his *Some Thoughts Concerning Education; The Reasonableness of Christianity;* and *The Three Epistles on Tolerance.*

Locke's Goals

In his method and approach to philosophy, Locke was strikingly different from the Continental thinkers. His mind was empirical rather than rationalistic; he relied on analytical observation; and his conclusions were held in a *tentative spirit.* He challenged the axioms and first principles of thinking. But to him skepticism was not an end in itself; it was a prelude to a more scientific philosophy. He wanted to destroy the idols of his time, to bring about intellectual clarity, to remove confusion, and to contribute to the flowering of the sciences.

It must be remembered that Locke was in close contact with the outstanding scientists of his time. Robert Boyle, the great physicist and chemist, was one of his friends; Thomas Sydenham, a renowned physician, stimulated his empirical thinking; Isaac Newton's mathematical theories excited his imagination. Both Boyle and Sydenham attacked the older traditions in science. Boyle fought a constant warfare against the alchemists and made an outstanding contribution to chemical analysis, while Sydenham emphasized the importance of observation in medicine rather than reliance upon the ancient authorities. Medicine should be learned empirically, he believed, not by the memorization of philosophical axioms. He wrote a brief book on medicine called *On Therapeutics,* which Locke greatly admired. Like Sydenham, Locke wanted to remove the cobwebs from man's mind; consequently he started his philosophy with an examination of the first principles of knowledge.

In his *Essay Concerning Human Understanding* Locke asked why men reason so poorly. He gives three answers to this question. In the first place, most people never reason at all. They are led in their thinking by the example of others and hold principles by faith, not by original investigation. This acceptance of authority creates certainty, but it is extremely dangerous, for it leads to a slavish imitation of the past. In the second place, reason is hindered by emotionalism. We feel before we think; we constantly cover up our real reasons, real intentions, and real motives. This habit leads to prejudice, bias, and obscurity in out mental processes and creates a closed mind, oblivious to new ideas and new truths. In the third place, our intellect is limited by partiality. We cannot grasp the complete aspect of truth. "We see but in part and we know but in part." We arrive at generalizations too quickly. If we were to examine all aspects of a problem, if we were more tentative in our conclusions, much progress could be made in science and philosophy.

Especially insistent was Locke's opposition to those who are led merely by emotionalism, or enthusiasm, as he called it. Enthusiasm in his time stood for a ready acceptance of revelation. How do men know, asked Locke, that they have a revelation from God? How can they be so certain in their beliefs? He answered that there can be no absolute certainty. Enthusiasm rises from the conceits of an arrogant brain; it mades men overbearing, self-satisfied, and smug. The philosopher must guard against this feeling and love truth for the sake of truth, not for the sake of substantiating theological doctrines.

In all intellectual discourse, according to Locke, words are significant. As a nominalist, he believed that general terms do not have a reality of their own but depend on particulars. Moreover, he maintained, words must be carefully examined and rigorously analyzed; otherwise our thinking exhibits confusion and obscurity. Yet words stand for general concepts. How do they become general? Locke answers, By being made the symbols of abstract ideas.

Beliefs

Above all, Locke opposed the system of scholastic philosophy that still prevailed in his period. Scholasticism created generalizations without a factual basis and prevented progress in the sciences. To regard Aristotle as the master of knowledge, to revere without criticism, was an act of folly, according to Locke.

At the same time, he opposed the prevalent stress upon the humanistic curriculum. The classical languages, he maintained, had only an ornamental value; they were of little use to the gentleman of leisure and to the merchant. Likewise, he had little use for rhetoric, for it created too many disputations and developed a false conceit on the part of the students.

He anticipated the modern science of semantics. Again and again he reminds us that words are emotionally charged and that they should be carefully defined if education is to advance. It is better, Locke maintained, to have a few definite ideas than to express many ideas in vague terms. An excellent stylist, he had contempt for the involved language he found so often in the philosophical and educational literature of his time.

Aims of Education

What is the aim of education? Locke replies that human beings should cultivate a sound mind in a sound body. Without physical health, our mental accomplishments would be secondary; without a wise mind, physical strength would create no lasting satisfactions. As Locke eloquently states:

> He whose mind directs not wisely will never take the right way; and he whose body is crazy and feeble will never be able to advance

in it. I confess there are some men's constitutions of body and mind so vigorous and well framed by nature that they need not much assistance from others; but by the strength of their natural genius, they are, from their cradles, carried towards what is excellent; and, by the privilege of their happy constitutions, are able to do wonders. But examples of this kind are but few; and I think I may say that of all the men we meet with, nine parts of ten are good or evil, useful or not, by their education. It is that which makes the great difference in mankind.

I imagine the minds of children as easily turned this or that way as water itself; and though this be the principal part, and our main care should be about the inside, yet the clay cottage is not to be neglected. How necessary health is to our business and happiness, and how requisite a strong constitution, able to endure hardships and fatigue, is to one that will make any figure in the world, is too obvious to need any proof. What concerns the body and health reduces itself to these few and observable rules: Plenty of open air, exercise, and sleep; plain diet, no wine or strong drink, and very little or no physic; not too warm and strait clothing.[1]

Self-control is a vital element in education, according to Locke:

The great mistake I have observed in people's breeding their children has been that this has not been taken care enough of in its due season; that the mind has not been made obedient to discipline, and pliant to reason, when at first it was most tender, most easy to be bowed. Parents being wisely ordained by nature to love their children are very apt, if reason watch not that natural affection very warily—are apt, I say, to let it run into fondness. They love their little ones, and it is their duty; but they often with them cherish their faults too. They must not be crossed, forsooth; they must be permitted to have their wills in all things: and they begin in their infancies not capable of great vices, their parents think they may safely enough indulge their little irregularities, and make themselves sport with that pretty perverseness, which they think well enough becomes that innocent age. But to a fond parent, that would not have his child corrected for a perverse trick, but excused

1. *Some Thoughts concerning Education.*

it, saying it was a small matter, Solon very well replied: "Aye, but custom is a great one."[2]

Locke favored reasoning rather than corporal punishment for children:

This they are capable of understanding; and there is no virtue they should be excited to, nor fault they should be kept from, which I do not think they may be convinced of; but it must be by such reasons as their age and understanding are capable of, and those proposed always in very few and plain words.

Beating is the worst, and therefore the last means to be used in the correction of children; and that only in cases of extremity, after all gentler ways have been tried, and proved unsuccessful: which, if well observed, there will be very seldom any need of blows. For, it not being to be imagined that a child will often, if ever, dispute his father's present command in any particular instance; and the father not interposing his absolute authority, in peremptory rules, concerning either childish or indifferent actions, wherein his son is to have his liberty; or concerning his learning or improvement, wherein there is no compulsion to be used: there remains only the prohibition of some vicious actions, wherein a child is capable of obstinacy, and consequently can deserve beating: and so there will be but very few occasions of that discipline to be used by any one who considers well, and orders his child's education as it should be.[3]

A good teacher, in Locke's system, is concerned with the book of the world:

That great work of a governor is to fashion the carriage and form the mind; to settle in his pupil good habits, and the principles of virtue and wisdom; to give him, by little and little, a view of mankind, and work him into a love and imitation of what is excellent and praiseworthy; and, in the prosecution of it, to give him vigor, activity, and industry. The studies which he sets him upon are but, as it were, the exercises of his faculties, and employment of

2. *Ibid.*
3. *Ibid.*

his time, to keep him from sauntering and idleness, to teach him application, and accustom him to take pains, and to give him some little taste of what his own industry must perfect. For who expects that under a tutor a young gentleman should be an accomplished critic, orator, or logician; go to the bottom of metaphysics, natural philosophy, or mathematics; or be a master in history or chronology? though something of each of these is to be taught him: but it is only to open the door that he may look in, and, as it were, begin an acquaintance, but not to dwell there; and a governor would be much blamed that should keep his pupil too long, and lead him too far in most of them. But of good breeding, knowledge of the world, virtue, industry, and a love or reputation, he cannot have too much; and if he have these, he will not long want what he needs or desires of the other.[4]

A teacher should love his student:

The great skill of a teacher is to get and keep the attention of his scholar: whilst he has that, he is sure to advance as fast as the learner's abilities will carry him; and without that, all his bustle and pother will be to little or no purpose (as much as may be) the usefulness of what he teaches him; and let him see, by what he has learned, that he can do something which he could not do before; something which gives him some power and real advantage above others, who are ignorant of it. To this he should add sweetness in all his instructions; and by a certain tenderness in his whole carriage, make the child sensible that he loves him, and designs nothing but his good; the only way to beget love in the child, which will make him hearken to his lessons, and relish what he teaches him.[5]

UPPER CLASSES According to Locke, education for the upper classes should have as its goal four major qualities: First, *virtue,* which implies a knowledge of right and wrong, thus following the dictates of conscience. Moral ideals, Locke maintained, depend on our religious training. We should study the Bible, be inspired by its lofty dictates, and follow the decrees of God.

4. *Ibid.*
5. *Ibid.*

The second quality that Locke cherished was *wisdom*. Unlike Spinoza, Locke did not believe that man could get a complete view of the universe. Wisdom was a practical rather than a theoretical activity; it meant the ability to conduct our affairs in a skillful manner and to be in control of our environment. Locke felt that most philosophers had been antisocial in their attitude, and he recommended public service as an excellent outlet for the gentleman.

The third quality that he recommended was *good breeding*, which is part and parcel of the English character. Good breeding implies a sense of dignity. The gentleman would be neither too proud nor too humble. His manners would be spontaneous and he would exhibit self-control under all situations.

The fourth quality that Locke favored was *learning*, but this to him was far less important than the others. Learning could only produce outward knowledge; what mattered was action and prudent behavior.

Locke made a clear distinction between the education of the scholar and that of a gentleman. The gentleman was to concentrate on practical matters, while the scholar would cultivate the classical languages.

LOWER CLASSES When Locke discussed the education of the lower classes, he showed limited vision. He favored a scheme whereby children of the poor are to be taken away from their parents, to be educated in working schools from the ages of three to fourteen. The advantage of such a plan would be its economy. Children would be disciplined, and they would not be delinquent. They should be taught simple handicrafts, and they should be encouraged in thrift and hard work. For their moral edification they would be instructed in the precepts of the Bible. At the same time, the mothers of the children would have enough time to earn a living. For the poor, Locke favored no academic learning; rather, he recommended apprenticeship training that would start early in the morning and end late at night.

CURRICULUM   There has been a debate among scholars as to whether Locke was a mental disciplinarian. It is evident that Locke wanted education to be interesting; he disliked memorization because it presents the mind with specific facts rather than with general knowledge.

In regard to the subjects of the curriculum Locke was especially impressed by the study of the English language. This was far more important to him than a knowledge of the classics. To speak one's mother tongue well was the first obligation of the gentleman.

He favored the study of both the physical and biological sciences. Anatomy had a special place in his educational scheme, for when we become conscious of our bodily structure we become more aware of our physical functions.

Mathematics he recommended because of its clarity and logical order. The lesson of mathematics is that we must overcome our prejudices and reason objectively. Locke believed that the progress of science would depend on the advancement of mathematics.

Geography Locke favored, because it broadens the outlook of the gentleman, who thus would become more cosmopolitan in his outlook on life. Furthermore, it stimulates our desire for adventure. For history Locke had a special fondness. It stirs our imagination and shows how the present is determined by the past. Locke was especially interested in the moralists of ancient times, like Seneca and Marcus Aurelius, who could be models for later periods.

In his discussion of the arts, Locke favored the applied rather than the fine arts. He had little use of poetry. A gentleman might enjoy painting, but Locke thought that cabinetmaking and gardening might be more practical on a country estate.

GENTLEMEN   How can we distinguish between the gentleman and the ordinary man? Locke would reply that the gentleman is interested in all aspects of life; he has a broad education. He has excellent manners. The ordinary man, on the other hand, is usually a specialist in one field of endeavor and generally lacks poise.

To become a gentleman, one must, above all, control one's passions. According to Locke, man naturally is a being who likes pleasure and hates pain. Yet his reason would tell him that some pleasures should be avoided so that life can have a maximum meaning. Nothing is so important as the curbing of our desires, so that we may live like free men rather than like serfs.

This ideal of education, according to Locke, should be started in early youth. Teachers should use the method of social approval, and reward those acts that are praiseworthy and punish those that are undesirable. A child does not like to be disgraced, and will therefore seek encouragement and approval from his elders. However, as Locke states, the teacher should not rely merely upon precept, but, if necessary, should enforce obedience. Respect for authority is the foundation of education and of civilization.

Evaluation

The weaknesses of Locke's philosophy are apparent. He was mainly concerned with the upper classes; he had little faith in the capacities of the common man. He represented the class spirit of seventeenth-century England.

Still, his work contributed to the educational emancipation of England. He destroyed the hold of humanism and scholasticism. He was influential in the spread of the sciences and in the practical application of educational ideals.

Locke asked fundamental questions regarding creativity in education. Should education produce scholars or educated individuals who were at home in the world? Which is more important, virtue or learning? Should the classics or the sciences be the foundation of the curriculum? Should formal logic be stressed or should the study of mathematics be cultivated? Should the teacher emphasize obedience or freedom on the part of the student? Is general education more important than the development of specific skills?

These questions are as important in our own time as they were in Locke's day.

15. Rousseau

The story of the life of Jean Jacques Rousseau (1712–1778) reads like a modern novel. He experienced fantastic adventures and in his emotional life exhibited great instability. He had one reckless love affair after another, and he was equally inconstant in his religious views. He started out as a Calvinist, became a Catholic, then returned to Calvinism. In his later years he developed his own form of religion, a mixture of deism and romanticism. His literary reputation was not established until his middle years, after he had won the prize for the best essay in a contest sponsored by the Academy of Dijon. But he never had a chance to enjoy his fame, for he was exiled from France because of his radical political opinions. He found refuge for awhile in Prussia and then in Switzerland; but he was always exposed to attacks, and his enemies were numerous. Suffering from a persecution complex, he could never be at rest. His friends found him very difficult to get along with; even Hume, who usually was tolerant, was glad to be rid of him.

Rousseau believed himself to be motivated by the noblest of impulses, as he revealed in his *Confessions,* letters, and other works, but even the most charitable evaluation of his character cannot support this opinion. To be sure, he was a genius and one of the most advanced thinkers of his time, and his influence on modern culture has been exceptional. But one can scarcely admire his personal life and personal inclinations.

Ironically enough, according to his own account, Rousseau, the father of modern progressive education, had his five children brought up in an orphanage. These children he had by a very unattractive woman, Thérèse le Vasseur, an ignorant inn servant, who when he first met her could neither read nor write. It is difficult to understand what drew Rousseau to a woman of no beauty, wit, or understanding. Perhaps it was his own sense of inadequacy, for he could completely dominate her and in her presence exhibit his intellect and wit in unrestrained fashion.

Rousseau's life was characterized by intense emotionalism. In every way he was a man of feeling and sensibility. He cried easily; he did not believe in self-control; nor did he accept the aristocratic code of the eighteenth century, which placed particular emphasis on moderation and reasonableness. To Rousseau the aristocracy seemed completely corrupt and degenerate; he glorified the homely virtues and ideals of the simple people. He had an abiding sympathy for bourgeois existence, for to him such a life, in its simplicity and unconcern, stood in vivid contrast to the moral depravity of the Parisian salons.

Thus Rousseau expressed the spirit of the rising middle class, which hated the dissipations of the French aristocracy, and was envious of the ostentatious luxury that the upper classes enjoyed. No wonder the middle class gladly welcomed Rousseau's philosophy!

In spite of his many love affairs, and strange as it may seem, Rousseau had a puritanical strain in his nature. He said he did not believe in sensuality; in his novel *La Nouvelle Héloïse* he celebrated the joys of married life and described the dignity that such a relationship develops. Love to him, he declared, was not a superficial emotion. It is not to be taken lightly, he advised; it transforms the inner being of man. While the French aristocrats looked lightly upon the institution of marriage, Rousseau felt differently, at least in his books. Marriage should be enduring, he wrote, and the source of all human relationships. Seldom in the history of philosophy has a moralist lived such an immoral life.

The Problem of Civilization

The problem of civilization was discussed by Rousseau most clearly in his *Discourse on the Origin of Inequality among Men,* in which he completely reversed the tenor of French and European philosophy. Before Rousseau, it had been almost universally accepted that the sciences and arts contribute to the perfection of man. Opposing this view, Rousseau showed that the life of man has been made miserable by the progress of knowledge. Civilization itself, insisted Rousseau, has only produced a wasteful leisure class, leading to oppression, inequality, and injustice.

Hobbes had maintained that the state of nature is a state of violence and war. This is not true, according to Rousseau; no, the state of nature is quite ideal. In the state of nature man lives in peace, unfettered by false conventions; he follows his natural feelings and is guided by innate goodness, while selfishness arises with civilization because it intensifies man's acquisitive instinct. Rousseau was quite emphatic in his belief that the least advanced cultures are the happiest. To some extent, his conclusions have been vindicated by Freud, who pointed to man's aggressive drive, which can never be satisfied because of the inhibitions of civilization.

Ever since Rousseau, the problem of civilization has been foremost in the discussions of historians and philosophers. At first, in the nineteenth century, the positivists, led by their founder, Auguste Comte, were triumphant. Without reason and science, according to Comte, man's condition is low and brutish. The road to progress, according to Comte's philosophy, lay in the direction opposite to that suggested by Rousseau—not back to nature, but forward to scientific control. The ills of mankind, claimed Comte, could be cured by a better scientific methodology and a more adequate understanding of society, not by a return to a primitive age.

However, as the spirit of optimism waned in the nineteenth century, and as wars became more threatening, Rousseau found new adherents. Thoreau in the United States counseled a return to nature; in Russia Tolstoy spoke rhapsodically about the delights of a simple peasant existence. In the twentieth century the pessimism of Rousseau regarding civilization found a willing echo in the works of Spengler. According to Spengler, civilization is in a state of decline and symbolizes a movement away from the real sources of our existence and our being. It represents a mechanical existence in which the city ultimately triumphs over the country, the proletariat rules supreme, and a life-negating philosophy is accepted.

Rousseau made a keen comparison between the state of civilized man and his savage ancestry:

> The savage and the civilized man differ so much in the bottom of their hearts and in their inclinations, that what constitutes the supreme happiness of one would reduce the other to despair. The former breathes only peace and liberty; he desires only to live and be free from labor. Even the ataraxia of the Stoic falls far short of his profound indifference to every other object. Civilized man, on the other hand, is always moving, sweating, toiling, and racking his brains to find still more laborious occupations; he goes on in drudgery to his last moment and even seeks death to put himself in a position to live, or renounces life to acquire immortality. He pays his court to men in power, whom he hates, and to the wealthy, whom he despises; he stops at nothing to have the honor of serving them; he is not ashamed to value himself on his own meanness and their protection; and, proud of his slavery, he speaks with disdain of those who have not the honor of sharing it. What a sight would the perplexing and envied labors of a European minister of state present to the eyes of a Caribbean! How many cruel deaths would not this indolent savage prefer to the horrors of such a life, which

is seldom even sweetened by the pleasures of doing good! But for him to see into the motives of all this solicitude, the words, power, and reputation would have to bear some meaning in his mind; he would have to know that there are men who set a value on the opinion of the rest of the world—who can be made happy and satisfied with themselves rather on the testimony of other people than on their own. In reality, the source of all these differences is, that the savage lives within himself, while the social man lives constantly outside himself, and only knows how to live in the opinion of others, so that he seems to receive the consciousness of his own existence merely from the judgment of others concerning him.[1]

The conclusion is quite clear. Inequality is the product of civilization, which heightens the misery of the masses and creates a wasteful aristocracy:

> It follows from this survey that, as there is hardly any inequality in the state of nature, all the inequality which now prevails owes its strength and growth to the development of our faculties and the advance of the human mind, and becomes at last permanent and legitimate by the establishment of property and laws. Secondly, it follows that moral inequality, authorized by positive right alone, clashes with natural right, whenever it is not proportionate to physical inequality; a distinction which sufficiently determines what we ought to think of that species of inequality which prevails in all civilized countries, since it is plainly contrary to the law of nature, however defined, that children should command old men, fools wise men, and that the privileged few should gorge themselves with superfluities while the starving multitude are in want of the bare necessities of life.[2]

Political Education

The political theories of Rousseau are contained in his *Social Contract*. In this book we can find the sources of both totali-

1. *Discourse on the Origin of Inequality among Men.*
2. *Ibid.*

tarian and democratic tendencies. The democratic spirit is indicated by Rousseau's belief that sovereignty belongs to the people
and that governments are not absolute ends in themselves. Bit-
terly he attacked the institution of monarchy, and he showed
kings to have been frequently dissolute and weak and enslavers
of the people. Most monarchs, he declared, are surrounded by
advisers who are not only corrupt but also lethargic and stupid,
who flatter the great in order to obtain preferment. Therefore,
said Rousseau, a man of real worth among the king's ministers is
extremely rare. A hereditary monarch, moreover, is constantly
plagued by the problem of succession. How many times have
monarchies been ruled by children, even by feeble-minded persons, just for the sake of continuous succession.

At the same time Rousseau attacked the concept of absolute
democracy, for he realized that in history we have examples of
only limited democracies. In Greece, slaves, women, and for-
eigners were not allowed to take part in political life. Even the
town meeting in New England was not completely democratic,
and the Puritan oligarchy used property and religious qualifications to exclude many people from participating in political
affairs. An absolute democracy, Rousseau cautioned, demands
vigilance on the part of the people for the preservation of their
liberties. But such vigilance obtains only in a small state where
all the citizens are acquainted with each other and where no
great degree of economic stratification exists. Rousseau believed
that luxury and wealth are inevitable enemies of democracy.
Whenever the class spirit develops, and whenever class-conscious-
ness triumphs, democracy is endangered.

Thus, Rousseau well understood the weaknesses of the democratic form of government. Democracies, he maintained, frequently are subject to indecision, too many men control the
affairs of state, and too much deliberation takes place. Therefore
democratic states move slowly and sometimes not at all. Under
more autocratic governments, on the other hand, action can be

taken quickly. Quick decisions can be made in place of prolonged indecisive negotiations. And democracy demands too much of human nature, he declared. It would be an ideal form of government for the gods, but since most men are unstable and guided by their passions, democracy most of the time leads to disintegration and civil strife.

Rousseau's ideal form of government is an elective aristocracy that approaches the English system of government. True, such a political system likewise has its imperfections; it requires moderation, a sense of balance, and it presupposes inequality in economic matters. The great advantage of this system, Rousseau believed, is its stability and lack of internal disorder. He made a clear distinction between the forms of government, which may vary, and the state, which is one. This concept is connected with his famous doctrine of the general will, which represents the sovereignty of the state. It is the symbol of common interests; it is inalienable and stands for the common good. On the other hand, the will of the citizens is subject to change and is usually guided by selfish desires. It is the general will that is the principle of political continuity and that makes for stability in political life. The general will, moreover, contains within itself the power of coercion; it can subject the desires of the individual to the public good. The doctrine of the general will had a decided influence on Hegel, and in modern times was highly regarded by the theorists of National Socialism, who glorified the absolute power of the state.

Rousseau was much more enthusaistic about the possibilities of revolution than was John Locke, who regarded a revolution as the very last alternative, mainly for the protection of property rights. In this respect, Rousseau influenced the modern Marxist theories, for he held that whenever a government becomes oppressive and whenever it ceases to represent the people, rebellion is necessary. Those who believe revolutions result only in violence and bloodshed are utterly mistaken, according to Rousseau, who thought revolutions bring about a constructive reorganization of human life and lead ultimately to human betterment.

The leaders of the French Revolution, especially Robespierre, held Rousseau in great esteem. Had not Rousseau attacked the existing institutions? Had he not glorified the genius of the French nation? Had he not exposed the villainy of the existing ecclesiastical system? Robespierre translated Rousseau's dogmas into actual legislation.

However, the conclusions of Rousseau's political theory are quite pessimistic: No political institution remains constant; all governments are in a state of flux. Naturally, the leaders of the various nations speak about a perpetual reign, but they are mistaken. Rousseau cited the example of Sparta and Rome; those nations perished, and he believed modern nations would experience the same fate.

Rousseau's Ethical Theories

In his ethical theories Rousseau championed the importance of feeling and conscience. This concept impressed Immanuel Kant, who likewise rebelled against the formal concepts of rationalism. Unlike Voltaire, Rousseau was an optimist with regard to God's providence. To believe in the majesty and goodness of God was a fundamental tenet of Rousseau's faith. His religion was directed against the existing orthodoxy, which claimed special privileges and a direct approach to God. But God, according to Rousseau, cannot be found through reason; he must be found through the heart. Faith thus gives a practical validity to our beliefs. This voluntaristic concept of religion was later echoed by William James in his classic work *The Will to Believe*.

The ideal government as conceived by Rousseau would have nothing to do with either Protestantism or Catholicism; instead, it would teach the doctrine of natural religion, which simplifies our experience of the supernatural. Rousseau's natural religion does not depend on an established priesthood, for it can be understood by every individual: It postulates the existence of God and teaches the immortality of man. But it does not promote tolerance. Indeed, Rousseau advocated that those who would not accept this natural religion should be banished from the state or, if necessary, put to death. While he objected to the fanaticism of others, his own prejudices were always apparent.

According to Rousseau, a study of moral philosophy only hinders the development of a real ethical and religious perspective and develops more pedantic scholarship. It makes man proud and arrogant instead of encouraging in him an attitude of humility. Conscience, Rousseau believed, is the infallible guide. Why, then, should we study Plutarch or Socrates? Why repeat the moral theories of Aquinas? Although he himself was a brilliant philosopher, Rousseau had a low opinion of the study of systematized thinking. Instead, he counseled his adherents to follow their hearts and their emotions.

Educational Background

Education in the time of Rousseau was still extremely formal. The schoolmaster was an absolute authority; memorization was encouraged and learning was notably stereotyped. Since the classics were the center of the curriculum, the sciences were slighted. Children were regarded as being naturally wayward beings who had to be disciplined and strictly controlled.

To be sure, there were progressive tendencies. The Jansenists urged a system of education based upon moral regeneration. François Fénelon, who was enthusiastic about the possibilities of education for women, was opposed to all forms of austerity; he wanted to make education as pleasant as possible. Abbé Jean Baptiste de la Salle (1651–1719), who founded the Institute of the Brothers of the Christian Schools (the Christian Brothers) at Rouen in 1684, held such advanced ideas that the interests of the pupils rather than those of the teacher became the center of the curriculum.

In Germany, Johann Basedow (1723–1790) had similar ideas. He believed that the poor and rich should enjoy the same education, and he urged that children be taught according to their interests and outlook. He wanted better trained teachers with a humanitarian concept of life and this explains his founding of a model school for children, the Philanthropinium, at Dessau in 1774.

In short, the ideas of Rousseau were part of the *Zeitgeist,* the spirit of the times. He stated these ideas in a stark form to make them dramatic. He made it clear that the beginning and end of education is not the adult, but the child; the child has his own interests and lives in his own world, and the values of children are completely different from those of adults. Society has erred in regarding its educational standards as absolutes; they were only postulates. More important than society was the individual, whose integrity should be cherished.

Rousseau, like many progressive thinkers who followed him, believed that we must start with the present in education. School is not a preparation for living; it is an exercise in living. The child, above all, must be shielded from the vices of society so that his virtues can develop.

Education can be regarded as either an external process or as internal development. Like Johann Pestalozzi (1746–1827), Rousseau believed that it is inward growth. We cannot impose standards; we cannot impart information mechanically; we can only develop the natural tendencies of children and excite their curiosity.

Rousseau pointed to four stages in the development of the child, who repeats the growth of the race. Till the child reaches the age of five the main emphasis should be upon *physical* activities, whereby we try to harden his body. Artificial conventions are to be avoided and the child is to experience life directly. In this stage the child is similar to an animal. Above all, Rousseau recommended the avoidance of rational activities, for knowledge only too often inhibits man.

The second phase, from age five to twelve, corresponds to the *savage* state of humanity. Now the child is aware of his separate identity. Book knowledge is to be curbed; Rousseau felt that it created pedants, unfit for life. He warns teachers not to reason with the youngster, who is to learn from experience. The keynote is "do nothing." At the same time, the child, with natural curiosity, will start to explore the world and his surroundings, and will pick up the first elements of language, writing, and reading.

The third phase of development, from age twelve to fifteen, corresponds to the *rational* stage of humanity. Now the youngster is able to evaluate and to form critical judgments. *Robinson Crusoe* should be the text for this period. The sciences, especially astronomy, agriculture, and the manual arts, are to be stressed; the child will learn by doing. Hence, the teacher should encourage manual activities. The test of the subjects studied lies in their utility; if they had only an ornamental value, Rousseau would eliminate them.

The *social* stage is from age fifteen to twenty. Now religious concerns are dominant for adolescents, who are to be taught a system of natural religion, whereby they may find God through nature, not through orthodox theology. At the same time, they would develop a natural interest in the opposite sex. Their studies should make use of real situations, for we learn best by acting in a natural way; we become philosophers by being reflective, and we develop religious ideals by acting in a charitable manner. Rousseau sounds like William Heard Kilpatrick, the famous American educator, when he says that we learn what we live in our daily existence.

Living, to Rousseau, implies action. As he states in *Émile:*

> In the natural order of things, all men being equal, the vocation common to all is the state of manhood; and whoever is well trained for that, cannot fulfill badly any vocation which depends upon it. Whether my pupil be destined for the army, the church, or the bar,

matters little to me. Before he can think of adopting the vocation of his parents, nature calls upon him to be a man. How to live is the business I wish to teach him. On leaving my hands he will not, I admit, be a magistrate, a soldier, or a priest; first of all he will be a man. All that a man ought to be he can be, at need, as well as anyone else can. Fortune will in vain alter his position, for he will always occupy his own.

Our real study is that of the state of man. He among us who best knows how to bear the good and evil fortunes of this life is, in my opinion, the best educated; whence it follows that true education consists less in precept than in practice. We begin to instruct ourselves when we begin to live; our education commences with the commencement of our life; our first teacher is our nurse. For this reason the word "education" had among the ancients another meaning which we no longer attach to it; it signified nutriment.

To live is not merely to breathe, it is to act. It is to make use of our organs, of our senses, of our faculties, of all the powers which bear witness to us of our own existence. . . .

O men, be humane! it is your highest duty; be humane to all conditions of men, to every age, to everything not alien to mankind. What higher wisdom is there for you than humanity? Love childhood; encourage its sports, its pleasures, its lovable instincts. Who among us has not at times looked back with regret to the age when a smile was continually on our lips, when the soul was always at peace? Why should we rob these little innocent creatures of the enjoyment of a time so brief, so transient, of a boon so precious, which they cannot misuse? Why will you fill with bitterness and sorrow these fleeting years which can no more return to them than to you? Do you know, you fathers, the moment when death awaits your children? Do not store up for yourselves remorse by taking from them the brief moments nature has given them. As soon as they can appreciate the delights of existence, let them enjoy them. At whatever hour God may call them, let them not die without having tasted life at all.[3]

We must in all our endeavors reverse the current practices, according to Rousseau. Moral instruction must be negative:

3. *Émile.*

We are now within the domain of morals, and the door is open to vice. Side by side with conventionalities and duties spring up deceit and falsehood. As soon as there are things we ought not to do, we desire to hide what we ought not to have done. As soon as one interest leads us to promise, a stronger one may urge us to break the promise. Our chief concern is how to break it and still go unscathed. It is natural to find expedients; we dissemble and we utter falsehood. Unable to prevent this evil, we must nevertheless punish it. Thus the miseries of our life arise from our mistakes. . . .

The only moral lesson suited to childhood and the most important at any age, is never to injure anyone. Even the principle of doing good, if not subordinated to this, is dangerous, false, and contradictory. For who does not do good? Everybody does, even a wicked man who makes one happy at the expense of making a hundred miserable; and thence arise all our calamities. The most exalted virtues are negative.[4]

Rousseau stated that we must respect children. Words without a knowledge of things are a waste of time:

Respect children, and be in no haste to judge their actions, good or evil. Let the exceptional cases show themselves such for some time before you adopt special methods of dealing with them. Let nature be long at work before you attempt to supplant her, lest you thwart her work. You say you know how precious time is, and do not wish to lose it. Do you not know that to employ it badly is to waste it still more, and that a child badly taught is farther from being wise than one not taught at all? You are troubled at seeing him spend his early years in doing nothing. What! is it nothing to be happy? Is it nothing to skip, to play, to run about all day long? Never in all his life will he be so busy as now.

Pedagogues, who make such an imposing display of what they teach, are paid to talk in another strain than mine, but their conduct shows that they think as I do. For after all, what do they teach their pupils? Words, words, words. Among all their boasted subjects, none are selected because they are useful; such would be the sciences of things, in which these professors are unskillful.[5]

4. *Ibid.*
5. *Ibid.*

Clarity is the goal of education:

> Bear in mind always that the life and soul of my system is, not to
> teach the child many things, but to allow only correct and clear
> ideas to enter his mind. I do not care if he knows nothing, so long
> as he is not mistaken. To guard him from errors he might learn, I
> furnish his mind with truths only. Reason and judgment enter
> slowly; prejudices crowd in; and he must be preserved from these
> last. Yet if you consider science in itself, you launch upon an
> unfathomable and boundless sea, full of unavoidable dangers.
> When I see a man carried away by his love for knowledge, hasten-
> ing from one alluring science to another, without knowing where to
> stop, I think I see a child gathering shells upon a seashore. At first
> he loads himself with them; then, tempted by others, he throws
> these away, and gathers more. At last, weighed down by so many,
> and no longer knowing which to choose, he ends by throwing all
> away, and returning empty-handed.[6]

Émile, instructed by Rousseau's concepts, leads almost a utopian
life:

> In a word, Émile has every virtue which affects himself. To have
> the social virtues as well, he only needs to know the relations which
> make them necessary; and this knowledge his mind is ready to
> receive. He considers himself independently of others, and is satis-
> fied when others do not think of him at all. He exacts nothing from
> others, and never thinks of owing anything to them. He is alone
> in human society, and depends solely upon himself. He has the
> best right of all to be independent, for he is all that anyone can be
> at his age. He has no errors but such as a human being must have;
> no vices but those from which no one can warrant himself exempt.
> He has a sound constitution, active limbs, a fair and unprejudiced
> mind, a heart free and without passions. Self-love, the first and
> most natural of all, has scarcely manifested itself at all. Without
> disturbing anyone's peace of mind he has led a happy, contented
> life, as free as nature will allow.[7]

6. *Ibid.*
7. *Ibid.*

Real democracy is to be practiced by the teacher. Education is to be measured by action, especially by our capacity to love and to engage in useful endeavors.

> In a word, teach your pupil to love all men, even those who despise them; let him not belong to any class, but be at home in all. Speak before him of the human race with tenderness, even with pity, but never with contempt. Man, do not dishonor man!
>
> When the critical age approaches, bring before young people scenes that will restrain and not excite them; give a chance to their nascent imagination by objects which, far from inflaming their senses, will repress the activity of them. Remove them from great cities where the dress and immodesty of women will hasten and anticipate the lessons of nature, where everything presents to their eyes pleasures which they ought to be acquainted with only when they know how to choose them. Take them back to their first dwelling place, where rural simplicity lets the passions of their age develop less rapidly; or if their taste for the arts still attaches them to the city, prevent in them, by this taste itself, a dangerous idleness. Carefully choose their associations, their occupations, and their pleasures; show them only touching but modest pictures, which will move without demoralizing them, and which will nourish their sensibilities without stirring their senses.[8]

Evaluation

What strikes the reader are the modern tendencies of Rousseau. He was the father of modern child psychology; he laid the foundations for a new curriculum; he emphasized the importance of play activities; he saw that the child must unfold from within; he knew that languages had to be taught in a new way; and he believed that curiosity and utility are the foundations of the curriculum.

Still, the weaknesses of his system are apparent; he restricted the activities of teachers who are to be only minor parts of education. We know today that firm guidance is one of the primary

8. *Ibid.*

tasks of education and that, if it is not exercised by teachers, it will be carried on by the agencies of communication and the cultural mores, which will lead to mediocre standards for the individual and society.

Furthermore, Rousseau overlooked the importance of reason. To be sure, reason may be perverted; intellectual discipline may be overdone, and the child may be taught useless facts; still, reason is man's most glorious possession; without it he is like an animal. "I think, therefore I am," remarked Descartes, and while reality may not be intellectual it is explored best through the resources of reason. This does not imply a separation of reason and emotion; this would be a major mistake. What is needed in a sound system of education is to make emotions rational and to intensify reason through the development of our creative drives. Of all the capacities of man reason has the most explosive potentialities; undoubtedly, Rousseau underestimated its possibilities.

There is a direct line between Rousseau, Kant, and Pestalozzi; Rousseau's impact on contemporary education, especially in the United States, is immense. He is the prophet of freedom and of *laissez-faire,* but we must realize that the freedom to be creative in education also demands a sense of responsibility and a sense of social dedication.

16. Pestalozzi

The educational ideals of Johann Pestalozzi (1746–1827) are a reflection of his own life. Since his father, a physician, passed away when the boy was five, he was brought up by his mother, who encouraged his sensitivity. He hated the Latin school that he attended in Zürich, but he enjoyed his college years at the Collegium Humanitatis and the Collegium Carolinum. He tried several professions, including the ministry, law, and politics, but in each he was unsuccessful. He then took up agriculture and developed a farm at Neuhof, but he was threatened by poverty, a fact that did not diminish his idealism.

His labors at Neuhof, where he established a school for orphans; at Stanz, where he was in charge of poor children and orphans; at Burgdorf; and, at last, at Yverdon, where he conducted a boarding school, convinced him that a new approach was needed in education. His last period was spent at Neuhof, after the Yverdun school developed financial difficulties. There he died in 1827.

His most significant works are *Leonard and Gertrude, How Gertrude Teaches Her Children, Swan-Song,* and *Evening Hours of a Hermit.*

The educational ideals of Pestalozzi rest upon his social philosophy. Unlike Rousseau, Pestalozzi did not glorify the state of nature for it was not an ideal utopia; rather, it tended to be brutish. Primitive man, according to Pestalozzi, often acted like an animal in a jungle. He even killed members of his own family if his own survival was threatened. Pestalozzi in his views of primitive man was far more scientific than Rousseau, who was carried away by vague romantic dreams.

The next stage of man, Pestalozzi maintained, is that of society, which is not a convenience but a dire necessity. Because man has animal drives and is a passionate creature, he has to be tamed. Thus, laws are invented and enforced; religion creates tabus and restrictions; we develop a sense of right and wrong. Often, however, society enforces the wrong laws and protects the guilty. Pestalozzi felt that the claims of society are not absolute, for only too often they conflict with our ethical ideals.

Like Comenius and Kant, Pestalozzi had utopian tendencies. He wanted to establish a truly ethical society in which God was worshipped, morality recognized, and human creativity stimulated.

Within all of us, according to Pestalozzi, there are three drives: we have primitive impulses, we are social beings, and we have ethical yearnings. Education was the process whereby ethics triumphed over our animal impulses. This did not imply artificial training; on the contrary, it meant inward development, for we all have sparks of creativity and a capacity for love and understanding.

The model for the school is the home, Pestalozzi taught. Let the teacher act like a loving father; let him develop initiative on the part of the student; let him stress the importance of ethical behavior; let him be an example in all activities. Just as cooperation and understanding govern a good home, so these ideals are to be applied to the schoolroom.

The ideal of love governs the educational philosophy of Pesta-

lozzi. Such love is to be unrestrained; it is to include the successful as well as the poor student; it is to be unfailing even when
students misbehave. Pestalozzi was especially fond of the children
of poor parents and he did everything in his power to improve their
lot.

The individual, Pestalozzi believed, develops through the
head, the hand, and the heart. The head stands for intellectual
development. Like Locke, Pestalozzi refuted the concept of innate ideas; we learn through sense expressions, but it must be
remembered that the mind is active in its adjustment to the
external world. Form, number, and language are the bases of the
educative process. This means that qualitative elements and the
power of communication should be stressed. Like Rousseau,
Pestalozzi approached education from the standpoint of the interests of the children rather than through the logic of adults.

He taught a new concept of geography. Often he would take
children on walks; and in this way his charges became conscious
of their environment. He used clay models to portray mountains
and rivers and he tried to make this study as dramatic as possible.
In mathematics he started with concrete objects; thus, he would
point to two students to develop a concept of the number two.
He showed that abstraction can come only when concrete ideas
have been mastered.

This is the basis of our contemporary instruction in arithmetic.
We do not force the child to remember by rote; rather, we try to
show how arithmetic is involved in daily living. Thus, the child
goes to the store and has to have the correct change. In the
schoolroom, a model of a bank is constructed, and children act
out the roles of bank president, tellers, and customers. In this
manner they learn the concrete meaning of arithmetical concepts. This type of instruction dates back to Pestalozzi.

Pestalozzi also emphasized the importance of art in the curriculum. This was not only an outlet for the creative talents of
children, but it also gave them a consciousness of their powers

and it developed intellectual discipline. Children had to partici-pate in art and not be mere bystanders. Instead of learning about melodies they should be encouraged to sing and play instru-ments. By necessity, their progress would be slow, and their ideas would differ from the ideas of adults, but the teacher should never exhibit an attitude of disapproval or condescension. Again, this meant a revolution in the curriculum. It implied an emphasis on the integrity of the student and placed stress on his creative abilities.

Pestalozzi stressed the importance of concrete situations. He felt that what we see and visualize we remember more vividly than what we hear. Thus, in language training he started with objects like apples and trees. He was certain that knowledge moved from the concrete to the abstract. He made several innova-tions: he put into use slates and pencils and taught the letters of the alphabet using cards. Instead of instructing one student at a time he organized specific classes.

He emphasized the need for manual training not just for the children of the laboring classes but for all, for he believed that our hands are just as important as our intellect, and that we develop excellent work habits when we are busy with manual activities.

However, without the development of the heart, education is incomplete, according to Pestalozzi. We must cultivate our capac-ity to love. This we first learn at home; hence, the ideals and attitudes of our parents, especially of the mother, are so impor-tant. The child must feel a sense of belonging; otherwise emo-tional difficulties will develop. Religion is to be part and parcel of education. It does not stand for any particular dogma, but rather for a feeling of dependence upon God; in this view Pesta-lozzi echoed the ideas of Friedrich Schleiermacher (1768–1834). Religion, he felt, is measured by its capacity to stimulate ethical action. Profession of faith meant nothing if it was not followed by constructive action.

In short, the test of education, according to Pestalozzi, is ethical actuality. Are we becoming more tolerant? Are we developing a spirit of compassion? Are we able to live in peace and charity with our neighbor? Are we becoming more spiritual in our philosophy of life?

The approach to education, Pestalozzi taught, must be that of integration: The head, hand, and heart should develop harmoniously. More important than specific instruction is *general education,* for we all meet life in its complexity. As we mature, we become the masters of our environment. Knowledge thus means power, not merely an abstract contemplation of the universe.

Critics might feel that Pestalozzi overlooked the importance of discipline and effort. Pestalozzi thought of the teacher as like a gardener and the pupil as like a plant which had to be carefully nurtured. It was so easy to destroy the creative capacities of the individual. Instruction should proceed step by step according to the ability of the child: nothing should be forced.

Pestalozzi was one of the originators of the modern idea of "readiness." Psychological research indicates that not all pupils are able to learn to read at the same time, that they mature at varying rates. To force them into one mold or one pattern would be a mistake. Pestalozzi was conscious of the importance of individual differences.

However, we must re-examine our concepts of readiness in the twentieth century. Today, children mature more rapidly; they are exposed to far more stimuli than they were in the time of Pestalozzi. They are conditioned by television and motion pictures; thus their readiness for intellectual labor has been intensified. By under-educating our students we only add to the cultural lag of our time.

The Ideals of Pestalozzi

Pestalozzi's educational philosophy is based on the ideal of liberty:

Be in no hurry to get on, but make the first step sound before moving; in this way you will avoid confusion and waste. Order, exactness, completion—alas, not thus was my character formed. And in the case of my own child in particular, I am in great danger of being blinded by his quickness and rapid progress, and, dazzled by the unusual extent of his knowledge, of forgetting how much ignorance lurks behind this apparent development, and how much has yet to be done before we can go farther. Completeness, orderliness, absence of confusion—what important points!

Lead your child out into Nature; teach him on the hilltops and in the valleys. There he will listen better, and the sense of freedom will give him more strength to overcome difficulties. But in these hours of freedom let him be taught by Nature rather than by you. Let him fully realize that she is the real teacher and that you, with your art, do nothing more than walk quietly at her side. Should a bird sing or an insect hum on a leaf, at once stop your walk; bird and insect are teaching him; you may be silent.

I would say to the teacher, be thoroughly convinced of the immense value of liberty; do not let vanity make you anxious to see your efforts producing premature fruit; let your child be as free as possible, and seek diligently for every means of ensuring his liberty, peace of mind, and good humor.[1]

Nature, Pestalozzi taught, is to be our guide:

Man! in thyself, in the inward consciousness of thine own strength, is the instrument intended by Nature for thy development.

The path of Nature, which develops the forces of humanity, must be easy and open to all; education, which brings true wisdom and peace of mind must be simple and within everybody's reach.

Nature develops all the forces of humanity by exercising them; they increase with use.

The exercise of man's faculties and talents, to be profitable, just follow the course laid down by Nature for the education of humanity.

This is why the man who, in simplicity and innocence, exercises

1. *Diary.*

his forces and faculties with order, calmness, and steady application, is naturally led to true human wisdom; whereas he who subverts the order of Nature, and thus the due connection between the different branches of his knowledge, destroys in himself not only the true basis of his knowledge, but the very need of such a basis, and becomes incapable of appreciating the advantages of truth.

Thou who wouldst be a father to thy child, do not expect too much of him till his mind has been strengthened by practice in the things he can understand; and beware of harshness and constraint.[2]

God is the measure of all education, and Jesus should be our main example:

> A man's greatest need is the knowledge of God.
>
> The purest pleasures of his home do not always satisfy him.
>
> His weak, impressionable nature is powerless without God to endure constraint, suffering, and death.
>
> God is the Father of humanity, and his children are immortal.
>
> Sin is both the cause and effect of want of faith, and is an act opposed to what a man's inmost sense of good and evil tells him to be right.
>
> It is because humanity believes in God that I am contented in my humble dwelling.
>
> I base all liberty on justice, but I see no certainty of justice in the world so long as men are wanting in uprightness, piety, and love.
>
> The source of justice and of every other blessing in the world, the source of all brotherly love amongst men, lies in the great conception of religion that we are the children of God.
>
> That man of God who, by his sufferings and death, restoreth to men the sense that God is their Father, is indeed the Saviour of the world. His teaching is justice itself, a simple philosophy of practical value for all, the revelation of God the Father to His erring children.[3]

Knowledge depends upon its motivational foundations; words are only secondary instruments:

2. *The Evening Hours of a Hermit.*
3. *Ibid.*

I have generally found that great, noble, and high thoughts are indispensable for developing wisdom and firmness of character. Such instruction must be complete in the sense that it must take account of all our aptitudes and all our circumstances; it must be conducted, too, in a truly psychological spirit; that is to say, simply, lovingly, energetically, and calmly. Then, by its very nature, it produces an enlightened and delicate feeling for everything true and good, and brings to light a number of accessory and dependent truths, which are forthwith accepted and assimilated by the human soul, even in the case of those who could not express those truths in words.

I believe that the first development of thought in the child is very much disturbed by a wordy system of teaching, which is not adapted either to his faculties or the circumstances of his life. According to my experience, success depends upon whether what is taught to children commends itself to them as true, through being closely connected with their own personal observation and experience. Without this foundation truth must seem to them to be little better than a plaything, which is beyond their comprehension, and therefore a burden."[4]

The deep compassion that Pestalozzi felt was expressed in an autobiographical comment, written when he was head of the orphanage at Stanz:

We wept and smiled together. They forgot the world and Stanz; they only knew that they were with me and I with them. We shared our food and drink. I had neither family, friends, nor servants; nothing but them. I was with them in sickness and health, and when they slept. I was the last to go to bed, and the first to get up. In the bedroom I prayed with them, and at their own request, taught them till they fell asleep.[5]

Significance

Pestalozzi's ideas had an international impact. He was made a citizen of the French Republic, and he was knighted by the Czar

4. *Ibid.*
5. *Letter on his work at Stanz,* 1799.

of Russia. Maine de Biran and M. A. Julien, spread his ideas in France; in England, Dr. Charles Mayo and Elizabeth Mayo experienced the impact of his concepts; the Prussian government sent teachers to be instructed by Pestalozzi; and in Switzerland, Baron von Fellenberg established an agricultural school at Hofwyl that reflected Pestalozzi's ideals.

In the United States, William Woodbridge, Joseph Neef, William McClure, Horace Mann, John Griscom, and especially Edward A. Sheldon, felt the power of Pestalozzi's educational concepts. Oswego, New York, where Sheldon was superintendent, became a center for the promotion of a progressive system of education.

Pestalozzi's impact ultimately cannot be defined. In his own time he was misunderstood. His contemporaries thought that he was a radical and a visionary. He was too emotional for them and took education too seriously. Scholars thought that his ideas were muddled and obscure. He was intoxicated by his fame and he lacked detachment.

Still, he had one of the most inspiring conceptions of education and life in the history of humanity. He believed in the greatness of the individual, who had unlimited possibilities if he developed harmoniously. Like Comenius, Pestalozzi called not only for a reconstruction of education, but also for a transformation of society. Creativity should prevail not merely in the schoolroom, he believed, but in all activities of life.

Thus, education cannot be separated from ethical instruction. As Pestalozzi states in eloquent terms:

> Do not hesitate to touch on the difficult questions of good and evil, and the words connected with them. And you must do this especially in connection with the ordinary events of every day, upon which your whole teaching in these matters must be founded, so that the children may be reminded of their own feelings, and supplied, as it were, with solid facts upon which to base their conception of the beauty and justice of the moral life.

The pedagogical principle which says that we must win the

hearts and minds of our children by words alone, without having recourse to corporal punishment, is certainly good, and applicable under favorable conditions and circumstances; but with children of such widely different ages as mine, children for the most part beggars, and all full of deeply rooted faults, a certain amount of corporal punishment was inevitable, especially as I was anxious to arrive surely, speedily, and by the simplest means, at gaining an influence over them all, for the sake of putting them all in the right road. I was compelled to punish them, but it would be a mistake to suppose that I thereby, in any way, lost the confidence of my pupils.

Elementary moral education, considered as a whole, includes three distinct parts: the children's moral sense must first be aroused by their feelings being made active and pure; then they must be exercised in self-control, and taught to take interest in whatever is just and good; finally, they must be brought to form for themselves, by reflection and comparison, a just notion of the moral rights and duties.[6]

Pestalozzi was a dreamer with a vivid sense of actuality. He noted how most individuals live unhappy and frustrated lives and how they are guided by irrational passions. For example, in his novel *Leonard and Gertrude,* Leonard is a serf to drunkenness and cannot control his appetites. We rise above our passions, according to Pestalozzi, when we identify ourselves with mankind, and when we see education as man's eternal quest for meaning, significance, and enlightenment.

6. *Ibid.*

17. Herbart

Johann Herbart (1776–1841), born in Oldenburg, Germany, became the champion of realism in education. Unlike Fichte and the Romantics, he was not given to an expression of emotional feelings. A university professor and successor to Kant, Herbart expressed the ideals of the academic life. In every way he was systematic, and his writings inspire more by their depth than by their emotional content. Among the works that are of significance to educational thought, we find *The Application of Psychology to the Science of Education, Outlines of Educational Doctrine, The Science of Education,* and *Textbook in Psychology.*

He founded an important teacher-training institution, in which he stressed his fundamental ideal of education: the development of character. Morality, to Herbart, was the foundation and end of education. It implied a sense of balance between reason and emotion, between today and the future, between the mandates of God and those of man. Extremes were to be avoided; in this viewpoint Herbart followed the ideals of Aristotle. But character development could not be accomplished without self-control, for man's passions and desires constantly stood in the way of philosophic enlightenment.

Freedom and authority should be combined, according to Herbart:

> Man from his youth onward must voluntarily accept restrictions, particularly as he has to live a communal life. Hence, first: Children must learn to obey. Their natural exuberance must meet enough resistance to avert offense.
>
> Immediately we meet a new difficulty. The easy means for a child not to offend his parents or teachers is concealment and lying!
>
> To cut the knot some teachers assume at once that children always lie if they can. Hence, they have to be so closely supervised and watched, and kept so busy from morning to evening, that they have no time for trickery. There is some truth in this, but if it is carried out with too much harshness and exactness one may fail in the first fundamental postulate we have set up, that children's vigor must be preserved! For this they need freedom! Those teachers who restrict freedom to such a degree that all the children's actions are calculated to please the observer, educate babies. Such creatures will have to learn to use their powers when they are grown up—and in spite of all their endeavors they will remain timid, helpless, and inferior to free personalities, until eventually they will try to compensate in whatever way they can.
>
> Consequently, as such a restricting form of education is dangerous, something better must be combined with supervision and occupation.
>
> One says rightly that well-bred children have not the heart to deceive their father and mother. Why not? They are used to rely on truth and confidence. This, then becomes the keynote of their lives.[1]

Education means development of man's character:

---

1. *Brief Encyclopedia of Practical Philosophy* (trans. by R. Ulich), from *Three Thousand Years of Educational Wisdom* (Cambridge, Mass.: Harvard University Press, 1954). Reprinted by permission.

In spite of a certain severity in your guidance, lead the children into a situation which they like and which invites them to be free and confident.

This is the supreme demand in education; all the rest, whatever one may call it, is only of secondary and tertiary importance; all instruction from the elements of learning to the highest levels of scholarship should tend to this. Hence those schools whose main function is merely teaching and learning cannot be considered as serving education in the deepest sense of the word. They are only of assisting value, and this only for such families as have already fulfilled the educational postulates mentioned above. . . .

It follows that education, in order to have a permanent effect, must try to use instruction not only for mere information but also for the formation of character.[2]

While Pestalozzi and Rousseau had emphasized the importance of the individual against society, Herbart tried to achieve a balance between the two. The individual should develop his own capacities; at the same time, he owes much to society and finds himself best in service to his fellow man.

Ethics does not imply the establishment of rigid rules, for life is an educational process that is forever incomplete. The moralist may be the enemy of virtue, for he sets up his own standards as ultimates. Rather, Herbart recommends that we constantly redefine our functions and that we retain an exploratory spirit. Nothing is more futile than to specialize in one field or to look at life from one standpoint. The more we cultivate wide interests and wide sympathy the more we shall grow in genuine morality.

To Herbart, ethics is the test of education. This means that pure reason is the prelude to practical reason, and that knowledge is the overture to action. Ideals are not abstractions to be admired platonically; they are patterns for meaningful activity. The educated man, according to Herbart, knows virtue and understands human aspirations; at the same time, he seeks ways and

2. *Ibid.*

means whereby ideals can be actualized. This demands both intelligence and emotional balance.

Educational Psychology

As a psychologist, Herbart left his most lasting mark upon the history of education. He revolutionized this field in his attempt to make it into an autonomous science and divorce it from metaphysics. Before his time, psychologists had stressed the separate faculties of the mind and had labored under the impact of Aristotle and Aquinas. Herbart's approach was experimental, and he showed that education depends on psychological functions.

Without a psychological background we cannot comprehend the learner:

> Those who have no true psychological insight, rarely understand anything of education. They may cherish the obsolete opinion that there reside in the human soul certain powers or faculties which have to be trained in one way or another. These people seemingly have in mind gymnastic exercises which strengthen the muscles, for man has only one kind of muscles. Indeed in each single apperceptive mass (mass or group of ideas) are contained so-called fantasy, memory, and intelligence, but they are not equally distributed. Rather, in one and the same person a certain mass of apperceptions may be of more intellectual, imaginative, or of reproductive character; one mass may be penetrated with profound feeling, another with an atmosphere of coolness, etc. Therefore, what educators call formal discipline (*Formelle Bildung*) would be an absurdity if it meant the training of isolated mental faculties which exist only in some people's imaginations.[8]

Teachers, according to Herbart, should be conscious of the plasticity of human behavior:

> It requires a great deal to raise knowledge to the level of erudition; it is a still more difficult task to combine the imparting of knowledge with the formation of character. To achieve this purpose,

3. *Ibid.*

knowledge must be deeply felt and experienced; in other words, the mere quantity of knowledge and the logical and practical training in notions, maxims, and principles must affect the whole emotional attitudes of a person. One may show how instruction has to proceed to produce such an effect. (I have shown this in my *Science of Education*.) The degree of success, however, depends largely on the pupil's individuality.

Only teachers of much experience can imagine how rapidly even carefully and cultivated knowledge vanishes under new conditions. They only can believe how rapidly new opinions and ambitions emerge and how irresistibly a person is attracted by temptations that appeal to his nature—in spite of all previous precautions. Even superficial experience teaches us that the results of an examination are valid only for the day when it is held. . . . Such facts, however, are truly explained through reference to the continual flow of ideas (apperceptive masses) in our mind. Those who consider the human soul as a fixed and concrete object will never understand the mutability of the human character; they will easily resort to false remedies which only aggravate the evil.[4]

In this respect, there are important similarities between Herbart and William James. Both viewed education and philosophy from a psychological standpoint; both were opposed to traditionalism; both had an experimental bent; both were important textbook writers; and both systematized the knowledge of their time. However, James was a voluntarist, fully aware of the impact of the will, while Herbart had a more rationalistic and mathematical conception of psychology.

To Herbart, man's mind is a battleground of ideas or presentations. They fight for dominance, and when they lose they become part of our subconscious. Consciousness is not a simple process; it is like a stage play in which new actors constantly enter, and occasionally the old performers reappear. In his concept of the subconscious, Herbart anticipates Freud; except that

4. *Ibid.*

to Herbart it lacked a sexual connotation and the process of repression was on a mechanical plane.

The mind, according to Herbart, has three functions: it knows, feels, and wills. However, the will is not a separate faculty; it is the desire which underlies our mental processes and our emotional reactions. The mind moves from sensation to memory, to imagination, and, at last, to conceptual thinking, its highest sphere. When a new concept enters the mind it can be rejected, and thus find its way into the subconscious; or it can be accepted and assimilated with other presentations.

To Herbart, there is no real intellectual creativity. An idea enters the mind and it has to be assimilated; what happens in creative thinking is a synthesis on a higher level. This can be verified by historical examples. There are no radically new inventions; they are usually built upon the past, and represent a redefinition on a more qualitative level. Toynbee uses the term etherialization to describe progress as a form of qualitative simplification in which past ways are modified by present experiences.

Implications for the Teacher

All this may sound extremely abstract and unrelated to the practical problems of teaching. However, the teacher can greatly benefit from Herbartian concepts. The teacher should be conscious of the fact, Herbart maintained, that learning involves an internal change. New ideas thus must strike a responsive chord in the mind of the student; they must be developed in his imagination, which can be accomplished only if the student is truly interested.

Instruction has four phases. It must (1) be concrete, (2) be continuous, (3) be elevating, and (4) have application to life. Herbart maintains that learning should start with illustrations, for our senses have to be stirred; then continuous exercise is needed, for without effort we do not progress. Yet, as Whitehead later pointed out, we also must be imbued with the adventure of ideas; thus, our imagination should invest facts with a romantic mantle. Lastly, knowledge is to be lived and experienced. This is the lesson of Goethe's *Faust;* action is superior to theoretical contemplation.

Herbart hints at the fact that the individual in his educational development repeats the development of the race. The young child, thus, is like the primitive and lives on a sensate level. The adolescent is like early society and his sense of romance and adventure is important. He needs, above all, disciplined thinking. The third stage corresponds to modern civilization when man achieves a balance between individuality and society, and when he is able to make evaluative judgments.

The difference between the scholar and the average person lies in concentration. Take the example of a scholar writing a book: his ideas are disciplined; his energies are focused on the project. He is scarcely conscious of the stimulus of his environment, of the room he is working in, or of what time of day it is. Take, on the other hand, a mediocre student of today studying for a test. He will daydream about his weekend; he may even listen to television; thus, his thoughts are broken up, and only scattered intellectual associations result.

The method of Herbart is formalized in five steps:

1. *Preparation.* The environment is created—both external and internal—for the development of ideas. Old ideas are recalled from the subconscious and attention is cultivated.

2. *Presentation.* The lessons are presented to children with the use of illustrations to make them as concrete as possible.

3. *Association.* Both similarities and differences between old and new ideas are stressed. This develops order and consistency in thinking.

4. *Generalization.* This is a method of qualitative simplification, so that more and more facts can be understood in their widening meaning.

5. *Application.* Knowledge must be used and become part of our daily existence.

What strikes the observer is the balanced viewpoint of Herbart. He is concerned with theory and practice, with ideal and actuality. The curriculum, he maintained, should cultivate both the sciences and the humanities. Through the sciences the students would gain "empirical knowledge," while the humanities would give him sympathy.

Our mind develops in two ways. It grows and expands through a systematic concentration upon facts which have to be mastered and explored. Thus, Herbart especially favored mathematics, which would create rigorous thinking. Yet, at the same time, we have to develop patterns of appreciation, for we are not merely intellectual beings or products of pure reason. Hence, we should study literature, philosophy, the arts, religion, and history. Now we become part of the life stream of humanity; our emotions are touched and we learn to identify ourselves with others.

In the American system of education in the twentieth century we overrate empirical knowledge, and we are seduced by facts. The "Quiz Kid" thus becomes the ideal of many teachers. However, far more important than facts are wisdom and the ability to judge. Life basically is an evaluative process. Without wisdom we become prisoners of practicality and victims of a false utilitarianism.

The ideal of balanced wisdom stamps the educational philosophy of Herbart:

If the teacher succeeds in developing in the pupil manifold interest, then the education becomes a noble task in that it helps mankind to realize the great practical ethical ideas. These ideas will become the more self-evident to the pupil the less it is necessary to teach him merely to swim on the waves of society as was the case with the unsusceptible type. On the other hand, it is necessary to combine exact methods of thinking and self-criticism with the enthusiasm which can be imparted to the susceptible pupil by such means as religion and history. Of particular use for such an examining attitude is the capacity of clear ethical discrimination. For by its own nature the human mind is not so well disposed as to apprehend clearly the ideas of justice, equity, perfection, and sympathy, and to act accordingly. In addition, a person with the capacity for inner freedom not rarely abandons traditional ideals and inclines towards eccentric claims and opinions for which, so he thinks, he has to fight and to bring sacrifices in order to carry off the crown of martyrdom. The striving for the unusual and the exceptional is in the spirit of the time, but it does not fit our country. Hence, what education has to do is to preserve in talented youth their natural courage and open-mindedness but not to inspire them with burning ambition.[5]

Evaluation

American educators who studied in Germany were impressed by the ideas of Herbart, and they tried to introduce his concepts into the American curriculum. Among these men were Charles McMurray as well as Charles de Gammo, who regarded Herbart as the new Aristotle. In 1892, the National Herbartian Society was founded; ten years later it changed its name to the National Society for the Scientific Study of Education. In later years Herbart's influence waned, as Dewey's concepts and the ideals of pragmatism were more widely accepted.

Still, the lasting contributions of Herbart should not be underestimated. He made the study of educational psychology paramount; he developed a more creative technique of classroom teaching; he showed the significance of methodology in instruction; he developed the social perspective in the study of history and the humanities; he pointed to the intimate connection between education and ethics; he had a balanced viewpoint regarding the responsibilities of the teacher and the student. As yet, our knowledge of the human mind is limited and, while we have progressed beyond Herbart, the psychology of learning is still in

5. *Ibid.*

its infancy. The more we learn about education, the more we appreciate the wisdom of Herbart, who insisted that education should be based upon sound psychological theory and that the human mind acts not according to faculties, but as a unitary whole.

It has often been pointed out, especially by Dewey, that Herbart concentrates too much on the intellectual side of man, and that he overlooks the importance of feeling, and that, furthermore, he makes too much of man's rationalistic processes and neglects the role of impulse. But the other extreme in education, which glorifies impulse and neglects rational control, is far more devastating in its social effects than Herbartianism.

To Dewey, as is well known, education has no external goal; it implies the constant reconstruction of experience. To Herbart, on the other hand, education has a moral purpose, which was to be determined by historical experience in the light of man's deepest spiritual longings. To state that education has no purpose is true from a semantic standpoint, but, viewed idealistically, the aims of educators define their effectiveness.

The greatness of Herbart lies in his faith that education ultimately could become a science. This may be impossible, for actually the teacher is a creative artist who attempts to cultivate sensitivity in his students and in society. But we shall never advance in education unless we subject its results to the test of scientific evidence, and unless we concentrate more upon the psychology of learning—a field in which Herbart was a master.

18. Froebel

The life of Friedrich Froebel (1782–1852) covers a stormy period in German history. He lived under the impact of the Napoleonic wars, and he witnessed the growing nationalism of the German states.

All his life Froebel suffered from the impact of his mother's death; she had passed away when he was only nine months old. His father, a pastor, remarried, but coldness prevailed between the boy and his stepmother. He studied at the University of Jena, and later at Göttingen and Berlin.

His educational capacities were stirred when he became a teacher of drawing at Frankfurt, when he worked with three boys at Keilhau, and, later, when he founded several schools in Switzerland. His most important achievement from the standpoint of education, took place in 1837, when he established a kindergarten at Blankenburg.

Among his works, special mention should be made of his *Autobiography, Education by Development, The Education of Man, Mother Play, and Pedagogies of the Kindergarten.*

Among the influences that conditioned his thinking, mention should be made of the Zend-Avesta, which pictured both unity and diversity; the philosophy of Friedrich von Schelling, who gave a speculative account of nature; the ideas of F. C. J. Krause, a Neo-Kantian who pictured the unity of man and God; and especially the impact of Comenius, Rousseau, H. G. Heusinger, Pestalozzi, and Schiller.

Most important was the impact of his own experiences. He felt that children frequently lack security and love in the home, and that education should start as soon as possible in order to develop warmth and understanding between parents and children. He was opposed to war and regarded it as an enemy of human culture and education. How could man progress when he was constantly threatened by destruction? How could creativity develop when society emphasized violence? How could family life be strengthened when war killed the best members of society?

His educational ideals rested upon a deep faith in religion. Spiritual ideals could not be defined; they could only be experienced. God, as the Absolute Power, included all parts of nature; man was part of God and God was part of man: this was a clear expression of pantheism.

God was not a static force; He revealed Himself in the universe, which thus achieved higher and higher levels. Man likewise moved from primitivism to maturity, and finally attained self-consciousness.

A law governs all of life:

In all things there lives and reigns an eternal law. This all controlling law is necessarily based on an all-pervading, energetic, living, self-conscious, and hence eternal, unity. This unity is God. All things have come from the divine Unity, from God, and have their origins in the divine Unity, in God alone. God is the sole source of all things. In all things there lives and reigns a divine Unity, God. All things live and have their being in and through the divine Unity, in and through God. All things are only through the divine effluence that lives in them. The divine effluence that lives in each thing is the essence of each thing.

It is the destiny and lifework of all things to unfold their essence, hence their divine being, and therefore the divine Unity itself—to reveal God in their external and transient being. It is the special destiny and lifework of man, as an intelligent and rational being, to become fully, vividly, and clearly conscious of his essence, of the divine effluence in him, and therefore of God; to become fully, vividly, and clearly conscious of his destiny and lifework; and to accomplish this, to render it (his essence) active, to reveal it in his own life with self-determination and freedom. *Education consists in leading man, as a thinking, intelligent being, growing into self-consciousness, to a pure and unsullied, conscious and free representation of the inner law of divine Unity, and in teaching him ways and means thereto.*[1]

Education depends on the cosmic purpose:

By education, then, the divine essence of man should be un-folded, brought out, lifted into consciousness, and man himself raised into free, conscious obedience to the divine principle that lives in him, and to a free representation of this principle in his life. Education as a whole, by means of instruction and training, should bring to man's consciousness, and render efficient in his life, the fact that man and nature proceed from God and are conditioned by him—that both have their being in God. *Education should lead and guide man to clearness concerning himself and in himself, to peace with nature, and to unity with God;* hence, it should lead him to a knowledge of himself and of mankind, to a knowledge of God and of nature, and to the pure and holy life to which such knowledge leads.[2]

The two most important aspects of man are creativity and freedom. Freedom implies the ability to make wise choices and to avoid evil. Goodness alone is real, according to Froebel, for evil is merely partiality and a distortion of goodness. Man is naturally creative; this is an expression of his basic nature.

These concepts have important educational implications. The

1. *The Education of Man.*
2. *Ibid.*

child is not evil; on the contrary, waywardness is usually a lack of vision and the result of false values. The child must be taught in such a way that the eternal spark of his soul becomes a living reality.

Education is most effective when it is based on the needs of children. Did not Jesus say that the Kingdom of Heaven is within man? This meant that, as nature unfolds, potentialities appear. It is a modern version of the dictum of Socrates that self-knowledge is the road to wisdom.

To Froebel, education depended on the unity of the family. The most important virtue for the mother was gentleness, whereas the father had to guide wisely. A home united by love would be the best institution for human progress. When the home failed in its responsiblities, the educator had the duty to instruct the parents in the paths of virtue.

This does not imply puritanism. To Froebel, moral laws were reflections of the Absolute and our human understanding was limited. Humility was a primary virtue. Still, God was our inspiration and we could find Him through the study of man, of nature, and of the universe. Like Emerson, Froebel believed in a fundamental unity. To study oneself and to study nature would lead to the same result: a recognition of the moral nature of the universe. The wise man is the good man, for virtue and knowledge are identical.

Our moral education, according to Froebel, is strengthened through association. Hence, children should be brought up in a wholesome environment. They should be imbued with the ideals of cooperation. To Froebel, play activities had primary significance; when a child played, he revealed his inner nature and at the same time developed patterns of socialization.

We learn best by doing; theorizing is a minor aspect of education, according to Froebel. For example, we can talk about the good life to children, and yet we will not influence them; what matters is, that we *live* the good life and that our school activities are constructive.

To become truly educated, Froebel asserted, we must cultivate our senses, especially hearing and vision. Too many children become indifferent because they are never aware of the beauties around them and because they do not play creatively.

Education, according to Froebel, means the cultivation of awareness, love, and independence:

> A child that plays thoroughly, with self-active determination, perseveringly until physical fatigue forbids, will surely be a thorough determined man, capable of self-sacrifice for the promotion of the welfare of himself and others. Is not the most beautiful expression of child life at this time a playing child?—a child wholly absorbed in his play?—a child that has fallen asleep while so absorbed?
>
> The aim and object of parental care, in the domestic and family circle, is to awaken and develop, to quicken all the powers and natural gifts of the child, to enable all the members and organs of man to fulfill the requirements of the child's powers and gifts. The natural mother does all this instinctively, without instruction and direction; but this is not enough: it is needful that she should do it consciously.
>
> The child—your child, ye fathers—follows you wherever you are, wherever you go, in whatever you do. Do not harshly repel him; show no impatience about his ever-recurring questions. Every harshly repelling word crushes a bud or shoot of his tree of life. Do not, however, tell him in words much more than he could find himself without your words. . . . To have found one fourth of the answer by his own effort is of more value and importance to the child than it is to half hear and half understand it in the words of another.[3]

The curriculum, Froebel made clear, should develop the foundations of perception. Facts are secondary and memorization is to be avoided. We are stirred only when we directly experience the greatness of life and of the universe.

Froebel was especially concerned with the problem of creativity. Is it an outward or an inward process? Does it demand disci-

3. *Ibid.*

pline or spontaneity? Froebel maintained that creativity is one of man's most important needs. We all seek self-expression; we all want self-realization. On the elementary level, it may be represented by a child building a castle in the sand; on a higher level, it may be a scientist developing a new theory of physics or an engineer building a new factory. Creativity is a process that starts in infancy and ends in the grave, and it can be furthered best if we understand the spontaneous nature of children. Froebel stated that if we encourage the child when he is young, the chances are that he will develop creative patterns in his mature years. Our interests, according to Froebel, are continuous; one builds upon another, and the wise teacher realizes that the first years of the child are the most important.

Life, Froebel taught, is lived on two levels. First, there is the level of actuality; then there is the realm of symbolism, which is a representation of inward urges and wishes. Objects used by children, such as toys, have an inner meaning. Nothing in the universe, according to Froebel, is without significance.

This is an expression of romantic mysticism that goes back to the ideals of St. Francis, who preached to the birds and who had a special love for children. It is part of the ideals of Jesus, who desired adults to have the openness of children. To Froebel, as to St. Francis and to Jesus, the universe was an allegory that taught a moral lesson to man.

Education implies the cultivation of the spirit. As he states:

> The debasing illusion that man works, produces, creates only in order to preserve his body, in order to secure food, clothing, and shelter, may have to be endured, but should not be diffused and propagated. Primarily and in truth man works only that his spiritual, divine essence may assume outward form, and that thus he may be enabled to recognize his own spiritual, divine nature and the innermost being of God. Whatever food, clothing and shelter he obtains thereby comes to him as an insignificant surplus. Therefore Jesus says, "Seek ye first the kingdom of heaven," that is, the

realization of the divine spirit in your life and through your life, and whatever else your finite life may require, will be added unto you.

Yet human power should be developed, cultivated, and manifested not only in inner repose, as religion and religious spirit; not only in outward efficiency, as work and industry; but also—withdrawing upon itself and its own resources—in abstinence, temperance, and frugality. Is it needful to do more than indicate this to a human being not wholly at variance with himself? Where religion, industry, and temperance, the truly undivided trinity, rule in harmony, in true pristine unity, there, indeed, is heaven upon earth— peace, joy, salvation, grace, blessedness.[4]

Instruction depends on example, communication, and the cultivation of a pure heart:

Will is the mental activity, ever consciously proceeding from a definite point in a definite direction toward a definite object, in harmony with the man's nature as a whole. This statement contains everything, and indicates all that parent and educator, teacher and school, should be or should give to the boy in example and precept during these years. The starting-point of all mental activity in the boy should be energetic and sound; the source whence it flows, pure, clear, living and life-giving, elevating, worthy of the effort, worthy of the destiny and mission of man, worthy of his essential nature, and tending to develop it and give it full expression.

Instruction in example and in words, which later on become precept and example, furnishes the means for this. Neither example alone nor words alone will do: not example alone, for it is particular and special, and the word is needed to give to particular, individual examples universal applicability; not words alone, for example is needed to interpret and explain the word, which is generally spiritual, and of many meanings. But instruction and example alone and in themselves are not sufficient; they must meet a good, pure heart, and this is the outcome of proper educational influences in childhood.[5]

4. *Ibid.*
5. *Ibid.*

The most lasting contribution of Froebel lay in his development of the kindergarten. This idea found a ready response in the United States. In 1873, W. T. Harris opened one of the first kindergartens as part of the educational system of St. Louis, Missouri. Today we realize the importance of the kindergarten as a socializing force, and we have made it a primary foundation of our educational system.

Critics often object that Froebel is too vague and indefinite in his ideas. There is a vast difference between him and Herbart. Froebel wrote like a poet and his philosophy was an expression of his heart, whereas Herbart was an analytical scientist. But Froebel was right in his belief that education was a transcendental function; it points not only to man's social nature, but also to his metaphysical ideals. Thus, education becomes an expression of man's ultimate hopes.

Such thoughts are important, but they cannot be presented systematically. They are like the intuitions of poetry or the melodies of music. They have primarily a symbolic, rather than a scientific, meaning.

Perhaps Froebel went too far in his child-centered system of education; perhaps he overrated play activities. In his period, such an emphasis was progressive. In our own time, it would not necessarily contribute to educational advancement.

In the twentieth century, we have gone to the other extreme. We often neglect intellectual discipline and try to make learning too easy. We underrate the importance of subject matter. Thus, part of our education may be an encounter with triviality.

For all this we must not blame Froebel, who had a basic faith in man's capacity for knowledge and culture. The sciences and the arts, religion and philosophy, all would contribute to create a harmonious world view.

In a period of disenchantment, the optimism of Freobel is refreshing. As he states:

> Man is by no means naturally bad, nor has he originally bad or evil qualities and tendencies, unless, indeed, we consider as naturally evil, bad, and faulty the *finite*, the *material*, the *transitory*, the *physical*, as such, and the logical consequences of the existing of these phenomena; namely, that man must have the possibility of failure in order to be good and virtuous; that he must be able to make himself a slave in order to be truly free. Yet these things are the necessary concomitants of the manifestation of the eternal in the temporal, of unity in diversity, and follow necessarily from man's destiny to become a conscious, reasonable, and free being.
>
> A suppressed or perverted good quality—a good tendency, only repressed, misunderstood, or misguided—lies originally at the bottom of every shortcoming in man. Hence, the only and infallible remedy for counteracting any shortcoming and even wickedness is to find the originally good source, the originally good side of the human being that has been repressed, disturbed, or misled into the shortcoming, and then to foster, build up, and properly guide this good side. Thus the shortcoming will at last disappear, although it may involve a hard struggle *against habit, but not against original depravity in man;* and this is accomplished so much the more rapidly and surely because man himself tends to abandon his shortcomings, for man prefers right to wrong . . . [6]

There are two types of idealism in the history of education. One type stresses the importance of authority and it plays a strong part in American educational history. From earliest Colonial times, the idealistic tradition was strong. It found an able representative in Jonathan Edwards, a New England theologian; later, in the nineteenth century, it was championed by Ralph Waldo Emerson and William T. Harris. In the twentieth century, Herman H. Horne, professor of philosophy at New York University, popularized some of the educational views of idealism. The idealists emphasized the importance of discipline and

6. *Ibid.*

they generally reacted unfavorably to the progressive measures of contemporary education. The idealists believe in tradition: there can be no sharp breaks with the past, and the classics are just as valid today as they were centuries ago.

Robert Hutchins, in his criticism of modern education, belongs to the idealistic tradition. Hutchins indicts education for its specialization, its scientific contents, and its neglect of history. To Hutchins, the ideal university would be Paris around A.D. 1200, instead of Harvard or Yale in the twentieth century. His ideas were formative in the establishment of St. John's College, whose educational philosophy is based upon the mastery of the Hundred Great Books of Western Civilization; here, professors and students learn together in seminars, and no electives are tolerated.

The idealists today in elementary and secondary education want to return to the three R's, which, they charge, are sadly neglected in contemporary education. They believe in a teacher-centered form of education, because they think that the student needs guidance and firmness, especially in the period of adolescence. Horne calls for an "ideal-centered" school—a reminder of Froebel's program.

19. Jefferson

Thomas Jefferson (1743–1826) was one of the most brilliant figures in the history of American education. He studied at William and Mary, where he majored in law. In 1769 he was elected to Virginia's House of Burgesses. There he was closely associated with Patrick Henry, the inveterate enemy of English imperialism. We note his work in the Continental Congress, where he helped draw up the Declaration of Independence. He was responsible for religious freedom in Virginia, and also aided in destroying the remains of feudalism there. He became the governor of Virginia, then ambassador to France; then Secretary of State, Vice-President, and finally President of the United States.

He promoted the cause of education as first rector of the University of Virginia. Not only was he a great statesman; he was also a thinker of unusual stature.

Influences

Philosophically, Jefferson drew upon a variety of sources. At William and Mary he was introduced to philosophy by Mr. Small, who, however, had little knowledge of metaphysics.

Small's lectures dealt mostly with scientific and moral problems. Philosophy at William and Mary occupied a rather minor place in the curriculum.

Among the thinkers who conditioned Jefferson's thinking, special attention should be given to Cicero, from whose writings he absorbed a faith in natural moral capacities and in the possibilities of education. Like Cicero, Jefferson was skeptical of supernatural truths.

Lord Kames' *Principles of Natural Religion* also had an impact on his thinking, as did Locke, Ferguson, Stewart, Ellis, and above all, Bolingbroke. While he stayed in France he was on friendly terms with Demeunier, Morellet, Mably, Condorcet, and Cabanis. He was well acquainted with Destutt de Tracy, whose system he admired greatly. In fact, he regarded Tracy as one of the most astute and able thinkers of all time.

While he respected the materialistic thinkers, he did not agree with their theories. He felt that they gave only a mechanistic account of man and he was opposed to their stress on self-interest. No valid moral system, according to Jefferson, could be based primarily on egoism.

Philosophical and Religious Ideals

Jefferson felt that moral ideals could not be reduced to a scientific basis:

> I think it lost time to attend lectures in this branch. He who made us would have been a pitiful bungler if he had made the rules of our moral conduct a matter of science. For one man of science, there are thousands who are not. What would have become of them? Man was destined for society. His morality, therefore, was to be formed to this object. He was endowed with a sense of right and wrong merely relative to this. . . . The moral sense, or conscience, is as much a part of man as his leg or arm. It is given to all human beings in a stronger or weaker degree, as force of members is given them in a greater or less degree. It may be strengthened by exercise,

as may any particular limb of the body. This sense is submitted indeed in some degree to the guidance of reason; but it is a small stock which is required for this: even a less one than what we call common sense. State a moral case to a ploughman and a professor. The former will decide it as well, and often better than the latter, because he has not been led astray by artificial rules. In this branch, therefore, read good books because they will encourage as well as direct your feelings.[1]

It is most important for us to be just and humane and to engage in activities that promote kindness and the brotherhood of man. Jefferson emphasized that the religion of Jesus is simple and can be applied to all men:

1. That there is one only God, and he all perfect.
2. That there is a future state of rewards and punishments.
3. That to love God with all thy heart and thy neighbor as thyself is the sum of religion. These are the great points on which he endeavored to reform the religion of the Jews.

But compare with these the demoralizing dogmas of Calvin:
1. That there are three Gods.
2. That good works, or the love of our neighbors, are nothing.
3. That faith is everything, and the more incomprehensible the proposition, the more merit in its faith.
4. That reason in religion is of unlawful use.
5. That God, from the beginning, elected certain individuals to be saved, and certain others to be damned; and that no crimes of the former can damn them; no virtues of the latter save.[2]

Jefferson held that Calvin had perverted the Christian faith:

Had the doctrines of Jesus been preached always as pure as they came from his lips, the whole civilized world now would have been Christian. I rejoice that in this blessed country of free inquiry and belief, which has surrendered its creed and conscience to neither kings nor priests, the genuine doctrine of one only God is reviving,

1. Letter to Peter Carr, August 10, 1787.
2. Letter to Dr. Benjamin Waterhouse, June 26, 1822.

and I trust that there is not a young man now living in the United States who will not die an Unitarian.

But much I fear that when this great truth shall be re-established, its votaries will fall into the fatal error of fabricating formulas of creed and confessions of faith, the engines which so soon destroyed the religion of Jesus, and made of Christendom a mere Aceldama.[3]

His political principles are summarized in his inaugural message of 1801:

It is proper you should understand what I deem the essential principles of this government and consequently those which ought to shape its administration.

I will compress them in the narrowest compass they will bear, stating the general principle, but not all its limitations.

Equal and exact justice to all men, of whatever state or persuasion, religious or political:

Peace, commerce, and honest friendship with all nations, entangling alliances with none.

The support of the State governments in all their rights, as the most competent administrations for our domestic concerns, and the surest bulwarks against anti-republican tendencies.

The preservation of the General government, in its whole constitutional vigor, as the sheet anchor of our peace at home, and safety abroad.

A jealous care of the right of election by the people, a mild and sage corrective of abuses, which are lopped by the sword of revolution, where peaceable remedies are unprovided.

Absolute acquiescence in the decisions of the Majority, the vital principle of republics, from which is no appeal but to force, the vital principle and immediate part of despotism.

A well-disciplined militia, our best reliance in peace, and for the first moments of war, till regulars may relieve them: The Supremacy of the Civil over the Military authority.

Economy in public expense, that labor may be lightly burthened.

The honest payment of our debts and sacred preservation of the public faith.

3. *Ibid.*

Encouragement of Agriculture, and of Commerce as its hand-maid.

The diffusion of information, and arraignment of all abuses at the bar of the public reason.

Freedom of Religion, freedom of the press, and freedom of Person under the protection of the Habeas Corpus: And trial by juries, impartially selected.[4]

Significance

In all his labors Jefferson was a true son of the Enlightenment. With his complete faith in science, reason, and progress, he represented the deistic ideal of life. As a supporter of peace, he was grateful that in the United States the bickerings and petty quarrels of Europe had no place. With all his power, he tried to keep the American colonies out of European entanglements.

To him democracy was almost a religious gospel. He felt that most of the evils of Europe could be traced to the crowned heads of the various countries; this distrust of kings has become part of the American tradition.

The keynote of the system of Jefferson was his insistent faith in freedom. He believed that the flame of freedom that had been kindled in the colonies would spread throughout the globe. Tolerant in his political and religious opinions, he zealously defended the right of others to differ, and even to assail him personally.

In education he followed the rule of Epicurus, together with the precepts of Jesus. Impatient with metaphysical disputes, he was interested above all in practical matters. He made it clear that Christianity must go back to its early purity and be purged of its Platonic content. He defended absolute freedom in religion; thus, he had no use for a state church.

To him all moral rules were summarized in the statement, "Fear God and love thy neighbor." The test of morality was utility, the way in which it promoted common happiness. He was

4. *First Inaugural Address,* 1801.

certain that no nation could violate moral rules and still prosper, since a disintegration of morality, he believed, inevitably led to tyranny.

To promote the welfare of mankind Jefferson urged above all the cultivation of education. Writing to Colonel Yancey in 1816, he stated: "If a nation expects to be ignorant and free in a state of civilization, it expects what never was and never will be."

Jefferson and the Twentieth Century

Jefferson is especially important in our era, which has seen a wholesale assault upon democracy. Two major world wars, depressions, and the rise of dictatorships in many countries have undermined the faith of many people in the possibilities of a free society. Fanatics of the left and right claim that in times of crisis democracy is an impossibility, that its machinery is too slow and too inefficient to meet the challenges of our time.

The twentieth century has been in a constant state of emergency. Violent military conflicts and ideological upheavals have cost the lives of millions of human beings. Jefferson, who was a careful student of history, pointed out that wars never aid democracies; they only strengthen the power of the elite and create an attitude of belligerency incompatible with peaceful living. Jefferson was opposed to entangling alliances because they curtail freedom of action and because they inevitably create counter alliances, and in this way spread the seeds of conflict.

Jefferson pointed out that the great problems of life cannot be solved by violence: Force would create a world of illusion; it would imply a compulsory return to the past. He believed that in the long run reason would prevail over force, for man's mind cannot be permanently curtailed. An opponent of militarism, Jefferson believed that civilian authority must be supreme; otherwise, a state of permanent emergency develops, with the result that prospects for mutuality are decreased.

The twentieth century has seen a vast concentration of mili-

tary power, especially in totalitarian societies. The influence of
the military extends not only to the government, but to economic
institutions and education. The military promise protection
against external aggression, but the security which they uphold is
never completely realized. In the armament race of the twentieth
century, all nations feel insecure because they are all equally
threatened with annihilation.

Ours has been an age of extremism. The extremists of the left
and the right are united by a common dislike for reason and by a
common prejudice against an objective discussion of public
affairs. They are so imbued with their respective causes that they
want to eliminate the freedom of their opponents. Jefferson reminds us that once freedom is curtailed, it can seldom be re-
gained, and that truth has nothing to fear in the open forum of
public debate. To Jefferson, no opinion was absolute and no
cause was sacred. This implied an emphasis on fallibility—an
important concept for twentieth-century man.

In a time when public opinion can easily be manufactured,
when stereotypes can be created almost overnight, when base
emotions can be aroused, when propaganda can triumph over
information, Jefferson reminds us that critical knowledge is a
foundation of decision-making in a democratic society. Jefferson
felt that it is not enough to be a specialist or a scholar; what
matters is participation in public life. Every man, he asserted,
owes an obligation to himself and to society to improve his mind
and study the issues that determine the fate of mankind.

He set an example to posterity by his own habits. He would
arise at dawn to write letters and reply to correspondence. In
fact, he wrote over 50,000 letters in his lifetime. His library was
one of the best of his time. Books, to him, were pathways to
emancipation. Before he went to bed at night he would read
great authors in their original language. Even in advanced age
he continued to read Greek, Latin, Italian, and French works.

To Jefferson, education implied a vital view of the present; it combined facts and values; it meant public service and the search for public enlightenment. He believed that education should be not only for the elite but also a means for the cultural advancement of all.

In an age of extreme specialization, Jefferson reminds us of the value of general education. He was as much interested in agriculture as in history. He treasured practical inventions and intellectual exercises, and could converse with equal ease with Dr. Benjamin Rush on medicine and with Thomas Paine on political theory. He believed that the human mind is capable of infinite improvement.

Jefferson believed that education was not to be gauged by the books that a student had read or by the grades he obtained, but by his growing understanding of himself and of society. If education alienated man from constructive relationships with others, then it had failed, and a sterile culture would result. If on the other hand education gave man an incentive to serve others and to improve humanity, then it was fulfilling its highest obligations.

Jefferson saw no opposition between the sciences and the humanities. The sciences he treasured because they added to man's control over nature and because they produced inventions that made life more exciting and that spread the impact of civilization. But to Jefferson science was not the goal of life; it was a method of understanding the external world. He valued the humanities because they enriched the mind; they represented the aristocracy of the spirit.

In a time when the past is often idolized, when some scholars want to return to the certainties of the thirteenth century, Jefferson reminds us that the past cannot be recovered and that traditionalism blocks the progress of education. Worship of the past leads to enslavement of the mind. The uniqueness of the present has to be explored if society is to advance and if democracy is to be safeguarded.

Jefferson was an excellent student of history and he had a special interest in Greek culture. Nevertheless, he maintained that students should be taught that the great ages lay ahead, not that their own period was only a footnote to antique glories.

The Puritan educators had looked on man as sinful, and preached the power of an arbitrary God who is enraged by the waywardness of man. Today many theologians are similarly enraptured by man's failings as they picture the awesome majesty of God. Jefferson, on the other hand, believed that religion is a simple matter, having a close relationship to education: Both are concerned with man's motivations; both are protests against pride and arrogance. Both are inward concerns that cannot be controlled by the state, and that have as their aim a closer union between ideal and reality.

Like Socrates, Jefferson was a moralist in his educational views. Morality implied, to Jefferson, a sense of obligation and a sense of humility. Jefferson asked penetrating questions as a way of clarifying complex issues and so that he could live a more examined existence. Morality, for private individuals, implied tolerance and understanding, sound habits, and the willingness to listen to various viewpoints.

For the nation, according to Jefferson, morality implied the avoidance of Machiavellianism. The end did not justify the means. Freedom could not be curtailed in times of crisis. Power was to be checked by progressive laws. Rulers were to be responsive to the desires of the people. Lies were never to be tolerated in public life. The expenses of government were to be kept to a minimum. Propaganda was to be avoided; instead, a careful deliberation of issues was to be stressed. More money was to be spent for institutions of education than for institutions of warfare. The rights of the opposition were to be safeguarded. The privileges of the individual were to be protected. Tyranny was to be combated, whether found in politics, religion, or education.

The evils that Jefferson fought against, such as organized ignorance, arbitrary government, authoritarianism, centralization of power, are even more significant in our own time than in his period. Today these evils threaten the survival of man; they could create a wasteland out of which escape may be impossible. Lincoln once remarked that Jefferson's ideas "represented the definitions and axioms of a free society."

The enemies of man, according to Jefferson, are not external; they are not represented by specific nations or civilizations, or by one religion or one philosophy; rather, the enemies of man reside in his own heart and permit his seduction by superstition and ignorance.

Education starts by liberating man from the tabus of the past; it removes him from the prejudice of his environment; it teaches him the value of freedom; it imbues him with a vast sense of social responsibility; it gives him an incentive to work for humanity; it stirs the resources of his intellect and his emotions; it appeals to his sense of purpose; it gives him a fervent sense of beauty; it gives him a genuine sense of morality that removes all social barriers.

Education in a Jeffersonian sense overcomes all forms of passivity and calls for strenuous participation in the drama of life. Education shows that democracy is not an unattainable ideal but an imperative reality. It points to the common rights of all individuals who are united in their quest for reason.

The task of the schools, according to Jefferson, is to inspire the young and the old, the rich and the poor with the possibilities of an open society. Thus democracy is to become a constant activity; it is to be the center of man's life; it is to dominate all his yearnings and ideals. It is to develop a genuine respect for individuality and for human integrity. It is to produce a new society which can look with confidence to the ideals of the future.

20. Emerson

Ralph Waldo Emerson (1803–1882) was probably the most eloquent apostle of transcendentalism. He was an individualist throughout his entire life. He resigned from his pastorate in the Second (Unitarian) Church of Boston when he lost faith in the symbols of religion, and when he could not tolerate any definite ritual. No party or religious sect could claim him.

In his age, individualism was much stronger than in the present century, when life has become more stereotyped. Comparing the attitude of the community of 1850 with that of the 1960's, one finds that intellectual tolerance has lessened. What would happen to Emerson today if he expressed his radical thoughts concerning the state?

Emerson's most famous contribution to American thinking was made in his address to the Phi Beta Kappa society of Harvard, in 1837, on the American scholar. Oliver Wendell Holmes said that it marked America's declaration of intellectual independence. This is an exaggeration—it was simply a prelude, the opening shot in the struggle for the liberation of the American mind.

The scholar, according to Emerson, derives his knowledge from three sources: first, from nature; second, from action; third, from books. The most important of these is nature. It is the first and formative influence which governs life. Nature is not mere disjointed and atomic force. It is not a realm in which merciless competition occurs, nor can it be explained solely by physical laws. Nature is the expression of a moral purpose; behind it is a spiritual fact, the Over-Soul, the principle of reality. In it is an undeniable identity, for all things are part of it. Thus, said Emerson, the ancient precept "Know thyself" and the modern maxim "Study nature" are at last united.

How different is this ideal from the concepts of modern schools of thought. Reading the books of Steinbeck, one finds a constant struggle between man and nature. The tragedy of existence, according to Sartre, is that there can be no common meeting ground between nature and man. Hence there is abroad today a feeling of despair and skepticism that has not only pervaded European literature, but has also made a powerful impression upon the American mind.

To Emerson, the scientific method is utterly inadequate. Like the Neoplatonists, he relied upon intuition. Truth, in Emerson's system, is to be discovered and envisioned; it cannot be gained through painstaking analysis.[1] Undoubtedly there is a strain of mysticism in his philosophy, but this element in his mental make-up was restrained and did not prevent him from having a sharp and penetrating social insight.

The task of the thinker, according to Emerson, is to be part of the rhythm of nature. To the twentieth-century world, this would lead to a gospel of skepticism; to Emerson it was an affirmation, because to him all of nature revealed an identical purpose and represented the perfection of the universe.

When Emerson turned to books, he showed how they could both stimulate and hinder the intellectual development of man. He reminded his listeners that the greatest works of the past, like

1. See Stewart G. Brown, "Emerson's Platonism," *New England Quarterly*, XVIII (1945), 325-45.

those of Cicero, Locke, and Bacon, were written in the youth of these authors; thus they could not be infallible guides to the problems of life. The professors in the audience, worshipping books for their own sake, must have disapproved most vigorously. Dr. John Pierce later compared Emerson's speech with the "misty, dreamy and unintelligible style of Swedenborg, Coleridge, and Carlyle."

It is unfortunate that the American intellectual has not listened to Emerson, for it is quite apparent that the academic life of the United States is still guided by medieval academic traditions. To read a list of dissertation topics for Ph.D. theses is a most disillusioning experience. Trivial subjects seem to rank high in this type of scholarship. The learned journals of American culture are almost scholastic in their endless debates concerning technical points.[2]

Emerson said that one must be creative to read well. There is too much respect in the United States for the printed word, too much intellectual conformity, too much tolerance for second- and third-rate political and economic ideas. And when these achieve oral expression, the lack of sophistication of American audiences is even more apparent.

Most important of all, Emerson urges the thinker to be a man of action. To be a recluse intellectually was distasteful to his mind. Living in the past as so many American intellectuals are wont to do is a betrayal, for their insight is needed by the man on the street. Scholarship that is confined to books is hopelessly incomplete and sterile, for it lacks the earthy touch of experience.

It was Emerson's belief that character has a higher role than intellect. It does not matter so much what a man thinks: more important is what he is. The Puritans were quite different in this respect. They were more concerned with the thoughts of a man

2. Regarding the separation of theory and practice and the medieval concept of learning, see John Dewey, *The School and Society*, pp. 41-44, 72-73.

than with his character development. Most Americans today would agree with Emerson; indeed, they distrust those who have too much intellect.

Here a definite danger arises. Critics like Dennis Brogan have seen the activistic aspects of American culture and pointed out how the modern American worships movement and change and dislikes to think about the goal of his endeavor. In such an atmosphere thinking is not welcome, for it may challenge the basic postulates of action.

Strangely enough, Emerson in his Phi Beta Kappa speech mentioned Swedenborg as a pattern for the future man.[3] Emerson had a great respect for this thinker because Swedenborg saw the symbolic spirit of nature and showed how close the bonds were between the material and the spiritual worlds. Swedenborg's greatness was based upon a combination of theology and mathematics. Emerson, perhaps, went too far in his enthusiasm. Certainly Swedenborg in his influence upon civilization has been a more regressive than liberating influence.

What are the duties of the scholar? Emerson replies:

They are such as become Man Thinking. They may all be comprised in self-trust. The office of the scholar is to cheer, to raise, and to guide men by showing them facts amidst appearances. He plies the slow, unhonored, and unpaid task of observation. Flamsteed and Herschel, in their glazed observatories, may catalogue the stars with the praise of all men, and the results being splendid and useful, honor is sure. But he, in his private observatory, cataloguing obscure and nebulous stars of the human mind, which as yet no man has thought of as such—watching days and months sometimes for a few facts; correcting still his old records;—must relinquish display and immediate fame. In the long period of his preparation

---

3. Besides Swedenborg, Emerson's technical philosophy owes much to Plato, Berkeley, Coleridge, Cousin, and Goethe. See Kenneth W. Cameron, *Emerson the Essayist: An Outline of His Philosophic Development Through 1836*, vol. 1. The Oriental influence on Emerson is fully discussed in F. I. Carpenter, *Emerson and Asia*, and A. Christy, *The Orient in American Transcendentalism*.

he must betray often an ignorance and shiftlessness in popular arts, incurring the disdain of the able who shoulder him aside. Long he must stammer in his speech; often forgo the living for the dead. Worse yet, he must accept—how often!—poverty and solitude. For the ease and pleasure of treading the old road, accepting the fashions, the education, the religion of society, he takes the cross of making his own, and, of course, the self-accusation, faint heart, the frequent uncertainty and loss of time, which are the nettles and tangling vines in the way of the self-relying and self-directed; and the state of virtual hostility in which he seems to stand to society, and especially to educated society. For all this loss and scorn, what offset? He is to find consolation in exercising the highest function of human nature. He is one who raises himself from private considerations and breathes and lives on public and illustrious thoughts. He is the world's eye. He is the world's heart. He is to resist the vulgar prosperity that retrogrades ever to barbarism, by preserving and communicating heroic sentiments, noble biographies, melodious verse, and the conclusions of history.[4]

The scholar is to resist the popular cry, Emerson continues:

These being his functions, it becomes him to feel all confidence in himself, and to defer never to the popular cry. He and he only knows the world. The world of any moment is the merest appearance. Some great decorum, some fetish of a government, some ephemeral trade, or war, or man, is cried up by half mankind and cried down by the other half, as if all depended on this particular up or down. The odds are that the whole question is not worth the poorest thought which the scholar has lost in listening to the controversy. Let him not quit his belief that a popgun is a popgun, though the ancient and honorable of the earth affirm it to be the crack of doom. In silence, in steadiness, in severe abstraction, let him hold by himself; add observation to observation, patient of neglect, patient of reproach, and bide his own time—happy enough if he can satisfy himself alone that this day he has seen something truly. Success treads on every right step. For the instinct is sure,

4. *The American Scholar.*

that prompts him to tell his brother what he thinks. He then learns that in going down into the secrets of his own mind he has descended into the secrets of all minds. He learns that he who has mastered any law in his private thoughts, is master to that extent of all men whose language he speaks, and of all into whose language his own can be translated. The poet, in utter solitude remembering his spontaneous thoughts and recording them, is found to have recorded that which men in crowded cities find true for them also. The orator distrusts at first the fitness of his frank confessions, his want of knowledge of the persons he addresses, until he finds that he is the complement of his hearers—that they drink his words because he fulfills for them their own nature; the deeper he dives into his privatest, secretest presentiment, to his wonder he finds that is the most acceptable, most public, and universally true. The people delight in it; the better part of every man feels, This is my music; this is myself.

In self-trust all the virtues are comprehended. Free should the scholar be—free and brave. Free even to the definition of freedom, "without any hindrance that does not arise out of his own constitution." Brave; for fear is a thing which a scholar by his very function puts behind him.[5]

5. *Ibid.*

The scholar is to promote the affirmative trends of his time:

I have dwelt perhaps tediously upon this abstraction of the scholar. I ought not to delay longer to add what I have to say of nearer reference to the time and to this country.

Historically, there is thought to be a difference in the ideas which predominate over successive epochs, and there are data for marking the genius of the Classic, of the Romantic, and now of the Reflective or Philosophical age. With the views I have intimated of the oneness or the identity of the mind through all individuals, I do not much dwell on these differences. In fact, I believe each individual passes through all three. The boy is a Greek; the youth, romantic; the adult reflective. I deny not, however, that a revolution in the leading idea may be distinctly enough traced.

Our age is bewailed as the age of Introversion. Must that needs be evil? We, it seems, are critical; we are embarrassed with second thoughts; we cannot enjoy anything for hankering to know whereof the pleasure consists; we are lined with eyes; we see with our feet; the time is infected with Hamlet's unhappiness—

"Sicklied o'er with the pale cast of thought."

It is so bad then? Sight is the last thing to be pitied. Would we be blind? Do we fear lest we should outsee nature and God, and drink truth dry? I look upon the discontent of the literary class as a mere announcement of the fact that they find themselves not in the state of mind of their fathers, and regret the coming state as un-tried; as a boy dreads the water before he has learned that he can swim. If there is any period one would desire to be born in, is it not the age of the Revolution; when the old and the new stand side by side and admit of being compared; when the energies of all men are searched by fear and by hope; when the historic glories of the old can be compensated by the rich possibilities of the new era? This time, like all times, is a very good one, if we but know what to do with it.[6]

Emerson calls for self-affirmation:

Another sign of our times, also marked by an analogous political movement, is the new importance given to the single person. Every thing that tends to insulate the individual—to surround him with barriers of natural respect, so that each man shall feel the world is his, and man shall treat with man as a sovereign state—tends to true union as well as greatness. "I learned," said the melancholy Pestalozzi, "that no man in God's wide earth is either willing or able to help any other man." Help must come from the bosom alone. The scholar is that man who must take up into himself all the ability of the time, all the contributions of the past, all the hopes of the future. He must be an university of knowledges. If there be one lesson more than another which should pierce his ear, it is,

6. *Ibid.*

The world is nothing, the man is all; in yourself is the law of all nature, and you know not yet how a globule of sap ascends; in yourself slumbers the whole of Reason; it is for you to know all; it is for you to dare all. Mr. President and Gentlemen, this confidence in the unsearched might of man belongs by all motives, by all prophecy, by all preparation, to the American Scholar. We have listened too long to the courtly muses of Europe. The spirit of the American freeman is already suspected to be timid, imitative, tame. Public and private avarice made the air we breathe thick and fat. The scholar is decent, indolent, complaisant. See already the tragic consequence. The mind of this country, taught to aim at low objects, eats upon itself. There is no work for any but the decorous and the complaisant.[7]

What is the solution? Emerson gave an optimistic answer:

They did not yet see, and thousands of young men as hopeful now crowding to the barriers for the career do not yet see, that if the single man plant himself indomitably on his instincts, and there abide, the huge world will come round to him. Patience—patience; with the shades of all the good and great for company; and for solace the perspective of your own infinite life; and for work the study and the communication of principles, the making those instincts prevalent, the conversion of the world. Is it not the chief disgrace in the world, not to be a unit;—not to be reckoned one character;—not to yield that peculiar fruit which each man was created to bear, but to be reckoned in the gross, in the hundred, or the thousand, of the party, the section, to which we belong; and our opinion predicted geographically as the north, or the south? Not so, brothers and friends—please God, ours shall not be so. We will walk on our own feet; we will work with our own hands; we will speak with our own minds. The study of letters shall be no longer a name for pity, for doubt, and for sensual indulgence. The dread of man and the love of man shall be a wall of defense and a wreath of joy around all. A nation of men will for the first time exist, because each believes himself inspired by the Divine Soul which also inspires all men.[8]

7. *Ibid.*
8. *Ibid.*

Freedom and Education

In his stress upon freedom Emerson became the spokesman of the American way of life. Could not a man rise in the United States regardless of social origin? In the twentieth century, however, realistic critics do not hold with this belief. While in the nineteenth century the social make-up of the United States had been fluid and had found a constant outlet through the frontier, definite class lines have appeared today, and opportunities have decreased with the closing of the frontier.

An institution, according to Emerson, is "the lengthened shadow of a great man." In his essay "Self-Reliance" he showed how the Reformation was a result of Luther, how Quakerism developed because of Fox, Methodism because of Wesley, and gave numerous other examples. History itself is a very simple matter to Emerson, for it represents the biography of greatness. However, with the development of sociology, economics, and a more scientific viewpoint of history, we could maintain the opposite: that man is only a shortened shadow of an institution. The latter view is much more sober and disillusioning, for if man is a product of immutable forces in his environment, his life is determined from the very beginning, and his struggle frequently merely becomes an expression of futility.

While Emerson believed in the theoretical greatness of democracy, he never shut his eyes to the actual shortcomings of the American system. For Jacksonian democracy he had little sympathy, he regarding it as a rule of the demagogue and of the untutored, although he approved of its principles. The Whigs, who represented the interests of business, he reproached for their subservience to the financiers and for their disregard for human rights, although he admired their cultured leadership.

Certainly Emerson was not a detached thinker when it came to the political issues of his time. He blasted the Fugitive Slave Bill and attacked Harvard College for being subservient to financial interests. Boston he dismissed as depressing to an emancipated mind.

How different from his utopian dreams were the actual political conditions; he envisaged a society in which the best and wisest would govern. He believed that the end of all governmental functions should be the welfare of the people, not the perpetuation of power. In place of Machiavellian principles in legislation, he looked forward to an age in which good will would triumph.[9]

Emerson reminds us that the state is an artificial institution.

> In dealing with the State we ought to remember that its institutions are not aboriginal, though they existed before we were born; that they are not superior to the citizen; that every one of them was once the act of a single man; every law and usage was a man's expedient to meet a particular case; that they all are imitable, all alterable; we may make as good, we may make better. Society is an illusion to the young citizen. It lies before him in rigid repose, with certain names, men and institutions rooted like oak trees to the centre, round which all arrange themselves the best they can. But the old statesman knows that society is fluid; there are such roots and centres, but any particle may suddenly become the centre of the movement and compel the system to gyrate around it.[10]

"The law is only a memorandum," he asserted in a famous phrase. He expected little from either the conservative or the radical party:

> The philosopher, the poet, or the religious man, will of course wish to cast his vote with the democrat, for free-trade, for wide suffrage, for the abolition of legal cruelties in the penal code, and for facilitating in every manner the access of the young and the poor to the sources of wealth and power. But he can rarely accept the persons whom the so-called popular party propose to him as

9. For an interesting interpretation of Emerson, see George Santayana, *Interpretations of Poetry and Religion*, pp. 217-33.
10. *Politics.*

representatives of these liberalities. They have not at heart the ends which give to the name of democracy what hope and virtue are in it. The spirit of our American radicalism is destructive and aimless; it is not loving; it has no ulterior and divine ends, but is destructive only out of hatred and selfishness. On the other side, the conservative party, composed of the most moderate, able and cultivated part of the population, is timid, and merely defensive of property. It vindicates no right, it aspires to no real good, it brands no crime, it proposes no generous policy; it does not build, nor write, nor cherish the arts, nor foster religion, nor establish schools, nor encourage science, nor emancipate the slave, nor befriend the poor, or the Indian, or the immigrant.[11]

Educational and Philosophical Contributions of Emerson

Though Emerson's system lacked systematic organization, its main outlines can be clearly described:

1. In his approach to knowledge and philosophy, he urged an independent and creative attitude. We are not to be guided by the past, but by the present. We learn not merely from books, but also from nature and people. Ideas must be applied functionally to reveal the moral purpose of the universe. Most famous is his call for a declaration of independence on the part of the American scholar.

2. In his epistemology he dwelt on intuition. Both reason and sensation are inferior compared with intuition. Reality cannot be defined; it can only be visualized and felt. Self-knowledge and knowledge of nature are not opposed to each other; rather, both belong together and supplement each other.

3. In his metaphysical system he starts with a dualistic assumption: Nature and the Soul, the One and the Many, Unity and Variety. However, this dualism is not metaphysically real; both nature and the soul and all other phenomenal manifestations are part of the Over-Soul, the principle of reality.

11. *Ibid.*

As for the categories of science, such as space, time, and causality, they do not characterize reality, which is beyond spatial and temporal determinations.

4. In religion Emerson was a mystic, but unlike the Eastern mystics he emphasized the pragmatic and concrete effects of contemplation. He rejected any type of religion based on tradition and revelation. To him the religious experience was dynamic and progressive and not confined to one sect, one nation, or one man. For its vitality it depended on the power of intuition, which precluded ritual.

5. In his ethical and political doctrines Emerson upheld the gospel of individualism. Thus, he preached self-reliance and indicated that governments exist for the sake of man; that, in fact, wise men need no governments at all. He taught that evil has no metaphysical reality; that the universe is based on invariable moral laws, which establish a definite system of cosmic justice.

6. His general philosophical viewpoint can best be described as idealism. This, however, did not lead Emerson to the subjectivism of Berkeley or to Hegel's absolute Idealism. Rather, it implied to him that mind is more significant than matter, and that nature reveals moral purposes and is symbolic of spiritual perfection.

This meant that Emerson did not welcome the gospel of naturalism. While there are evolutionary features in his system, they are on a qualitative plane. Emerson asserted that it is the task of man to realize the purity of the soul; in short, to find the Over-Soul, in which all his doubts will be abolished and all his conflicts resolved.

The idealism of Emerson demanded a new type of education: not a system dedicated to the past, but one that explored the day after tomorrow: not one that stressed analytical knowledge but one that explored the wisdom of the heart.

21. Mann

Among the pioneers of American education Horace Mann
(1796–1859) deserves an honored place. His own career illustrates the importance of the educative process. Born in Franklin,
Massachusetts, he received only the most rudimentary training
until he was fifteen. A traveling schoolmaster gave him a few
lessons during the year, but most of his learning he acquired
himself. He studied day and night and was able to enter Brown
University, where he made a brilliant record. At this time, law
was his major interest. In 1827 he was elected to the Massachusetts House of Representatives. A notable political career seemed
to have opened up for him. But he became more interested in
education than in law. Indeed, he was responsible for the establishment of the Board of Education of Massachusetts and served
as its first secretary. When asked why he exchanged law for education, he replied that "the interests of a client are small compared with the interests of the next generation."

With single-minded dedication he labored for the cause of
education. One of his aims was to abolish the cruel punishments
that were current in his time. In most schools of that day there
were at least ten to twenty floggings a day. Schoolmasters, influ-

enced by the Calvinist doctrine, believed that it was their duty to drive the devil out of their students. Was the child not a creature of sin? Was not hell-fire a fitting punishment for the child who disobeyed his teachers and parents? Was not flogging an aid to learning?

Horace Mann was brought up as a Calvinist, but became a Unitarian. He believed that human nature is basically good, that all human beings have the potential for creativity and growth. Excessive punishment only meant a stifling of individualism. It encouraged sadism and disregarded the rights and integrity of the students. In a report on Prussian education he noted that physical punishments were rarely used, and yet Prussia had excellent discipline.

The schoolmasters of Mann's time were not convinced by his arguments. They felt that abolishment of corporal punishment would open the door to chaos. Such a step could diminish their authority and might be a prelude to open rebellion. Nevertheless, the ideals of Horace Mann prevailed and education has been elevated because of him.

The school buildings in his time were often like hovels. They symbolized the community's disrespect for education. Lighting was inadequate; many of the school buildings were unsafe and unsanitary. Mann saw to it that numerous new buildings were created, that they embodied better standards of planning and beauty, and were more conducive to learning. Through his reports, through many letters, through speeches and lectures, and lobbying in the state legislature and Congress he publicized the need for better public education. Often the response was hostile. Once when he and the Governor of Massachusetts were to address an audience they arrived to find the hall dark and its floor unswept. Mann promptly took off his coat and swept the hall.

Education must be more than intellectual training, more than an exercise of one's abilities or a mere study of the past. Mann saw education as a tool of liberation, whereby the poor could rise on the social ladder; a tool whereby the Negro could become emancipated and the handicapped child learn to adjust to his environment and find a meaningful life.

To Horace Mann, the school was the foundation of democracy. Here rich and poor could learn together; here the young and the old were united in a common search; here were no frontiers to learning; here intellect and character merged and the past became the prelude to a more meaningful future.

Like Pestalozzi, who had a great impact on his thinking, Mann believed in training by vocational experience. He felt that the child should learn to use his senses, that he should take nature as the point of departure. He enriched the curriculum with such subjects as hygiene, drawing, and music. Rather than a classical basis, learning should have a utilitarian purpose so that man and society could be improved.

All this demanded a new conception of instruction. Mann was responsible for lengthening the school term and raising teachers' salaries. To make learning as enjoyable as possible, he helped to introduce new textbooks designed to show a relationship between intellectual knowledge and the practical problems of society.

When he was a boy, he read almost all the 116 volumes in the library in Franklin, Massachusetts. Most schools of his time had inadequate library facilities. Mann organized many school libraries so that books could become part of the student's daily life. He believed less in formal assignments than in individual learning. What the student discovers for himself when his own interests govern his reading is of more value to him than stereotyped assignments.

The basis of education, Mann argued, was reading. This meant an exercise of intellectual curiosity. It implied a knowledge of the great authors of the past. Books, to him as to Thoreau, are the real wealth of mankind, their function being to liberate man from the narrow limitations of his environment.

Mann was responsible for the establishment of the first normal school in America, which opened its doors in 1839 in Lexington, Massachusetts. Only three students attended, but the idea soon spread to many parts of the nation, and the Lexington school was widely imitated. Mann believed that teachers' training should be intellectual, moral, and esthetic. Intellectually, they ought to have specific competence and a wide knowledge of the humanities. Morally, they should be models in their enthusiasm for education; indeed, to Mann education was the supreme embodiment of morality. Esthetically, teachers were to develop a sense of beauty in their students, who could eventually transform their own communities, so that ugliness would be eliminated through real esthetic appreciation.

Mann's greatest controversy was with orthodox members of the clergy. He himself regarded Jesus as a supreme teacher whose ideals of love ought to be imitated, but he had no use for religion in the classroom. Did not ecclesiasticism lead to regression and was not dogmatism incompatible with the open mind that ought to prevail in education? Were not the basic religious concepts, such as original sin and eternal punishment, replicas of an obsolete age? Should not education be safeguarded from any outside interference?

The result was that Horace Mann was attacked in many sermons in Boston. The Reverend Mr. Smith regarded him as a representative of evil and viewed his ideas as being subversive both to religion and to morality. To the minister, Horace Mann was a radical reformer whose concepts would lead to the decline of society, and whose ideals of democracy might open the door to revolution.

Thus, the Reverend Mr. Smith wrote to Mann:

1. I regard you as the representative of a system, or its head which seeks to change, slowly, perhaps, but surely, the whole system of education in common schools—the result of which will be to elevate the intellectual over the moral, and man above God. In

detail and in element I conceive your notions, in this matter, to be crude, their fruits destructive; and the more I have seen your system explained, the worse, to my mind, it appears.

2. Are you in favor of the use of the rod as the principal means of enforcing obedience? That you tolerate it in deference to public sentiment, I do not dispute. But I am misinformed if you are not against its use, and do not, as you have opportunity, discountenance its use.[1]

In a sermon, Smith charged that "even now, in our best city schools, insubordination and licentiousness abound." All this he attributed to the heretical opinions of Horace Mann.

Ideals

In his 1848 report as Secretary of the Board of Education, Mann stressed the importance of the schoolroom:

I proceed, then, in endeavoring to show how the true business of the schoolroom connects itself, and becomes identical, with the great interests of society. The former is the infant, immature state of those interests; the latter, their developed, adult state. As "the child is father to the man," so may the training of the schoolroom expand into the institutions and fortunes of the State.[2]

Next he turns to intellectual education as an aid to equality:

According to the European theory, men are divided into classes, —some to toil and earn, others to seize and enjoy. . . .

Our ambition as a State should trace itself to a different origin, and propose to itself a different object. Its flame should be lighted as the skies. Its radiance and its warmth should reach the darkest and coldest abodes of men. It should seek the solution of such problems as these: To what extent can competence displace pauperism? How nearly can we free ourselves from the low-minded and the vicious, not by their expatriation, but by their elevation? To what extent can the resources and powers of Nature be converted

1. Smith, *The Ark of God on a New Cart,* pp. 23 ff.
2. *Report of the Secretary of the Board of Education of Massachusetts for 1848.*

into human welfare, the peaceful arts of life be advanced, and the vast treasures of human talent and genius be developed? How much of suffering, in all its forms, can be relieved? or, what is better than relief, how much can be prevented? Cannot the classes of crimes be lessened, and the number of criminals in each class be diminished? Our exemplars, both for public and private imitation, should be the parables of the lost sheep and of the lost piece of silver. When we have spread competence through all the abodes of poverty, when we have substituted knowledge for ignorance in the minds of the whole people, when we have reformed the vicious and reclaimed the criminal, then may we invite all neighboring nations to behold the spectacle, and say to them, in the conscious elation of virtue, "Rejoice with me," for I have found that which is lost.

Now, surely nothing but universal education can counterwork this tendency to the domination of capital and the servility of labor. If one class possesses all the wealth and the education, while the residue of society is ignorant and poor, it matters not by what name the relation between them may be called; the latter, in fact and in truth, will be the servile dependents, and subjects of the former. But if education be equally diffused, it will draw property after it by the strongest of all attractions; for such a thing never did happen, and never can happen, as that an intelligent and practical body of men should be permanently poor. . . .[3]

Intelligence, he stated, is the condition of wealth:

For the creation of wealth, then, for the existence of a wealthy people and a wealthy nation, intelligence is the grand condition. The number of improvers will increase as the intellectual constituency, if I may so call it, increases. In former times, and in most parts of the world even at the present day, not one man in a million has ever had such a development of mind as made it possible for him to become a contributor to art or science. Let this development precede, and contributions, numberless, and of inestimable value, will be sure to follow. That political economy, therefore, which busies itself about capital and labor, supply and demand, interest

3. *Ibid.*

and rents, favorable and unfavorable balances of trade, but leaves out of account the element of a widespread mental development, is nought but stupendous folly. The greatest of all arts in political economy is to change a consumer into a producer; and the next greatest is to increase the producer's producing power,—an end to be directly attained by increasing his intelligence.[4]

Then he turns to political education:

The necessity of general intelligence,—that is, of education (for I use the terms as substantially synonymous, because general intelligence can never exist without general education, and general education will be sure to produce general intelligence),—the necessity of general intelligence under a republican form of government, like most other very important truths, has become a very trite one. It is so trite, indeed, as to have lost much of its force by its familiarity. Almost all the champions of education seize on this argument first of all, because it is so simple as to be understood by the ignorant, and so strong as to convince the skeptical.[5]

Education, Mann believed, involves controversy:

Shall all teaching relative to the nature of our government be banished from our schools? and shall our children be permitted to grow up in entire ignorance of the political history of their country? In the schools of a republic, shall the children be left without any distinct knowledge of the nature of a republican government, or only with such knowledge as they may pick up from angry political discussions, or from party newspapers, from caucus speeches, or Fourth-of-July orations,—the Apocrypha of Apocrypha?

Surely, between these extremes, there must be a medium not difficult to be found. And is not this middle course, which all sensible and judicious men, all patriots, and all genuine republicans, must approve?—namely, that those articles in the creed of republicanism which are accepted by all, believed in by all, and which form the common basis of our political faith shall be taught

4. *Ibid.*
5. *Ibid.*

to all. But when the teacher, in the course of his lessons or lectures on the fundamental law, arrives at a controverted text, he is either to read it without comment or remark; or, at most, he is only to say that the passage is the subject of disputation, and that the school-room is neither the tribunal to adjudicate, nor the forum to discuss it.

Such being the rule established by common consent, and such the practice observed with fidelity under it, it will come to be universally understood that political proselytism is no function of the school, but that indoctrination into matters of controversy between hostile political parties is to be elsewhere sought for, and elsewhere imparted. Thus may all the children of the Commonwealth receive instruction in all the great essentials of political knowledge,—in those elementary ideas without which they will never be able to investigate more recondite and debatable questions; thus will the only practicable method be adopted for discovering new truths, and for discarding, instead of perpetuating, old errors; and thus, too, will the pernicious race of intolerant zealots, whose whole faith may be summed up in two articles—that they themselves are always infallibly right, and that all dissenters are certainly wrong—be extinguished.[6]

He advocated moral education:

Moral education is a primal necessity of social existence. The unrestrained passions of men are not only homicidal, but suicidal; and a community without a conscience would soon extinguish itself. . . .

Education has never been brought to bear with one-hundredth part of its potential force upon the natures of children, and, through them, upon the character of men and of the race. In all the attempts to reform mankind which have hitherto been made, whether by changing the frame of government, by aggravating or softening the severity of the penal code, or by substituting government-created for a God-created religion—in all these attempts, the infantile and youthful mind, its amenability to influences, and the

6. *Ibid.*

enduring and self-operating character of the influence it receives, have been almost wholly unrecognized. Here, then, is a new agency, whose powers are but just beginning to be understood, and whose mighty energies hitherto have been but feebly invoked; and yet from our experience, limited and imperfect as it is, we do know, that, far beyond any other earthly instrumentality, it is comprehensive and decisive. . . .[7]

But it will be said that this grand result in practical morals is a consummation of blessedness that can never be attained without religion, and that no community will ever be religious without religious education. Both these propositions I regard as eternal and immutable truths. . . .[8]

Religious education, Mann felt, adds to public education:

He describes his own religious feelings.

. . . I was originally a member, and from which I have always sought counsel and guidance; and in justice to thousands of the most wise, upright, and religious-minded men in Massachusetts, who have been my fellow-laborers in advancing the great cause of popular education, under the auspices of this system,—I have felt bound to vindicate it from the aspersions cast upon it, and to show its consonance with the eternal principles of equity and justice. I have felt bound to show, that so far from its being an irreligious, an anti-Christian, or an un-Christian system, it is a system which recognizes religious obligations in their fullest extent; that it is a system which invokes a religious spirit, and can never be fitly administered without such a spirit; that it inculcates the great commands upon which hang all the law and the prophets; that it welcomes the Bible, and therefore welcomes all the doctrines which the Bible really contains; and that it listens to these doctrines so reverently, that, for the time being, it will not suffer any rash mortal to thrust in his interpolations of their meaning, or overlay the text with any of the "many inventions" which the heart of man has sought out. It is a system, however, which leaves open all other

7. *Ibid.*
8. *Ibid.*

means of instruction—the pulpits, the Sunday schools, the Bible classes, the catechisms, of all denominations,—to be employed according to the preferences of individual parents. It is a system which restrains itself from teaching that what it does teach is all that needs to be taught, or that should be taught; but leaves this to be decided by each man for himself, according to the light of his reason and conscience, and on his responsibility to that Great Being, who, in holding him to account for the things done in the body, will hold him to the strictest account for the manner in which he has "trained up" his children. . . .[9]

He praises the Pilgrim Fathers, who felt that

. . . if they could give knowledge and virtue to their children, they gave them all things . . . *We have our futurity as they had theirs,*—a futurity rapidly hastening upon us,—a futurity now fluid, —ready, as clay in the hands of the potter, to be moulded into every form of beauty and excellence; but so soon as it reaches our hands, so soon as it receives the impress of our plastic touch, whether this touch be for good or evil, it is to be struck into the adamant of the unchanging and unchangeable past. Into whose form and likeness shall we fashion this flowing futurity,—of Mammon, of Moloch, or of Jesus? Clear, and more clear, out of the dimness of coming time, emerge to the visions of faith the myriad hosts of the generations that shall succeed us. Those generations are to stand in our places, to be called by our names, and to accept the heritage of joy or of woe which we shall bequeath them. Shall they look back upon us with veneration for our wisdom and beneficent forecast, or with shame at our selfishness and degeneracy? Our ancestors were noble examples to us; shall we be ignoble examples to our posterity?[10]

Fighter for Freedom

Horace Mann did not remain neutral regarding the great issues of his time. When he was elected to Congress in 1848 he

9. *Ibid.*
10. *Ibid.*

denounced slavery in bitter terms. He attacked the ravages of the industrial system. He urged that workers be better paid, that child labor be curbed, that factories become more sanitary and that slums be eliminated. No educator, he said, could remain neutral about social injustice. His ideals and aspirations were to be applied to society; otherwise, education would be mere theory.

How was the new society to be established? Mann rejected the doctrine of revolution. This would only create counterviolence; it would not abolish fundamental evils. A better way was through education, which would open new doors to the underprivileged.

While Thoreau viewed the machine as an aid to enslavement, Mann felt that it would enlarge human powers. Science and technology would aid the emancipation of the poor, who would use machines to achieve higher economic standards and more leisure. The machine, Mann predicted, would control nature and would increase human power so that human beings could become the kings of creation.

When Horace Mann became the first president of Antioch College, Yellow Springs, Ohio, in 1852, he again displayed his independent genius. Antioch College was to be a unique institution; there were to be no class barriers. Women were to be admitted—a radical step for his time. There were to be no color bars. Students, he believed, ought to have both intellectual and work experiences. The college was to be a truly democratic institution; indeed, the students were to share in its administration.

In the classroom at Antioch the professor was not to be an oracle of truth, but rather a friendly guide to knowledge. Discussion and the seminar method were to be encouraged. Mann believed that a rigid curriculum was incompatible with intellectual democracy; hence, he urged a stress upon electives. This meant that students could pursue their own interests and that their differences could be explored.

While most educators of Mann's time stressed an exclusively

mental training, Mann urged the cultivation of physical training. Would not the mind suffer when the body was neglected? Was not physical education a preparation for an active life? Did not physical exercises increase the enjoyment of human existence?

He had little regard for the lessons of the past. To him, history was a record of human errors and follies. Like Jefferson, he believed that every generation had to make its own history.

He remarked that at Antioch many of the students had more brilliance than the professors. The task of the college, he felt, was to keep their interests alive, to intensify their curiosity, and not to stifle their identity. To him, administration meant gentle encouragement and unwavering humanitarianism. In a commencement speech in 1859 he summarized his philosophy by saying: "Be ashamed to die until you have won some victory for humanity."

22. Thoreau

Thoreau's Significance in American Culture

Henry David Thoreau (1817–1862) was less appreciated during his lifetime than Mann or Emerson. For many years afterwards, his works were not read widely, but in the twentieth century he has attracted a growing following, and his voice has been heard as far away as Gandhi's India. His anarchistic ideals appeal to many moderns more strongly than the humanistic culture of Emerson. The life of nature Thoreau advocated appears to be an excellent antidote to the confusion and oppression of a mechanistic culture.

Like Emerson, Thoreau was a Harvard graduate, but he had no definite profession. When he graduated, he tried to be a teacher; he did this just to make a living, as he confessed later on. Being idealistic, he believed that his task in life was not just to support himself, but to improve his fellow men, and so he gave up teaching. He later turned to manufacturing pencils, but this occupation did not satisfy him.

Most of his life was spent living close to nature. His experiences at Walden have become as famous as Tolstoy's life amidst the poor Russian serfs. Occasionally Thoreau would do odd jobs, helping his neighbors and assisting Emerson in his editing of the

Dial. Otherwise, his life was not at all noteworthy except for his refusal to pay the poll tax, which landed him in jail.

If his life was uneventful by conventional standards, it was picturesque as an intellectual pilgrimage. The problem of Thoreau was how to attain a meaning in life. His neighbors were intent upon amassing wealth, and they thought that the greatest goal lay in comfortable living. To them happiness was to be gained from material things; their aim was to get as far away as they could from the country and live a luxurious city existence.

Thoreau would have nothing to do with such a spirit. He deserted society. He never married, never was a slave to convention, never supported a church, never took any interest in political life, and was an anarchist when it came to the state. In every way his life was a protest.

While Americans of Thoreau's period, like those of more recent times, were incessantly traveling to other nations, he stayed near Concord. Here he found everything: a magnificent countryside, abundant wild life, stimulating friends—what more could a man ask?

The Puritan heritage was strong in Thoreau. He used neither tobacco nor alcohol. As for women, his conduct was retiring, and he never seemed to partake of the pleasures of the flesh. He was remarkable for his self-sufficiency.

To some extent he underestimated the European tradition. He had contempt for England. He said he would rather go to Oregon than to London. He was proud of the fact that in Massachusetts the civilization had not been built on the ashes of a previous culture.

Philosophy of Life and Knowledge

Thoreau was an individualist, concerned about his own salvation and his own way of life rather than the reform of society. That is why he undertook his Walden experiment.

I went to the woods because I wished to live deliberately, to front only the essential facts of life, and see if I could not learn what it had to teach, and not, when I came to die, discover that I had not lived. I did not wish to live what was not life, living is so dear; nor did I wish to practice resignation, unless it was quite necessary. I wanted to live deep and suck out all the marrow of life, to live so sturdily and Spartan-like as to put to rout all that was not life, to cut a broad swath and shave close, to drive life into a corner, and reduce it to its lowest terms, and, if it proved to be mean, why then to get the whole and genuine meanness of it, and publish its meanness to the world; or if it were sublime, to know it by experience, and be able to give a true account of it in my next excursion. For most men, it appears to me, are in strange uncertainty about it, whether it is of the devil or of God, and have somewhat hastily concluded that it is the chief end of man here to "glorify God and enjoy Him forever."[1]

He felt melancholy when he looked at the manner in which most people spend their lives:

This world is a place of business. What an infinite bustle! I am awaked almost every night by the panting of the locomotive. It interrupts my dreams. There is no sabbath. It would be glorious to see mankind at leisure for once. It is nothing but work, work, work. I cannot easily buy a blank-book to write thoughts in; they are commonly ruled for dollars and cents. An Irishman, seeing me making a minute in the fields, took it for granted that I was calculating my wages. If a man was tossed out of a window when an infant, and so made a cripple for life, or scared out of his wits by the Indians, it is regretted chiefly because he was thus incapacitated for—business! I think that there is nothing, not even crime, more opposed to poetry, to philosophy, ay, to life itself, than this incessant business.

There is a coarse and boisterous money-making fellow in the outskirts of our town, who is going to build a bank-wall under the hill along the edge of his meadow. The powers have put this into his head to keep him out of mischief, and he wishes me to spend

1. *Walden* or *Life in the Woods.*

three weeks digging there with him. The result will be that he will perhaps get some more money to hoard, and leave for his heirs to spend foolishly. If I do this, most will commend me as an industrious and hard-working man; but if I choose to devote myself to certain labors which yield more real profit, though but little money, they may be inclined to look on me as an idler.[2]

We labor without any real goals, according to Thoreau:

If a man walk in the woods for love of them half of each day, he is in danger of being regarded as a loafer; but if he spends his whole day as a speculator, shearing off those woods and making earth bald before her time, he is esteemed an industrious and enterprising citizen. As if a town had no interest in its forests but to cut them down!

Most men would feel insulted if it were proposed to employ them in throwing stones over a wall, and then in throwing them back, merely that they might earn their wages. But many are no more worthily employed now. For instance: just after sunrise, one summer morning, I noticed one of my neighbors walking beside his team, which was slowly drawing a heavy hewn stone swung under the axle, surrounded by an atmosphere of industry,—his day's work begun,—his brow commenced to sweat,—a reproach to all sluggards and idlers,—pausing abreast the shoulders of his oxen, and half turning round with a flourish of his merciful whip, while they gained their length on him. And I thought, Such is the labor which the American Congress exists to protect,—honest, manly toil, —honest as the day is long,—that makes his bread taste sweet, and keeps society sweet,—which all men respect and have consecrated; one of the sacred band, doing the needful but irksome drudgery. Indeed, I felt a slight reproach, because I observed this from a window, and was not abroad and stirring about a similar business.[3]

The wise man, advised Thoreau, will treasure his own independence:

The community has no bribe that will tempt a wise man. You may raise money enough to tunnel a mountain, but you cannot

2. *Miscellanies, Life Without Principle.*
3. *Ibid.*

raise money enough to hire a man who is minding *his own* business. An efficient and valuable man does what he can, whether the community pay him for it or not. The inefficient offer their insufficiency to the highest bidder, and are forever expecting to be put into office. One would suppose that they were rarely disappointed.

Perhaps I am more than usually jealous with respect to my freedom. I feel that my connections with an obligation to society are still very slight and transient. Those slight labors which afford me a livelihood, and by which it is allowed that I am to some extent serviceable to my contemporaries, are as yet commonly a pleasure to me, and I am not often reminded that they are a necessity. So far I am successful. But I foresee that if my wants should be much increased, the labor required to supply them would become a drudgery. If I should sell both my forenoons and afternoons to society, as most appear to do, I am sure that for me there would be nothing left worth living for. I trust that I shall never thus sell my birthright for a mess of pottage.[4]

Like Socrates, he was critical of organized education:

I hardly know *an intellectual* man, even, who is so broad and truly liberal that you can think aloud in his society. Most with whom you endeavor to talk soon come to a stand against some institution in which they appear to hold stock—that is, some particular, not universal, way of viewing things. They will continually thrust their own low roof, with its narrow skylight, between you and the sky, when it is the unobstructed heavens you would view. Get out of the way with your cobwebs; wash your windows, I say! In some lyceums they tell me that they have voted to exclude the subject of religion. But how do I know what their religion is, and when I am near to or far from it? I have walked into such an arena, and done my best to make a clean breast of what religion I have experienced, and the audience never suspected what I was about. The lecture was as harmless as moonshine to them. Whereas, if I had read to them the biography of the greatest scamps in history, they might have thought that I had written the lives of the deacons of their church. Ordinarily, the inquiry is, Where did you come from? or, Where are you going? That was a more pertinent ques-

4. *Ibid.*

tion which I overheard one of my auditors put to another once, —"What does he lecture for?" It made me quake in my shoes.

To speak impartially, the best men that I know are not serene, a world in themselves. For the most part, they dwell in forms, and flatter and study effect only more finely than the rest. We select granite for the underpinning of our houses and barns; we build fences of stone; but we do not ourselves rest on an underpinning of granitic truth, the lowest primitive rock. Our sills are rotten.[5]

Thoreau had reverence for books:

I kept Homer's Iliad on my table through the summer, though I looked at his page only now and then. Incessant labor with my hands, at first, for I had my house to finish and my beans to hoe at the same time, made more study impossible. Yet I sustained myself by the prospect of such reading in future. I read one or two shallow books of travel in the intervals of my work, till that employment made me ashamed of myself, and I asked where it was then that I lived.

The student may read Homer or Aeschylus in the Greek without danger of dissipation or luxuriousness, for it implies that he in some measure emulate their heroes, and consecrate morning hours to their pages. The heroic books, even if printed in the character of our mother tongue, will always be in a language dead to degenerate times; and we must laboriously seek the meaning of each word and line, conjecturing a larger sense than common use permits out of what wisdom and valor and generosity we have. The modern cheap and fertile press, with all its translations, has done little to bring us nearer to the heroic writers of antiquity. They seem as solitary, and the letter in which they are printed as rare and curious, as ever. It is worth the expense of youthful days and costly hours, if you learn only some words of an ancient language, which are raised out of the trivialness of the street, to be perpetual suggestions and provocations. It is not in vain that the farmer remembers and repeats the few Latin words which he has heard. Men sometimes speak as if the study of the classics would at length make way for more modern and practical studies; but the adventurous student will always

5. *Ibid.*

study classics, in whatever language they may be written and however ancient they may be. For what are the classics but the noblest recorded thoughts of man? They are the only oracles which are not decayed, and there are such answers to the most modern inquiry in them as Delphi and Dodona never gave. We might as well omit to study Nature because she is old. To read well, that is, to read true books in a true spirit, is a noble exercise, and one that will task the reader more than any exercise which the customs of the day esteem. It requires a training such as the athletes underwent, the steady intention almost of the whole life to this object. Books must be read as deliberately and reservedly as they were written.[6]

He placed the written word above oratory:

The one is commonly transitory, a sound, a tongue, a dialect merely, almost brutish, and we learn it unconsciously, like the brutes, of our mothers. The other is the maturity and experience of that; if that is our mother tongue, this is our father tongue, a reserved and select expression, too significant to be heard by the ear, which we must be born again in order to speak. The crowds of men who merely *spoke* the Greek and Latin tongues in the Middle Ages were not entitled by the accident of birth to *read* the works of genius written in that Greek or Latin which they knew, but in the select language of literature. . . .

No wonder that Alexander carried the Iliad with him on his expeditions in a precious casket. A written word is the choicest of relics. It is something at once more intimate with us and more universal than any other work of art. It is the work of art nearest to life itself. It may be translated into every language, and not only be read but actually breathed from all human lips;—not be represented on canvas or in marble only, but be carved out of the breath of life itself.[7]

He attacked the reading done by his contemporaries:

The best books are not read even by those who are called good readers. What does our Concord culture amount to? There is in this

6. *Walden.*
7. *Ibid.*

town, with a very few exceptions, no taste for the best or for very good books even in English literature, whose words all can read and spell. Even the college-bred and so-called liberally educated men here and elsewhere have really little or no acquaintance with the English classics; and as for the recorded wisdom of mankind, the ancient classics and Bibles, which are accessible to all who will know of them, there are the feeblest efforts anywhere made to become acquainted with them. I know a woodchopper, of middle age, who takes a French paper, not for news as he says, for he is above that, but to "keep himself in practice," he being a Canadian by birth; and when I ask him what he considers the best thing he can do in this world, he says, beside this, to keep up and add to his English. This is about as much as the college-bred generally do or aspire to do, and they take an English paper for the purpose. One who has just come from reading perhaps one of the best English books will find how many with whom he can converse about it? Or suppose he comes from reading a Greek or Latin classic in the original, whose praises are familiar even to the so-called illiterate; he will find nobody at all to speak to, but must keep silence about it. Indeed, there is hardly the professor in our colleges, who, if he has mastered the difficulties of the language, has proportionately mastered the difficulties of the wit and poetry of a Greek poet, and has any sympathy to impart to the alert and heroic reader; and as for the sacred Scriptures, or Bibles of mankind, who in this town can tell me even their titles? Most men do not know that any nation but the Hebrews have had a scripture. A man, any man, will go considerably out of his way to pick up a silver dollar; but here are golden words, which the wisest men of antiquity have uttered, and whose worth the wise of every succeeding age have assured us of;—and yet we learn to read only as far as Easy Reading, the primers and class-books, and when we leave school, the "Little Reading," and story-books, which are for boys and beginners; and our reading, our conversation and thinking, are all on a very low level, worthy only of pygmies and manikins.[8]

Like Emerson, Thoreau called for an educational renaissance:

8. *Ibid.*

Shall the world be confined to one Paris or one Oxford forever? Cannot students be boarded here and get a liberal education under the skies of Concord? Can we not hire some Abelard to lecture to us? Alas! what with foddering the cattle and tending the store, we are kept from school too long, and our education is sadly neglected. In this country, the village should in some respects take the place of the nobleman of Europe. It should be the patron of the fine arts. It is rich enough. It wants only the magnanimity and refinement. It can spend money enough on such things as farmers and traders value, but it is thought Utopian to propose spending money for things which more intelligent men know to be of far more worth. This town has spent seventeen thousand dollars on a town-house, thank fortune or politics, but probably it will not spend so much on living wit, the true meat to put into that shell, in a hundred years. The one hundred and twenty-five dollars annually subscribed for a Lyceum in the winter is better spent than any other equal sum raised in the town. If we live in the Nineteenth Century, why should we not enjoy the advantages which the Nineteenth Century offers? Why should our life be in any respect provincial? If we will read newspapers, why not skip the gossip of Boston and take the best newspapers in the world at once?—not be sucking the pap of "neutral family" papers, or browsing "Olive-Branches" here in New England. Let the reports of all the learned societies come to us, and we will see if they know anything. Why should we leave it to Harper & Brothers and Redding & Co., to select our reading? As the nobleman of cultivated taste surrounds himself with whatever conduces to his culture,—genius—learning—wit—books—paintings—statuary—music—philosophical instruments, and the like; so let the village do,—not stop short at a pedagogue, a parson, a sexton, a parish library, and three select-men, because our Pilgrim forefathers got through a cold winter once on a bleak rock with these. To act collectively is according to the spirit of our institutions; and I am confident that, as our circumstances are more flourishing, our means are greater than the nobleman's. New England can hire all the wise men in the world to come and teach her, and board them round the while, and not be provincial at all. That is the *uncommon* school we want. Instead of noblemen, let us have noble villages of men.[9]

Real education, Thoreau stated, transcends poverty:

The setting sun is reflected from the windows of the alms-house as brightly as from the rich man's abode; the snow melts before its door as early in the spring. I do not see but a quiet mind may live as contentedly there, and have as cheering thoughts, as in a palace. The town's poor seem to me often to live the most independent lives of any. Maybe they are simply great enough to receive without misgiving. Most think that they are above being supported by the town; but it oftener happens that they are not above supporting themselves by dishonest means, which should be more disreputable. Cultivate poverty like a garden herb, like sage. Do not trouble youself much to get new things, whether clothes or friends. Turn the old; return to them. Things do not change; we change. Sell your clothes and keep your thoughts. God will see that you do not want society. If I were confined to a corner of a garret all my days, like a spider, the world would be just as large to me while I had my thoughts about me. The philospher said: "From an army of three divisions one can take away its general, and put it in disorder; from the man the most abject and vulgar one cannot take away his thought." Do not seek so anxiously to be developed, to subject yourself to many influences to be played on; it is all dissipation. Humility like darkness reveals the heavenly lights. The shadow of poverty and meanness gather around us, "and lo! creation widens to our views." We are often reminded that if there were bestowed on us the wealth of Croesus, our aims must still be the same, and our means essentially the same. Moreover, if you are restricted in your range by poverty, if you cannot buy books and newspapers, for instance, you are but confined to the most significant and vital experiences; you are compelled to deal with the material which yields the most sugar and the most starch. It is life near the bone where it is sweetest. You are defended from being a trifler. No man loses ever on a lower level by magnanimity on a higher. Superflu-

9. *Ibid.*

ous wealth can buy superfluities only. Money is not required to buy one necessary of the soul.[10]

With such a philosophy Thoreau could not accept the theological dogmas of orthodox Christianity, which to him represented a religion of negation rather than of joy. He had much more understanding of the gods of Greece, for they were part of nature.

When he saw the New Englanders worshipping in their churches, he felt a sense of pity, for the God they adored was a magnified image of a ruthless industrial system. As for himself, he literally followed the precepts of Christ. Had Christ not said, "Seek ye first the kingdom of heaven; lay not up for yourself treasures on earth"? Thoreau knew the meaning of Christ's insight that a man would gain nothing if he conquered the world and lost his own soul.

Thoreau believed in man expressing himself in a complete and thoroughgoing manner; those who prostrated themselves before an arbitrary God had no understanding of the real meaning of religion; Thoreau found his religious experience much more readily in nature than in the churches of New England.

The more one reads Thoreau—not merely his *Walden* but also his *A Week on the Concord and Merrimack Rivers,* his *Excursions, The Main Woods, Cape Cod, The Yankee in Canada*—the more one gets the impression of a saintlike nature. Though he detested formal theology and had only scorn for the clergy of his time, he had a basically religious interpretation of life. He measured all philosophy, all thinking, according to their contribution to the actual improvement of man's existence.

What did philosophy mean to Thoreau? It was not merely a systematized view of the world, nor an insight into its metaphysical structure; not an adherence to definite dogmas, but a love of wisdom that made it possible to give a practical solution to life's problems. To Thoreau, thought was an auxiliary to action. In this view he echoed the practices of the Stoic philosophers.

10. *Ibid.*

Political Doctrines and Education

Politically, Thoreau's doctrines were out of tune with the faith of his time. While great fortunes were being made in New England, the United States expanded in the war with Mexico, and Webster was defending high tariffs and the federal union, Thoreau detested the power of the state and preached a gospel of nonresistance.

The use of force was completely abhorrent to him, for he recognized clearly that modern society is based upon coercion. From the exaction of the tax collectors to the waging of war, governments usually use tyrannical means. Thoreau thought that it was his duty to protest against this trend. He was not willing to be coerced by the majority; in his system everyone was equipped with inalienable rights, given to him by nature.

His philosophy resembled that of Rousseau in his scorn for laws. He emphasized that the law "will never make men free; it is men who have got to make the law free." As for the defenders of the law, he was extremely suspicious of them:

> The government can have no pure right over my person and property but what I concede to it. The progress from an absolute to a limited monarchy, from a limited monarchy to a democracy, is a progress toward a true respect for the individual. Even the Chinese philosopher was wise enough to regard the individual as the basis of the empire. Is a democracy, such as we know it, the last improvement possible in government? Is it not possible to take a step further towards recognizing and organizing the rights of man? There will never be a really free and enlightened State until the State comes to recognize the individual as a higher and independent power, from which all its own power and authority are derived and treats him accordingly. I please myself with imagining a State at last which can afford to be just to all men, and to treat the individual with respect as a neighbor; which even would not think it inconsistent with its own repose if a few were to live aloof from it, not meddling with it, nor embraced by it, who fulfilled all the duties of neighbors and fellowmen. A State which bore this kind of fruit,

and suffered it to drop off as fast as it ripened, would prepare the way for a still more perfect and glorious State, which also I have imagined, but not yet anywhere seen.[11]

Like Carlyle and Ruskin, Thoreau vigorously attacked the abuses of the industrial system. How different life was at Walden from that of Boston! How different fate was for him than for the wage earner in the textile mills! To Thoreau it appeared an undeniable truth that the industrial system was based upon serfdom. The majority of the people had only a bare existence, for which they slaved enormously; for a few it meant wealth at a terrible price.

No wonder that Thoreau objected furiously to the capitalistic values. He thought that eventually the condition of the American worker would be as pitiful as that of the English wage earner, and he foresaw a period in which the United States would be covered with slums.

What was the solution? Could it be found through cooperative experiments like Brook Farm and Fruitlands? The answer was No, for this would have made him a part of society and he wanted to live by himself. He was not dogmatic about his solutions. He knew that he had found a satisfying way of life; others would differ in their methods.

The story goes that when Thoreau was on his deathbed he was asked if he could see anything of the world beyond. "One world at a time," he replied, "one world at a time."

This statement characterizes his educational outlook, for he never gave sweeping and categorical answers; in fact, if judged by his solution of the problems of modern society, he appears to be hopelessly inadequate. It is impossible for man in the Atomic Age to give up his scientific undertakings, desert his family, and live the type of life that Thoreau enjoyed at Walden. Thoreau's ideals were influenced too much by the gospel of anarchy.

This is especially evident in his attitude regarding political events:

11. *Civil Disobedience.*

Those things which now most engage the attention of men, as politics and the daily routine, are, it is true, vital functions of human society, but should be unconsciously performed, like the corresponding functions of the physical body. They are *infra*-human, a kind of vegetation. I sometimes awake to a half-consciousness of them going on about me, as a man may become conscious of some of the processes of digestion in a morbid state, and so have the dyspepsia, as it is called. It is as if a thinker submitted himself to be rasped by the great gizzard of creation. Politics is, as it were, the gizzard of society, full of grit and gravel, and the two political parties are its two opposite halves,—sometimes split into quarters, it may be, which grind on each other. Not only individuals, but states, have thus confirmed dyspepsia, which expresses itself, you can imagine by what sort of eloquence. Thus our life is not altogether a forgetting, but also, alas! to a great extent, a remembering, of that which we should never have been conscious of, certainly not in our waking hours.[12]

His lasting significance for the American thinker lies in his penetrating question about the meaning and function of human life. It is not enough, according to Thoreau, to be an adherent to worthwhile causes if one neglects the inner self. Real leadership can come about only if the individual has an immediate awareness of nature.

In this respect no thinker can neglect Thoreau. Too frequently the intellectual in the twentieth century is tempted by the importance of reforms to overlook his inner self. Consequently, his ideas are academic, his outlook upon the world is stereotyped, and his personality is maladjusted. Educators must learn that lasting reform can be brought about only if there is a correspondence between outward action and personal development.

12. *Ibid.*

23. Tolstoy

Significance

One of the leading spokesmen for the pre-Soviet Russian civilization and education is Count Leo Tolstoy (1828–1910). In his realism, based upon minute and penetrating observation, and in his propensity for self-examination, Tolstoy represents typical Russian traits. His concept of love is much more sweeping than that of the Western mind, for love to him means more than affection, more than compassion; it stands for complete self-abnegation. To find a parallel the reader would have to turn to the concept of Bhakti, as found in the *Bhagavad-Gita*. Tolstoy is not alone among pre-Soviet writers in stressing the importance of sacrificial love; Dostoevsky is possessed by the same burning passion, even in the cold despair of Siberia.

Combined with love in Tolstoy is an unsparing frankness. He analyzes society in anatomical terms, penetrates through the veil of social convention and human rationalizations, and investigates the darkest caverns of the institutional system. This candid observation is extended to human emotions. Seldom have they been portrayed more vividly and more picturesquely. Occasionally, the description becomes physiological, as in the *Kreutzer Sonata,* in which he describes the sensations of sex with Augustinian clarity. He never spares himself in this process of analysis, and there is an element of autobiography in all of his major works. Usually the conclusions he reaches regarding his own motives are somber and melancholy. He constantly seems to be asking himself: "Why am I doing this? Why do I not live up to my ideals?" And as a result, his life is full of torment and anguish.

Someone has remarked that genius is characterized by perpetual melancholy. In some geniuses this is merely an esthetic gesture, like the tragic declamations of a great actor; in others it has an emotional basis. Tolstoy belongs to the second class. And again, here he is more Oriental than European. Like Buddha, he felt the full weight of existence, the futility of life, and the ever-present reality of evil. Undoubtedly, there is a strain of cosmic pessimism in the works of the major Russian writers, from Chekhov to Gorky, mainly because these men felt and pondered so deeply the fundamental problems of existence.

What makes Tolstoy especially human is his sympathy for the oppressed, his identification with the underprivileged members of society, and his willingness to sacrifice for them. Gogol wrote, "Pity for a fallen creature is a very natural trait," and the truth of this claim is illustrated by the life of Tolstoy. He belonged to the aristocracy; yet he found the greatest meaning in life in the peasants' type of existence; he betrayed the ideals, the expressions, and the interests of his class. Later in life he regretted that he had not been born a simple peasant. He wanted to overcome all the barriers that separated him from the lowliest man on his estate, and since this was never quite possible, Tolstoy lived in two worlds and experienced the full twilight of human existence.

Finally, in his proclivity for extremes, Tolstoy exhibits another Russian trait. It takes a certain mellowness in civilization to produce moderation, a spirit shown by the Athenians in the Periclean age. The feudalism and the autocracy of the Russian state did not lead to moderation. The harshness of the climate also made life more somber. Very often we find in Russian writers and educators an alternation between extreme sensuality and extreme asceticism, with periods of conversion following soul-shaking crises. Tolstoy experienced the full measure of emotional storms. He did not hesitate to follow his ideas, regardless of the consequences.

But Tolstoy represents more than the Russian mind; he represents the spirit of world brotherhood. What is more important, he teaches that peace demands more than a new adjustment in international relations, more than institutional reorganization; it requires a new philosophy of life and a new system of education.

Major Ideas

Tolstoy was born in 1828. In his youth he enjoyed all the advantages of the aristocracy. He received an excellent education, mostly by private tutors, and was surrounded by all the luxuries of life. As a boy, he was strong and passionate, and already had a keen power of observation. His memories of early childhood were distinct and clear. When his mother died in 1830, he writes, "During the service I wept decently, crossed myself, and bowed down to the floor, but I did not pray with my soul, and I was rather indifferent; I was troubled because the little new dress coat that they had made me wear was very tight under the arms. I was careful not to soil overmuch the knees of my trousers and I stealthily made observations on all who were present.[1]

He attended the University of Kazan, where he majored in natural science, law, and philosophy. He was bored by the curriculum of the University, which was too formal and stereotyped, and his real education came through discussions with his fellow students. Already he had taken a liking to Rousseau, who was to

1. Tolstoy, *Childhood*, chap. 27.

become a powerful influence in his life. The ambition of young Tolstoy can be seen in a plan of study he outlined for himself when he left the University. Within two years he desired to master the fundamentals of law, of practical and theoretical medicine, French, German, English, Latin, and Italian, the principles of agriculture, history, geography, statistics, the principles of mathematics, and to advance his knowledge in music, painting, and natural science. In addition to these efforts, he planned to write a dissertation and treatises on all the subjects he studied— certainly an ambitious program for a young man. He failed to accomplish these gols in the next two years, since he devoted his life to gay social activities. He wrote to his brother a year later, after he went to St. Petersburg, "I did nothing useful there, merely squandered heaps of money and got into debt." But the ambition for learning persisted and his knowledge later on became truly encyclopedic.

In 1851 he entered the army as an officer, rapidly advanced in rank, and fought through the Crimean campaign, during which he took part in the storming of Sevastopol. His three sketches about the campaign, *Sevastopol in December, 1854, and in May and August, 1855,* portray the full horror of war. These sketches are very different from the patriotic exhortations of Tennyson. He pictures fear in all its dimensions: the fear of the army officers leaving for the front, the cowering dread of the common soldiers crawling on all fours, the mute despair of the hospitals.

The awareness of death is one of the distinguishing traits of Tolstoy. Perhaps he is one of the most skillful biographers of death in the history of world literature. As Tolstoy became older, he spoke more fearfully about death, and his desire for immortality became more insistent. It is well to remember that not for a moment of his life did the awareness of the transitory aspects of human existence desert him. Like Buddha, Tolstoy wanted to conquer not only life but death itself.

He gave up his army career, joined a brilliant literary circle in

St. Petersburg, and resolved to become a great author. He traveled abroad, visited France, Switzerland, Germany, and Italy. Like Schopenhauer, he saw the darker aspects of existence in those countries; for instance, the picture of a man being executed in Paris remained in his mind. In Switzerland he observed the life of the idle rich, parasites without any constructive purpose in life.

When he returned to Russia he devoted himself to improving the lot of the serfs who had just been emancipated by the order of the Czar. He conducted an experimental school, which tried to put into practice individualistic theories of education. "I should give two rules for education," he said, "not only to live well oneself, but to work over oneself, constantly perfecting oneself and to conceal nothing about one's own life from one's children." He also edited an educational journal, *Yasnaya Polyana,* which reflected his indebtedness to Rousseau.

He married when he was thirty-four. His wife was more practical than he, and, while they were devoted to each other, there was no close intellectual comradeship. With his passionate mind, he made a very difficult partner in marriage. It was at this time that he wrote *War and Peace.* The fundamental purpose of this book was educational: to show the fallacy of war. Unlike Carlyle, Tolstoy did not believe in hero-worship. Napoleon appears as a vain puffed-up individual. Kutuzov is pictured as a stodgy, impotent general; both are puppets in the hands of Fate. Tolstoy shows no respect for the military strategy of Napoleon, and with alacrity exposes his mistakes. The battles are viewed by Tolstoy as parts of a gigantic chaos, in which organization and the best-made plans count for nothing. The real heroes of *War and Peace* are the common soldiers. Their endurance, their sacrifices, their comradeship, are described with profound sympathy. The leading character of the story is not Prince Andrey or his friend Count Pierre Bezukhov, but an illiterate, simple peasant, Platon Karatayev. Instinctively, Tolstoy shows, this man fulfilled the requirements of Christianity: "He loved all and lived lovingly with all with which life brought him into contact, and in particular with man—not with any special man, but with men who were before his eyes." To Tolstoy, Platon is the unattainable and eternal embodiment of the spirit of simplicity and real education; he represented a fulfillment in life for which he himself was constantly striving.

In *Anna Karenina* Tolstoy reaches the full height of his genius. Here we have a philosophy of life crystallized into emotional terms, and a tale of the inevitable decline of a social order. The world of Anna is destined to fall; nothing can prevent that collapse. All those who are identified with this world are doomed. Almost prophetic in his warning, Tolstoy understood the full significance of his time. But there is also the promise of a new society, symbolized by the efforts of Levin and by his pure love for Kitty.

Anna, as the story opens, is securely married to a high government official. She is a pillar of respectability. Marriage has brought not great emotional upheaval but steady security. Then Anna meets Vronsky, a handsome army officer, and her love for him becomes the overwhelming feature of her life. She gives herself to him completely, becomes an outcast from society, and finally finds that Vronsky is unworthy of her love. The result is suicide.

Quite different from Anna is Levin, who shuns society, lives a peasant existence, and like Platon, is imbued with the spirit of Christianity. Some critics have called him a Sunday school type, uninteresting and boring. Nevertheless, he has qualities that give him depth and reality; his sense of unworthiness, his tormenting doubts, and his humility. The spirit of Levin is expressed by Tolstoy in the last paragraph of *Anna Karenina*:

> Just as before, I shall get angry with Ivan the coachman, I shall dispute, I shall express my thoughts at the wrong time; there will be the same wall between the holy of holies of my soul and other people, even my wife; just in the same way as before I shall blame

her for my own terror and repent doing so; just as before I shall fail to understand with my reason why I pray, and yet I shall continue to pray—but my life now, my whole life, independently of anything that can happen to me, every moment of it, is not only not bereft of meaning, as it was before, but has the undoubted meaning of good, which I have power to implant in it!

In spite of the success of *War and Peace* and *Anna Karenina,* Tolstoy felt dissatisfied. Not only was he critical of his works (he wrote *Anna Karenina* seven times; and would wake up at night and start changing sentences that did not seem perfect), but he was tortured by doubts, and by a feeling of hopelessness. He began to take stock: He was rich; he owned 16,000 acres in the province of Samara; he had a devoted wife; he was famous as an author. But something was lacking. Buddha felt the same way when he surveyed the treasures of his kingdom. Tolstoy, with almost Faustian ferocity, longed to know the answers that had tortured philosophers and educators for thousands of years. In 1879, he summarized the questions that are central in education:

1. "Why live at all?" 2. "What is the cause of my existence, and of everyone else's?" 3. "What is the purpose of my existence and of everyone else's?" 4. "What is the meaning of the cleavage into good and evil which I feel within myself, and why does this cleavage exist?" 5. "What should be the plan of my life?" 6. "What is death—how can I transcend it?"

To find the answers to these problems Tolstoy turned to science. More avidly than ever he studied books on biology, chemistry, physics, and psychology. The scientists had reduced qualitative relationships to their quantitative constituents. They had measured nature, and created order out of chaos; but they had not solved the basic problems of life. Technical philosophy had even less to offer; it restated the problem in a more complicated form, and in obscure terminology concealed its essential ignorance. Tolstoy's despair grew as he turned to Socrates, Buddha, the book of Ecclesiastes, Schopenhauer. In unison they seemed to stress the vanity of life. Were not Buddha's Four Truths a commentary on the inescapable sorrow of man's existence? Did not Schopenhauer's philosophy end in nihilism? Did not Ecclesiastes stress the utter vanity of man's strivings? Tolstoy tried to turn to God, but he did not have a living awareness of Him; he also considered that Kant had demolished all the purely intellectual proofs of the existence of God.

So volcanic was this rebellion that Tolstoy could not find solace in the mysticism and the superstition of the Greek Orthodox Church. He was disgusted with the corruption of the priests, their support of the state, and their tacit approval of war. How different this organization was from the primitive Christian church! How it neglected the practices of Christ! Thus Tolstoy started a revolution against formalism and ritual. He desired to find the faith of the common man, the essential spirit of religion that could be universalized and applied to all times. From the Sermon on the Mount he drew the substance of his new beliefs.

Faith brought about a transvaluation of values. Riches, fame, physical love—all these things were obstacles in the quest for salvation. Like St. Augustine, Tolstoy examined his past actions and came to the conclusion that they had been sinful. Naturally, he exaggerated. In his *Confessions,* he tells about the people he killed in war, the money he lost at cards, the acts of lying, stealing, drunkenness, violence, murder, and above all of lust, which he had committed. He tells of an aunt who advised him to have a liaison with a married woman, and who later urged him to marry a rich girl so that he could have many servants. That, according to his *Confessions,* was his environment. "There was not a crime I did not commit, and for all that I was praised, and my contemporaries have regarded me as a comparatively moral man." The self-accusation does not stop here. Asked why he started to write books, he replied that it was not for the benefit of the community, but that he was driven by vanity, avarice, and pride. With pitiless clarity he observed his fellow authors; not only were most of them immoral and of weak character, but they were also complacent; they believed that they had found the avenue to education, when in reality they were only portraying insignificant aspects of life.

New Values Through Spiritual Education

Thus, the author of *Anna Karenina* became a writer of moral and theological tracts. In *Resurrection* we have perhaps the greatest expression of the new Tolstoy. It is the tale of Prince Nekhludoff, who falls in love with a servant girl. First, their relationship is innocent and very poetic, guided by the idealism of youth. Later, the army spoils his code of ethics. She has a child and he deserts her, according to the code of his class. When her condition is discovered, she has to leave the estate; she sinks lower and lower, and enters the darkest stratum of society. The climax of the story occurs when she is accused of a crime of which she is innocent. It happens that Prince Nekhludoff takes part in the trial. He recognizes her, and now realizes his own guilt. An innocent woman is being condemned. He tries to help her because his conscience hurts him, and he wants to save his own soul. She laughs at him. He realizes that he must make a more complete sacrifice; consequently, he abandons his class and his property and joins her exile in Siberia. There she becomes a real woman again because of his kindness and sacrifice.

One might interpret this story theologically as an allegory of the transforming power of love. But the meaning is much deeper. Man must atone, says Tolstoy, not just for the deeds he has committed, but for his indifference and neglect. He wrote from his own personal experiences, seeing as he did for the first time the naked horror of the existence of the lower classes. Moscow in his early period had been a gay city, and he used to drive past the miserable huts of the proletariat without pondering on the meaning of poverty. Siberia was an indifferent word; that people were exiled to this wasteland was a natural act of justice. Now his imagination expanded, and he spoke for the mute sufferings of millions of Russians—for the serfs, laboring under the yoke of the landlords; for the prisoners slaving under the guard of sadistic wardens; for the opponents of the Czar who languished in Siberia; in short, for all the outcasts of society.

It was small wonder that, in 1901, Tolstoy was excommunicated. The official notice stated that Tolstoy, with the zeal of a fanatic, had advocated the overthrow of all the dogmas of the Orthodox Church, and of the very essence of the Christian faith —a strange attack against one of the most religious men in Russia. The ministers of the Czar advised action against the radical theories of Tolstoy, but Alexander III was more judicious; he said that he had no intention of making a martyr out of the famous author.

How could this new order that he envisaged be established? By the help of the intellectuals and educators? Tolstoy claimed that most of them were supporters of the *status quo*. He turned to the artists, and found that they lived in ivory towers. One might suppose that he would appeal to political parties. However, when he analyzed the program of the socialists, he realized that they were trying to do the impossible: cure a condition that could not be bettered by evolutionary political means. The revolutionary forces appealed to him for aid. Was he not preaching against the wickedness of property, against the oppressions of the state? Did he not favor nationalization of the land and labor for all? Did he not speak of a new Utopia for the common man? Yes, there were many similarities between him and the revolutionaries. But Tolstoy hated violence, and he knew that to overthrow the system by revolt would mean the application of force and bloodshed. He wanted to reform humanity through education; his method, to borrow Koestler's terms, was that *of the Yogi, not of the Commissar*. But intellectually, he contributed to the growth of the eventual revolution, for he undermined the foundations of the Czarist government. His attacks corresponded with those of Rousseau against absolutism in France. Both weakened the internal strength of the existing institutional system.

Tolstoy extended his searching analysis to international relations. What is the cause of war? Not acts of aggression or injustice on the part of one nation against another, not the pressure of population, but the existence of statehood itself. He denounced in bitter terms the Russian war with Turkey, England's campaigns against the Boers, America's conflict with Spain, and Russia's war with Japan in 1904. He spoke against patriotism in all its forms, and saw the full danger of the suspicious attitude of the European nations. How could wars be abolished? In his time, treaties of arbitration were being made. The Hague Conferences were giving new hopes to mankind. But Tolstoy was far more realistic: he urged a more thoroughgoing reform, abolition of violence itself. He writes: "Bethink yourselves and understand that not the Boers, English, French, Germans, Bohemians, Finns, Russians are your enemies, but that the only enemies are you yourselves, who with your patriotism support the governments, which oppress you and cause your misfortune."

Conflicting Ideals

In his later years, Tolstoy's missionary zeal rose to an extreme. In an essay on art, he condemned the idea that art was designed for pleasure. Here he reminds us of Plato. He speaks of "Shakespeare's meaningless twaddle," of Beethoven as a "seducer to sensuality." Again he goes to an extreme, but his essay is justified in striking at the root of the impoverishment of modern art, in attacking the sensationalistic and superficial content of much of the art of his time, and in his insistence on the wider mission of the artist, who should be an apostle for humanity. "The best works of art of our time," he writes, "transmit religious feelings urging toward the union and the brotherhood of man." Hence, he praises the books of Dickens, Hugo, and Dostoevsky, for they are preachers of a universal brotherhood.

There was an abiding conflict in Tolstoy's existence. Although he worked like a peasant, laboring in the fields, he did not abandon his property, and was still living in a luxurious home. Around him was ignorance and abject misery; people were being sent to Siberia; and what did he do? He received interviewers, wrote pamphlets, and enjoyed the comforts of his class. Until the last days of his life, he carried on this process of self-examination. More and more he wrote of leaving his home, renouncing his property, abandoning his art, and walking as a pilgrim on the roads of Russia. Conflict with his family deepened, and in 1910 he left his home in a final dramatic gesture of trying to live up to his ideals. He died from exposure at the wayside railroad station of Astapovo.

Tolstoy as Educator

To criticize Tolstoy is like criticizing the New Testament. We may object to the asceticism of his later years, to his opposition to urban existence, to his Puritanical interpretation of art, to the impractical aspects of his social program, to the fanaticism of his beliefs, to his exaggerated faith in nonviolence, but all these things are insignificant when viewed in the total perspective of his life. For there are several Tolstoys: the Tolstoy of *Sevastopol*, the Tolstoy of *Anna Karenina*, and *War and Peace*, the Tolstoy of the *Confessions*, the Tolstoy of the *Resurrection*, and the Tolstoy as seen by his wife—the last, a passionate, idealistic, opinionated, unpredictable man.

Maxim Gorky said that Tolstoy's influence, like all that is alive, is growing, forever and ever. Upon Gandhi and Romain Rolland the imprint of his ideas is certainly evident. The love that he advocated overleaps the barriers of race, creed, and nationality. His religion is designed not for the West only, but also for the East. His constant search, his accomplishments, and his frailties make him a brother to human struggles everywhere. Above all, Tolstoy is important today because the new world society requires a transformation of existing values, a genuine educational reformation.

The age of Tolstoy was one of educational ferment. Especially important was K. D. Ushinsky (1824–1870), father of the Russian primary school and a proponent of scientific training for teachers. A liberal, he was influenced by Bacon, Locke, and Spencer, and he stressed the personality of the teacher, who was to have an intense faith in his vocation. Other Russian leaders who shared his ideas and those of Tolstoy were V. I. Vodovozov (1825–1886), V. Ya. Stoyunin (1826–1888), V. P. Ostrogorsky (1840–1902), D. I. Pisarev (1841–1868), and P. I. Makushin (1844–1926).

Tolstoy believed that education should cultivate a love of country, but it was not to encourage nationalism. There was no superior nation; patriotism had often been perverted by the teacher. Children were to be taught to love mankind and to look beyond the frontiers of race, nation, and civilization.

While some Russian educators emphasized the superiority of the West and glorified the advances of Western technology, Tolstoy, like Ushinsky, stressed the values of Russian civilization. The intellectual had to find deep roots in his own nation and become part of its spirit and its ideals.

Tolstoy believed that education had a spiritual meaning. The ideal was not merely to know, but to apply knowledge in a critical way. He maintained that "only a freely developed personality armed with information and scientific knowledge can change life." The dignity of the individual was to be safeguarded. He was *not* to be indoctrinated; he was never to become the tool of the state. Censorship and suppression of new ideas were to be regarded as absolute evils, for to Tolstoy freedom was the highest good.

Tolstoy demanded that scholars accept a sense of social responsibility. They were not just models of information, but they were to be models of enlightenment. The acquisition of truth and wisdom was to be an intensely personal process. How much could the scholars learn from the simplicity of the common man! How much could they benefit from the virtue of ordinary people!

Tolstoy stressed the personality of the teacher. It was far more significant that the teacher be imbued with the importance of his vocation than that he should be an expert. The teacher should be interested in all aspects of life. He was to be concerned with the problems of man rather than with those of technical science.

The type of school that Tolstoy favored would abolish marks and would have no use for class distinctions. It would be child-centered rather than teacher-centered. Students would learn from experience, and the classroom would be like a laboratory. Students would be guided in all their activities by the spirit of kindness and compassion.

In his educational theories, Tolstoy laid stress on the importance of the teacher's personality. If he was cold and hostile toward his students, he would become a negative influence, and would be only a taskmaker. On the other hand, if he really loved his vocation and had regard for the personality of the student, and if he saw education as a continuing process, he would become a pillar of enlightenment and civilization.

Knowledge was not to be restricted to the few. Tolstoy felt that all human beings yearned for truth, and wanted a better way of life. Thus, he felt that adult education should be emphasized and that culture was to be universalized.

Tolstoy taught through precepts. "Be frank with yourselves and be frank with children" was the basis of his educational philosophy. He made it clear that man can progress only through self-examination.

PART III

24. G. Stanley Hall

Evolutionary ideas found an educational application in the work of G. Stanley Hall (1844–1924). Hall, an American, studied in Leipzig under Wilhelm Wundt, the famous German psychologist. He himself not only became a noted child psychologist, but also attracted international attention as president of Clark University. His main books on education include *Aspects of Child Life and Education, Educational Problems,* and *Adolescence,* in two volumes. He edited *Pedagogical Seminary,* an important educational magazine, which later became the *Journal of Genetic Psychology.*

Hall's interest in evolution made him champion the theory of acquired characteristics. Thus, he extended the realm of heredity: The individual in his development repeats the development of his species. The growth of the individual is biological, mental, and cultural.

Influenced by romanticism, he placed feeling above intellect, and intuition above reason. He maintained that education fails if it does not appeal to the emotions of children.

Hall believed that sex is man's fundamental drive. This means that our unconscious urges will often triumph over our conscious desires. He popularized the ideas of Freud and Jung, but he was more influenced by the latter in his mysticism and his advocacy of a sound family life.

He stressed the biological differences between men and women. Women should not enter the professions; their main task is that of motherhood. The emancipated woman who escapes from her responsibilities is to be pitied. Motherhood is both a physical and spiritual responsibility; Hall described its glories in mystical terms.

Philosophy and Education

To Hall, philosophy has more than a theoretical meaning. Its function is to serve humanity and to provide a foundation for action. In the past, philosophy overemphasized theory and logic; it had established closed systems; it had often overlooked ethical problems. The philosophy of the future, on the other hand, will have an open perspective; it will be based on the insights of life and on concrete realities.

A valid philosophy must be in agreement with common sense. It cannot mistake appearance for reality; it cannot uphold a subjective reality and project it upon the universe. Philosophy should do more than explain the world; it has to become a platform for inspiration. Thus Hall opposed the pessimism typified by Schopenhauer's philosophy. If we teach that this is the worst of all possible worlds, then we cannot inspire our youth and we end in moral paralysis. Philosophy grows out of feelings and temperamental preferences. Ideas are footnotes to experience. This means that abstraction is to be avoided and that psychological knowledge is more significant than metaphysical explanation.

Hall's philosophy implies that neither conventional idealism nor conventional materialism is a valid guide for action. Philosophical idealism overlooks the concrete setting of our drives, whereas philosophical materialism does not stress sufficiently the importance of motivation and noble aspiration.

Philosophy should make youth enthusiastic; it should lead to a love of knowledge; it should never develop a premature sophistication or cynicism. It should increase our interest in life and enhance our awareness of our own powers. It should not destroy the sense of mystery basic to the development of esthetic and scientific imagination. Truth has to pass a practical test; it must not lead away from action and involvement; it must not develop an ascetic attitude so that life becomes an endurance contest. Indeed, to Hall, "truth becomes a tool of evolution," it urges individuals to apply their insights to concrete matters.

Conventional philosophy, according to Hall, is too far removed from life. It is imbued with too much logic. It analyzes so much that it neglects the realm of feelings and it does not give the student an affirmative view of the self and of society. It upholds artificial first principles that inhibit inquiry. It has too much faith in tradition, which blocks man's educational advancement.

A valid philosophy of education, Hall stated, can learn more from psychology than from conventional philosophy. For psychology studies the drives of man and examines his motives. Psychologists realize that man is a feeling animal intent upon significance and meaning. Psychology points to the need for constructive values that make life more abundant. Whether we are students or teachers, according to Hall, we need a wholesome perspective that combines interest in the self and humanitarianism.

To Hall, the universe is composed of space and motion. Space is the setting for energy. The world is guided by laws that can be understood by man. Evolution is the law of life that indicates that man can be perfected. Evolution implies growth, not merely in the physical realm but in morals and spiritual values. In fact,

Hall believed that the weak and the ineffective are destroyed by nature, while the strong prevail and create a great culture.

Basic in his educational ideals is a persistent faith in a progress that governs all areas of life. Progress can be seen in physical life when new species appear; in science new laws are discovered, whereas in education our enlightenment is spreading to other nations.

Education, to Hall, is a tangible evidence of man's perfectibility. Education indicates that man's goodness outweighs his negative capacities. It is the task of the teacher to inspire youth with the thought that greatness belongs to the future, not to the past.

Man lives in two worlds. On the one hand, man is part of a physical setting and surrounded by objects. On the other hand, he lives in a world of imagination in which feeling and intellect meet. Imagination, which should be the center of education, is symbolized by the play activities of children and is climaxed by the artistic and scientific creativity of adulthood.

Hall points to specific needs in the development of the individual. First comes infancy, a stage between birth to the end of the second year. This phase sees the rapid physical development of the child, whose senses are being stirred. The infant becomes aware of his own identity, and he becomes conscious of his environment. At the same time, he is dependent on parental love, help, and understanding.

Next comes the stage of childhood, which lasts until the eighth year. Now imagination should dominate and it should be carefully cultivated. This implies no artificial restraints and discipline and no restrictive curriculum. Precise knowledge is to be avoided; fairy tales are the center of childhood, for they indicate that children yearn for an ideal realm.

Between eight to thirteen a different phase prevails for youth, for now education should stress drill and obedience. Good habits are to be cultivated. Exactness is to be stressed in school. Hall believed that youngsters of this age group need firm guidance. This period should therefore be carefully supervised by teachers, who are to stress the significance of hard work and are to be strict disciplinarians.

Between fourteen and twenty-two a flexible educational system is to prevail. Now the youngster is ready to enter the stage of civilization. He needs little drill; rather, he requires inspiration. Now the arts and the humanities become especially important, and interest is to prevail in the classroom. Intuition rather than analysis is to be developed and the inward development of the student is to be attained.

Hall was opposed to examinations in this phase of the student's development. Instead, he urged that stress be placed on a complete view of life. The young student is to correlate the physical, spiritual, and moral elements in education. He is to become conscious of the beauty of ideas. Ultimately, he is to become his own teacher and develop patterns of autonomy. What is needed now is not accuracy of perception but creativity, which unites the ideal and the practical realm and which makes a unique contribution to civilization.

Contributions

Hall popularized the concepts of Jung and Freud and stimulated an interest in child psychology. He realized that the interests of children are different from those of adults; and that the integrity of childhood must be protected.

He believed that the group is more important than the individual, and he emphasizes common activities and the development of altruistic drives toward the service of humanity.

Intellect is less important than temperament. Hall's pragmatic philosophy looked to the consequences of ideas and made activity central in the educational experience. Like James, he opposed intellectualism as an obsolete view of life.

Education, to Hall, was the supreme study of man. It included the arts and the sciences, philosophy as well as religion. He felt that the history and philosophy of education should have a primary place in the college curriculum.

His evolutionary theories tended to be optimistic. He felt that the individual in his development recapitulated the history of the race, and like Rousseau, he urged a curriculum that would be appropriate to the various phases in the development of man.

He stimulated interest in higher education by his emphasis on research and the creation of a genuine academic community. Knowledge was not to imitate the past but to anticipate the frontiers of the future. Knowledge was to serve the interests of democracy and emancipate man from tribal taboos.

He called for a creative system of education that would explore all the powers of individuals. Teachers must be well trained in subject matter and infectious in their enthusiasm.

Like Dewey, Hall favored more elastic instruction. He regarded the idea of uniformity in the curriculum as a roadblock. Let children advance according to their own needs and explore with fervor, he urged. Let them use all their gifts; the body as well as the mind should be stimulated. Science and art should be correlated. The entire curriculum ought to be based on the needs of the children, not on adult authority.

Hall idolized the period of childhood, which he believed should become the center of education. Through numerous questionnaires and unflagging study he sought to explore the attitudes and motivations of children.

Like Rousseau, Hall had an overly romantic vision of childhood. It is doubtful whether his questionnaires actually clarified the dilemmas and the perplexities of children. But his influence was vast. It extended to scholars like Dewey, Kilpatrick, Starbuck, Terman, Cattell, and Bode.

25. William James

William James (1842–1910) was born into a wealthy family. His father traveled a great deal and was able to give an excellent education to his children, who spent several years in exclusive boarding schools in Europe. William James became very proficient in languages, and international in his outlook on life.

At first he aspired to be a painter and studied under William Hunt in Newport. But he changed his mind, and in 1861 he entered Harvard Medical School. His study there was helpful, for it gave him a scientific foundation for philosophy. One of his teachers was Louis Agassiz, whom he assisted in various experiments and whom he accompanied on an expedition to the Amazon. In 1869, James received his M.D. from Harvard, to which he returned four years later as instructor in anatomy and physiology. Gradually his interests again shifted, this time to the field of psychology, and in 1876 he organized the first psychological laboratory in the United States. He became a professor of philosophy at Harvard in 1881.

James did not neglect his scientific labors during this entire period. He was still interested in physiology, but now his main love was philosophy. He approached it, not from the standpoint of idealism, but from a common-sense, down-to-earth viewpoint.

In his last years he suffered from ill-health. He wanted to work on a systematic treatise to expound his viewpoint, but found neither the time nor the energy to fulfill this ambition.

The Works of James

The most notable treatise of James in the field of psychology is to be found in his *Principles of Psychology* (1890), which constituted almost a major revolution in that field. In its two volumes he discussed such subjects as "Functions of the Brain," "Association," "Perception of Space," "Perception of Reality," "Hypnotism," "The Effects of Experience." Another significant work by James is *The Will to Believe,* in which he treated such topics as "Is Life Worth Living?" "The Dilemma of Determinism," "Great Men and Their Environment," "The Importance of Individuals," and "What Psychical Research Has Accomplished." In 1899 he published his *Talks to Teachers in Psychology.* In this book he stressed the laws of habit and the association of ideas.

In the *Varieties of Religious Experience* (1902), he dealt with such topics as "Religion and Neurology," "The Sick Soul," "Conversion," "Saintliness," and "Mysticism." In 1907 he published *Pragmatism.* Here he defined his philosophical method, showing how pragmatism is related to religion and life. Two years later *The Meaning of Truth* was published. In this book he expanded some of his pragmatic concepts, and answered his critics.

The Hibbert Lectures appeared in 1909 under the title *A Pluralistic Universe.* In this work James attacked Hegel, and showed how any type of monistic idealism is bound to fail. He also devoted much space to Bergson's criticism of intellectualism.

Memories and Studies, published posthumously, expounds his concept of the moral equivalent of war. Ralph Barton Perry edited James's *Essays in Radical Empiricism*. This volume is especially significant from a technical standpoint, for it contains among other subjects James's views on "Consciousness," "The Essence of Humanism," and "Absolutism and Empiricism."[1]

The Purpose of James

James ushered in a new tradition in American education. Instead of definitions and abstractions, *experience* is made the criterion for truth. Concrete problems of life are emphasized. This makes the philosophy of James intelligible to the layman and accounts for its popularity.

He waged philosophical warfare against Hegelian idealism: The universe is not determined by ideas. It is not a dialectical process; rather, it can be understood through experience. Since it is not a deterministic whole, *freedom* has a place in it.

James describes his philosophy as radical empiricism. This means that it has no place for the thing-in-itself, for an Absolute Ego, or for a transcendental unity of apperception. Experience is continuous; it needs no substratum. Through it we perceive not merely objects but also *relations*.

Compare the view of James with that of Josiah Royce. To James, experience is autonomous and needs no transcendent explanation. To Royce, experience refers to a higher principle of unity—the Absolute. Truth has meaning, according to Royce, only when it is part of a coherent whole. This view James rejected categorically.

Philosophy and Psychology

Throughout his life, James was concerned with the relationship between philosophy and psychology. Philosophers are not concerned with eternal truths; their ideas arise out of concrete

1. For an evaluation of James, consult H. Kallen, *William James and Henry Bergson*; R. B. Perry, *In the Spirit of William James*; T. Flournoy, *The Philosophy of William James*.

circumstances and are dependent upon their temperament. We start to think when we have a problem to solve. If our life were completely perfect, if we faced no obstacles, there probably would be no philosophical speculation at all.

James realized that no complete agreement is possible in philosophy any more than in religion. The various philosophical and religious systems that we find in the world are expressive of emotional needs and emotional desires.

The pragmatic philosopher, in short, regards change as a necessary aspect of civilization, and will not try to coerce the opinions of those who come after him. It is merely pretentious to establish a completely systematic philosophical system, for ideas are subject to evolution. There can be no eternal truth in philosophy or in any other area of inquiry.

In every way, the philosophy of James differs from that of rationalism, which upholds universals and stresses the validity of logic. James, on the other hand, regards the *specific* fact as ultimate; the universal is merely "an abstraction." In many ways his philosophy resembles that of David Hume; consequently, he had no use for an absolute mind. But, unlike Hume, James stressed the fact that the relations that connect experiences must themselves be real. This faith in the validity of relations saves James from skepticism. In fact, in his own life doubt was never the ultimate standpoint. He rejected any philosophy that did not leave room for faith and for a spiritual explanation of life.

In his philosophy James made a famous distinction between two types of philosophers: the *tender-minded* and the *tough-minded*. The tender-minded are the idealists, who believe in free will, who are intellectual in their approach to the problems of life, and who favor optimism as against pessimism. They interpret the universe according to their own desires; in fact, in their philosophies the world appears as an expanded classroom. Their most unpleasant trait is their dogmatism. Frequently they pretend to know everything, and they explain the ways of the Absolute in exhaustive detail. Their style is pompous and dry, but their conclusions tend to be edifying to the religious minded.

Quite different are the tough-minded philosophers, who tend to be pessimistic, and who regard science as the ultimate principle of explanation. They favor the materialistic viewpoint and have only contempt for the gospel of freedom as taught by the idealists.

To some extent James favors the tough-minded thinkers; he had a great respect for the conclusions of science. Nevertheless, his basic purpose is to picture a universe consistent with his religious hopes and expectations.

By using a psychological approach to philosophy, James changed our perspective regarding technical thinkers. Instead of looking on their systems as expressions of logic and pure reason, we now tend to regard them according to their psychological presuppositions. We ask such questions as the following: What is the purpose of the thinker? How does he reflect the ideals of his period? Is he tough-minded or tender-minded? How do his educational views mirror his own experience?

With James, metaphysics and epistemology come down to earth, where they can be related to definite psychological motives. They become valuable if they have definite consequences; otherwise, they are disregarded.

Philosophy of Education

James opposed traditional instruction, which stressed memorization and relied on the classics. Instead, he favored functional training in laboratory work, which he thought would make for precision of thought and sharpness of observation.

In his period, moral philosophy frequently occupied the center of the curriculum, and it usually was taught by the college president, who usually was also a minister of the gospel. James opposed such instruction; he thought it cultivated mythologies and obscured the realities of our existence. Let the student explore life, he urged. Let him obtain a versatile view of science. Above all, let there be no fixed dogmas, traditional concepts, or obsolete superstitions.

James's educational philosophy rests upon psychology, not upon metaphysics. It is the task of the educator to study the laws of learning and become acquainted with the psychological facts that explain our nervous system. We must make habitual "as many useful actions as possible"; as in other realms of life, indecision is our great enemy. James despises the man who constantly frets over little things and who can never make up his mind. Education should see to it that such a type does not emerge; rather, education should develop bold leaders.

William James praised the structure of American education:

> In the general activity and uprising of ideal interests which every one with an eye for fact can discern all about us in American life, there is perhaps no more promising feature than the fermentation which for a dozen years or more has been going on among the teachers. In whatever sphere of education their functions may lie, there is to be seen among them a really inspiring amount of searching of the heart about the highest concerns of their profession. The renovation of nations begins always at the top, among the reflective members of the State, and spreads slowly outward and downward. The teachers of this country, one may say, have its future in their hands. The earnestness which they at present show in striving to enlighten and strengthen themselves is an index of the nation's probabilities of advance in all ideal directions. The outward organization of education which we have in our United States is perhaps, on the whole, the best organization that exists in any country. The State school systems give a diversity and flexibility, an opportunity for experiment and keenness of competition, nowhere else to be found on such an important scale.[2]

To James education is *"the organization of acquired habits of conduct and tendencies to behavior."* In explanation, he wrote:

2. *Talks to Teachers,* pp. 3-4.

To illustrate. You and I are each and all of us educated, in our several ways; and we show our education at this present moment by different conduct. It would be quite impossible for me with my mind technically and professionally organized as it is, and with the optical stimulus which your presence affords, to remain sitting here entirely silent and inactive. Something tells me that I am expected to speak, and must speak; something forces me to keep on speaking. My organs of articulation are continuously innervated by outgoing currents, which the currents passing inward at my eyes and through my educated brain have set in motion; and the particular movements which they make have their form and order determined altogether by the training of all my past years of lecturing and reading. Your conduct, on the other hand, might seem at first sight purely receptive and inactive,—leaving out those among you who happen to be taking notes. But the very listening which you are carrying on is itself a determinate kind of conduct. All the muscular tensions of your body are distributed in a peculiar way as you listen. Your head, your eyes, are fixed characteristically. And, when the lecture is over, it will inevitably eventuate in some stroke of behavior, as I said on the previous occasion: you may be guided differently in some special emergency in the schoolroom by words which I now let fall.—So it is with the impressions you will make there on your pupil. You should get into the habit of regarding them all as leading to the acquisition by him of capacities for behavior,—emotional, social, bodily, vocal, technical, or what not. And, this being the case, you ought to feel willing, in a general way, and without hairsplitting or farther ado, to take up for the purposes of these lectures with the biological conception of the mind, as of something given us for practical use. That conception will certainly cover the greater part of your own educational work.[3]

James correlated reception and reaction:

No reception without reaction, no impression without correlative expression,—this is the great maxim which the teacher ought never to forget.

An impression which simply flows in at the pupil's eyes or ears,

3. *Ibid.,* pp. 29-30.

and in no way modifies his active life, is an impression gone to waste. It is psysiologically incomplete. It leaves no fruits behind it in the way of capacity acquired. Even as mere impression, it fails to produce its proper effect upon the memory; for, to remain fully among the acquisitions of this latter faculty, it must be wrought into the whole cycle of our operations. Its *motor consequences* are what clinch it. Some effect due to it in the way of an activity must return to the mind in the form of the *sensation of having acted* and connect itself with the impression. The most durable impressions are those on account of which we speak or act, or else are inwardly convulsed.[4]

James stressed the power of emulation:

Imitation shades imperceptibly into *Emulation*. Emulation is the impulse to imitate what you see another doing, in order not to appear inferior; and it is hard to draw a sharp line between the manifestations of the two impulses, so inextricably do they mix their effects. Emulation is the very nerve of human society. Why are you, my hearers, sitting here before me? If no one whom you ever heard of had attended a "summer school" or teachers' institute, would it have occured to any one of you to break out independently and do a thing so unprescribed by fashion? Probably not. Nor would your pupils come to you unless the children of their parents' neighbors were all simultaneously being sent to school. We wish not to be lonely or eccentric, and we wish not to be cut off from our share in things which to our neighbors seem desirable privileges.

In the schoolroom, imitation and emulation play absolutely vital parts. Every teacher knows the advantage of having certain things performed by whole bands of children at a time. The teacher who meets with most success is the teacher whose own ways are the most imitable.[5]

Teaching depends on example, according to James:

Children admire a teacher who has skill. What he does seems easy, and they wish to emulate it. It is useless for a dull and

4. *Ibid.*, pp. 33-34.
5. *Ibid.*, pp. 49-50.

devitalized teacher to exhort her pupils to wake up and take an interest. She must first take one herself; then her example is effective as no exhortation can possibly be.

Every school has its tone, moral and intellectual. And this tone is a mere tradition kept up by imitation, due in the first instance to the example set by teachers and by previous pupils of an aggressive and dominating type, copied by the others, and passed on from year to year, so that the new pupils take the cue almost immediately. Such a tone changes very slowly, if at all; and then always under the modifying influence of new personalities aggressive enough in character to set new patterns and not merely to copy the old. The classic example of this sort of tone is the often quoted case of Rugby under Dr. Arnold's administration. He impressed his own character as a model on the imagination of the oldest boys, who in turn were expected and required to impress theirs upon the younger set. The contagiousness of Arnold's genius was such that a Rugby man was said to be recognizable all through life by a peculiar turn of character which he acquired at school. It is obvious that psychology as such can give in this field no precepts of detail. As in so many other fields of teaching, success depends mainly on the native genius of the teacher, the sympathy, tact, and perception which enable him to seize the right moment and to set the right example.[6]

James stressed both discipline and interest:

It is certain that most schoolroom work, till it has become habitual and automatic, is repulsive, and cannot be done without voluntarily jerking back the attention to it every now and then. This is inevitable, let the teacher do what he will. It flows from the inherent nature of the subjects and of the learning mind. The repulsive processes of verbal memorizing, of discovering steps of mathematical identity, and the like, must borrow their interest at first from purely external sources, mainly from the personal interests with which success in mastering them is associated, such as gaining of rank, avoiding punishment, not being beaten by a difficulty and the like. Without such borrowed interest, the child could not attend them at all. But in these processes what becomes inter-

6. *Ibid.*, pp. 50-51.

esting enough to be attended to is not thereby attended to *without effort*. Effort always has to go on, derived interest, for the most part, not awakening attention that is *easy,* however spontaneous it may now have to be called. The interest which the teacher, by his utmost skill, can lend to the subject, proves over and over again to be only an interest sufficient to *let loose the effort.* The teacher, therefore, need never concern himself about *inventing* occasions where effort must be called into play. Let him still awaken whatever sources of interest in the subject he can by stirring up connections between it and the pupil's nature, whether in the line of theorectic curiosity, of personal interest, or of pugnacious impulse. The laws of mind will then bring enough pulses of effort into play to keep the pupils exercised in the direction of the subject.[7]

James had little use for examinations, as the following extract attests:

> The boy who tells us, "I know the answer, but I can't say what it is," we treat as practically identical with him who knows absolutely nothing about the answer at all. But this is a great mistake. It is but a small part of our experience in life that we are ever able articulately to recall. And yet the whole of it has had its influence in shaping our character and defining our tendencies to judge and act. Although the ready memory is a great blessing to its possessor, the vaguer memory of a subject, of having once had to do with it, of its neighborhood, and of where we may go to recover it again, constitutes in most men and women the chief fruit of their education. This is true even in professional education. The doctor, the lawyer, are seldom able to decide upon a case off-hand. They differ from other men only through the fact that they know how to get at the materials for decision in five minutes or half an hour; whereas the layman is unable to get at the materials at all, not knowing in what books and indexes to look or not understanding the technical terms.
>
> Be patient, then, and sympathetic with the type of mind that cuts a poor figure in examinations. It may, in the long examination

7. *Ibid.,* pp. 109-11.

which life sets us, come out in the end in better shape than the glib and ready reproducer, its passions being deeper, its purposes more worthy, its combining power less commonplace, and its total mental output consequently more important.[8]

James contrasts negative and positive motivation:

For instance, your pupils are wandering in mind, are listening to a sound outside the window, which presently grows interesting enough to claim all their attention. You can call the latter back again by bellowing at them not to listen to those sounds, but to keep their minds on their books or on what you are saying. And, by thus keeping them conscious that your eye is sternly on them, you may produce a good effect. But it will be a wasteful effect and an inferior effect; for the moment you relax your supervision the attractive disturbance, always there soliciting their curiosity, will overpower them, and they will be just as they were before: whereas, if, without saying anything about the street disturbances, you open a counterattraction by starting some very interesting talk or demonstration yourself, they will altogether forget the distracting incident, and without any effort follow you along. There are many interests that can never be inhibited by the way of negation. To a man in love, for example, it is literally impossible, by any effort of will, to annul his passion. But let "some new planet swim into his ken," and the former idol will immediately cease to engross his mind.

It is clear that in general we ought, whenever we can, to employ the method of inhibition by substitution. He whose life is based upon the word "no," who tells the truth because a lie is wicked, and who has constantly to grapple with his envious and cowardly and mean propensities, is in an inferior situation in every respect to what he would be if the love of truth and magnanimity positively possessed him from the outset, and he felt no inferior temptations. Your born gentleman is certainly, for this world's purposes, a more valuable being than your "Crump, with his grunting resistance to his native devils," even though in God's sight the latter may, as the Catholic theologians say, be rolling up great stores of "merit."[9]

8. *Ibid.*, pp. 142-43.
9. *Ibid.*, pp. 193-94.

He turns to Spinoza, who

wrote in his *Ethics* that anything that a man can avoid under the notion that it is bad he may also avoid under the notion that something else is good. He who habitually acts *sub specie mali*, under the negative notion, the notion of the bad, is called a slave by Spinoza. To him who acts habitually under the notion of good he gives the name of freeman. . . . Make freemen of your pupils by habituating them to act, whenever possible, under the notion of a good. Get them habitually to tell the truth, not so much through showing them the wickedness of lying as by arousing their enthusiasm for honor and veracity. Wean them from their native cruelty by imparting to them some of your own positive sympathy with an animal's inner springs of joy. And, in the lessons which you may be legally obliged to conduct upon the bad effects of alcohol, lay less stress than the books do on the drunkard's stomach, kidneys, nerves and social miseries, and more on the blessings of having an organism kept in lifelong possession of its full youthful elasticity by a sweet, sound blood, to which stimulants and narcotics are unknown, and to which the morning sun and air and dew will daily come as sufficiently powerful intoxicants. . . .

If to some of you the things I have said seem obvious or trivial, it is possible that they may appear less so when, in the course of a year or two, you find yourselves noticing and apperceiving events in the schoolroom a little differently, in consequence of some of the conceptions I have tried to make more clear. I cannot but think that to apperceive your pupil as a little sensitive, impulsive, associative, and reactive organism, partly fated and partly free, will lead to a better intelligence of all his ways. Understand him, then, as such a subtle little piece of machinery. And if, in addition, you can also see him *sub specie boni*, and love him as well, you will be in the best possible position for becoming perfect teachers.[10]

James believed that progress could be achieved only through functional application. The education of the past, he thought, was too much occupied with the noble maxims. It had been too

10. *Ibid.,* pp. 194-96.

contemplative, and had neglected the everyday realm of action. The schoolroom must be equated with life and must become the center of action. Only in this way can education become constructive and dynamic in the experience of the individual.

There is a danger, James noted, that the teacher may moralize too much, that he may give too many sermons. Instead, he should appeal to the emotional drives of his students, and should make the process of knowledge as dramatic as possible. He should show that ideas can be as adventurous and as thrilling as other activities that at first may appear more interesting to the students.

If learning is to be effective, James taught, it must be based upon daily exercise. We should not postpone our intellectual efforts. By devoting a few hours every day to poetry and philosophy we can increase our intellectual proficiency, and we can actualize our mental potentialities. Nothing worthwhile is accomplished without constant effort, which at first we regret, for we believe we have abandoned some of our most cherished pleasures. But the more we indulge in intellectual effort, the more we improve ourselves and the more delightful life becomes.

At the same time, James was not an unqualified proponent of activism. He realized the weaknesses of the American type of education. For example, he mentioned the reaction of Hindu visitors who noticed the spiritual vacuity of education in the United States. James agreed with them, for like them, he felt that our life was becoming too tense and that anxiety was dominating our character. He taught that we must not be overcome by constant motion and by an unending expenditure of energy.

Many critics have been harsh with James because they have seen him merely as an apostle of utilitarianism. They have neglected the critical side of his dynamic ideas. He was also interested in higher personal ideals, in a wider perspective, and he thought that education could develop a more adequate set of attitudes by which we can improve civilization.

Action to him was not an end in itself. It was to be supplemented by self-discipline, and by meditation on the nature and destiny of man.

Education Against War

The social philosophy of James was much concerned with the problem of war. He had no illusions about the pacifistic drives of man. Has not war been a constant aspect of civilization, glorified by the ministers of God? Is not a man a beast of prey?

Since our culture is becoming more monotonous, we continually need excitement. Wars, consequently, especially for noncombatants, have been periods of relief from the tediousness of our existence. Furthermore, war fever is stimulated by the newspapers, which specialize in sensationalism and which dramatize the conflicts of nations.

James believed that to some extent people actually want war. This may be disillusioning for the sentimentalist, but they do not understand human nature. War has a religious motive: it is part of our savage background, and it adds a certain intoxication to life.

James believed that universal disarmament is not the correct answer to war, or its cure; we must put peaceful statesmen into power; we must educate the public, especially those who manufacture public opinion.

The best antidote is to find a substitute for war. Instead of military conscription, we should organize young men into battalions to build dams, to diminish the ravages of nature, and to expand our industrial system. Adventure would still remain with us. There would still be the thrill of new experiences, but our task would be constructive instead of destructive, and peace would reign supreme.

To bring about a better civilization, James looked to the outstanding individual. History is made not by the masses but by the outstanding leader. To establish peace, we must cultivate the type of statesman who abhors all militaristic notions and dedicates himself to the welfare of humanity.

26. Dewey

....

John Dewey (1859–1952), the outstanding student of William James, studied at the University of Vermont and at Johns Hopkins University; later he taught at the Universities of Minnesota, Michigan, and Chicago, and finally, from 1904, at Columbia University. He traveled to China, Japan, Mexico, Russia, and Turkey. His philosophical theories exerted a wide influence abroad; he was instrumental in reorganizing the Turkish educational system.

Among his most important works are *Experience and Nature, The Quest for Certainty, Logic, Essays in Experimental Logic,* and *Reconstruction in Philosophy.* In esthetics he wrote *Art as Experience.* To religious philosophy he contributed *A Common Faith.* To ethics and social philosophy, he added *Human Nature and Conduct* and *Freedom and Culture.* In political theory he gave voice to a pluralistic concept of the state in *The Public and Its Problems.*

Dewey continued the pragmatic tradition of William James, but his interest was mainly in education, whereas James's main interest was religion. Dewey had a powerful effect upon America's education development. His *Democracy and Education* became a sort of Magna Charta of the American school system.[1]

Among the influences that conditioned Dewey's thinking, Hegelian philosophy occupies a prominent place. W. T. Harris thought that Dewey might become the foremost interpreter of Hegel in America. Dewey found in Hegel a sweeping explanation of history that appealed to his imagination; he noticed, however, that Hegel's scientific views were defective, that they rested upon a superficial acquaintance with the experimental method.

More important than Hegel to John Dewey's development was the impact of Huxley, Spencer, and Darwin. The theory of evolution became the cornerstone of Dewey's educational system. Like Darwin, Dewey believed in a *biological approach to knowledge*. Darwinism did not make a pessimist out of Dewey; he thought that science could control nature and that the struggle for existence could be modified by the judicious use of man's intelligence.

At the same time, Dewey had a pronounced interest in ancient philosophy. In his eighties he continued to be an avid reader of Plato. Like Plato, Dewey had a lifelong interest in social problems; he was also interested in the establishment of a new society. However, he did not appreciate Plato's authoritarian tendencies. Dewey believed in the common man and had no use for dictators, either in philosophy, politics, or education.

The most significant single influence on Dewey was the work of William James, who had great respect for Dewey's philosophical insight. Dewey, in fact, became the St. Paul of pragmatism. There had arisen heresies in the pragmatic ranks. C. S. Peirce, founder of pragmatism, in his later views disliked the anti-intellectualism of James, and adopted the term pragmaticism to distinguish his own philosophy from that being developed from his original

1. For a critical survey of Dewey, see Hook, *John Dewey, an Intellectual Portrait;* Leander, *The Philosophy of John Dewey: A Critical Study;* Feldman, *The Philosophy of John Dewey: A Critical Analysis.*

views. F. C. S. Schiller, who never liked an orthodox cause, styled his particular system humanism and devoted most of his time to an onslaught on the Aristotelian syllogism. Giovanni Papini, the young Italian thinker, for whom James had great hopes, turned to Catholicism and devoted most of his labors to a defense of the Catholic saints, whose virtues and greatness he espoused. Dewey, however, remained faithful to pragmatism and defended its tenets against all opponents.

Like James, Dewey believed in an open universe, and he felt that traditional philosophy could not provide an adequate answer to the problems of education and human conduct. What matters, then, is not the goals of philosophy, but the *methods* utilized by the thinker.

But there are significant differences between the philosophies of Dewey and James. James was essentially religious. Dewey approached religion from the standpoint of the laboratory scientist, and had a strong bias for agnosticism. Dewey's system was more deterministic. Thus it reflected the growing stratification of American society. In James's time, individualism was the guiding voice of American culture; but in Dewey's era there was a strong trend in the direction of social action and social control.

Dewey dreamed of a welfare state that would provide economic security for its citizens and lift their standard of living.

Both James and Dewey were liberals; both hated oppressive authority, but Dewey's liberalism was more sober and scientific than James's. He expected no miracles; he had no faith in automatic solutions or in the laissez-faire spirit; instead, he urged the extension of democratic principles into the economic field.

Why did Dewey exert such an enormous influence on American life? First, he represented the down-to-earth tradition of pragmatism. He was not abstruse and theoretical like Royce and Edwards; rather, he discussed *concrete* and living issues.

Second, he had immense faith in democracy. He did not look down on the masses; he had no sympathy for the upper classes, nor any respect for old-world culture. In Dewey the American way of life found an eloquent spokesman.

Third, he was an activist. He stressed constantly his belief that mere contemplation is not sufficient, and that activity ennobles man. This spirit could easily be appreciated by the average American, who likewise had disdain for contemplation and whose energy was boundless. Americans are perhaps the most activist of all people; this spirit frequently produces anti-intellectualist currents in America.

Fourth, Dewey became the spokesman of the rebellion against authority. In education, students were demanding greater freedom and were trying to break away from the traditional curriculum; in religion, liberal Christianity was dissatisfied with the old supernaturalism, and was attempting to establish a universal foundation for religion. In politics, the progressive movement was trying to reform federal and local government so that American democracy would be closer to Lincoln's ideal of a government of the people, by the people, and for the people. In art the same rebellion could be noted. American artists tried their best to be up to date; with enthusiasm they adopted such European movements as cubism, surrealism, and dadaism, which they regarded as extremely progressive.

All these trends were reflected in Dewey's philosophy, which looked upon most of history as a dark and useless adventure. Instead, he urged his fellow countrymen to look to a new scientific age which would not tolerate any type of dogmatism and which would witness the full triumph of the pragmatic method.

Educational Ideals

Dewey's theory of education cannot be understood without a comprehension of his opposition to a merely cultural education, by which he understands the training of a parasitical leisure class. He opposed mere book knowledge in any area. He stressed actual practice, democratic cooperation, the fellowship of occupations, and the interests of the student, which are to be measured by his growth.

In *My Pedagogic Creed,* Dewey turned to what the school is:

The school is primarily a social institution. Education being a social process, the school is simply that form of community life in which all those agencies are concentrated that will be most effective in bringing the child to share in the inherited resources of the race, and to use his own powers for social ends.

Education, therefore, is a process of living and not a preparation for future living.

The school must represent life, as real and vital to the child as that which he carries on in the home, in the neighborhood, or on the playground.

That education which does not occur through forms of life, forms that are worth living for their own sake, is always a poor substitute for the genuine reality, and tends to cramp and to deaden.

The school, as an institution, should simplify existing social life; should reduce it, as it were, to an embryonic form. Existing life is so complex that the child cannot be brought into contact with it without either confusion or distraction; he is either overwhelmed by the multiplicity of activities which are going on, so that he loses his own power of orderly reaction, or he is so stimulated by these various activities that his powers are prematurely called into play and he becomes either unduly specialized or else disintegrated.

As such simplified social life, the school should grow gradually out of the home life; it should take up and continue the activities with which the child is already familiar in the home.

It should exhibit these activities to the child, and reproduce them in such ways that the child will gradually learn the meaning of them, and be capable of playing his own part in relation to them.

This is a psychological necessity, because it is the only way of securing continuity in the child's growth, the only way of giving a background of past experience to the new ideas given in school.

It is also a social necessity because the home is the form of social life in which the child has been nurtured and in connection with which he has had his moral training. It is the business of the school to deepen and extend his sense of the values bound up in his home life.[2]

He attacks contemporary views:

> Much of present education fails because it neglects this fundamental principle of the school as a form of community life. It conceives the school as a place where certain information is to be given, where certain lessons are to be learned, or where certain habits are to be formed. The value of these is conceived as lying largely in the remote future; the child must do these things for the sake of something else he is to do; they are mere preparations. As a result they do not become a part of the life experience of the child and so are not truly educative.
>
> The moral education centers upon this conception of the school as a mode of social life, that the best and deepest moral training is precisely that which one gets through having to enter into proper relations with others in a unity of work and thought. The present educational systems, so far as they destroy or neglect this unity, render it difficult or impossible to get any genuine, regular moral training.
>
> The child should be stimulated and controlled in his work through the life of the community.
>
> Under existing conditions far too much of the stimulus and control proceeds from the teacher, because of neglect of the idea of the school as a form of social life.
>
> The teacher's place and work in the school is to be interpreted from this same basis. The teacher is not in the school to impose certain ideas or to form certain habits in the child, but is there as a member of the community to select the influences which shall affect the child and to assist him in properly responding to these influences.
>
> The discipline of the school should proceed from the life of the school as a whole and not directly from the teacher.
>
> The teacher's business is simply to determine, on the basis of

2. *My Pedagogic Creed* (pamphlet issued in 1900).

larger experience and riper wisdom, how the discipline of life shall come to the child.

All questions of the grading of the child and his promotion should be determined by reference to the same standard. Examinations are of use only so far as they test the child's fitness for social life and reveal the place in which he can be of the most service and where he can receive the most help.[3]

Regarding the subject matter of education, Dewey stated:

The social life of the child is the basis of concentration, or correlation, in all his training or growth. The social life gives the unconscious unity and the background of all his efforts and of all his attainments.

The subject matter of the school curriculum should mark a gradual differentiation out of the primitive unconscious unity of social life.

We violate the child's nature and render difficult the best ethical results by introducing the child too abruptly to a number of special studies, of reading, writing, geography, etc., out of relation to this social life.

The true center of correlation on the school subjects is not science, nor literature, nor history, nor geography, but the child's own social activities.

Education cannot be unified in the study of science, or so-called nature study, because apart from human activity, nature itself is not a unity; nature in itself is a number of diverse objects in space and time, and to attempt to make it the center of work by itself is to introduce a principle of radiation rather than one of concentration.

Literature is the reflex expression and interpretation of social experience; hence it must follow upon and not precede such experience. It, therefore, cannot be made the basis, although it may be made the summary of unification.

Once more that history is of educative value insofar as it presents phases of social life and growth. It must be controlled by reference to social life. When taken simply as history it is thrown into the

3. *Ibid.*

distant past and becomes dead and inert. Taken as the record of man's social life and progress it becomes full of meaning. I believe, however, that it cannot be so taken excepting as the child is also introduced directly into social life.

The primary basis of education is in the child's powers at work along the same general constructive lines as those which have brought civilization into being.

The only way to make the child conscious of his social heritage is to enable him to perform those fundamental types of activity which make civilization what it is.

In the so-called expressive or constructive activities is the center of correlation.

This gives the standard for the place of cooking, sewing, manual training, etc., in the school.

They are not special studies which are to be introduced over and above a lot of others in the way of relaxation or relief, or as additional accomplishments. I believe rather that they represent, as types, fundamental forms of social activity; and that it is possible and desirable that the child's introduction into the more formal subjects of the curriculum be through the medium of these constructive activities.[4]

He emphasizes science and literature:

The study of science is educational insofar as it brings out the materials and processes which make social life what it is.

One of the greatest difficulties in the present teaching of science is that the material is presented in purely objective form, or is treated as a new peculiar kind of experience which the child can add to that which he has already had. In reality, science is of value because it gives the ability to interpret and control the experience already had. It should be introduced, not as so much new subject matter, but as showing the factors already involved in previous experience and as furnishing tools by which that experience can be more easily and effectively regulated.

At present we lose much of the value of literature and language

4. *Ibid.*

studies because of our elimination of the social element. Language is almost always treated in the books of pedagogy simply as the expression of thought. It is true that language is a logical instrument, but it is fundamentally and primarily a social instrument. Language is the device for communication; it is the tool through which one individual comes to share the ideas and feelings of others. When treated simply as a way of getting individual information, or as a means of showing off what one has learned, it loses its social motive and end.

There is, therefore, no succession of studies in the ideal school curriculum. If education is life, all life has, from the outset, a scientific aspect, an aspect of art and culture, and an aspect of communication. It cannot, therefore, be true that the proper studies for one grade are mere reading and writing, and that at a later grade, reading, or literature, or science, may be introduced. The progress is not in the succession of studies, but in the development of new attitudes towards, and new interests in, experience.

Education must be conceived as a continuing reconstruction of experience; that the process and the goal of education are one and the same thing.

To set up any end outside of education, as furnishing its goal and standard, is to deprive the educational process of much of its meaning, and tends to make us rely upon false and external stimuli in dealing with the child.[5]

Dewey's ideal is that the school should mirror the activities, interests, and aspirations of society. How foolish it is to divorce education from action, to make a monastery out of the school. Education is a *continuous* process. It does not start at any given time, and it certainly does not stop when we leave school. More than any other thinker, Dewey realized how important education is for the development of a free society.

While the Greek thinkers, especially Plato and Aristotle, had too much respect for merely cultural subjects, and disdained manual labor, John Dewey and his followers emphasized perhaps too

5. *Ibid.*

strongly the importance of manual work and industrial activity. The task of a genuinely progressive education should be to restore the balance between thinking and manual labor. America especially needs more concentrated courses in the fundamentals of modern civilization.

In fairness to John Dewey it should be pointed out that the weakness of progressive education is mostly due to *faulty application*. Many teachers who had no adequate educational training allowed their classes to do whatever they pleased. The lack of discipline they introduced bordered on anarchy; and Dewey's progressive ideal of education was constantly negated by the authoritarian tendencies both of the home and of social institutions.

Scientific Method

In Dewey's philosophy, the scientific method plays an important role. He feels that philosophers can learn much from scientists; they should be open-minded and experimental in their approach to intellectual problems. Thus, Dewey eliminates the consideration of metaphysical ideals from his system, and instead views life from a secular standpoint.

Dewey demands a *reconstruction of philosophy*. Thinkers must abandon belief in eternal realities and avoid useless epistemological controversies; instead they should deal with the social and moral problems of their time.

Any one of you who arrives at such a view of past philosophy will of necessity be left to entertain a quite definite conception of the scope and aim of future philosophizing. He will inevitably be committed to the notion that what philosophy has been unconsciously, without knowing or intending it, and so to speak, under cover, it must henceforth be openly and deliberately. When it is acknowledged that under disguise of dealing with ultimate reality, philosophy has been occupied with the precious values embedded in social traditions, that it has sprung from a clash of social ends and from a conflict of inherited institutions with incompatible contemporary tendencies, it will be seen that the task of future philosophy is to clarify men's ideas as to the social and moral strifes of their day. Its aim is to become so far as is humanly possible an organ for dealing with these conflicts.[6]

Applying this viewpoint to logic, Dewey points out that logic is not the key to reality and that it should follow an *experimental path*. Logic thus becomes a progressive discipline, occupied not with static syllogisms, but with the ever-changing data of experience.

Dewey's philosophy is characterized by *instrumentalism*, which is activistic and holds that growth is the main criterion for a meaningful life. There is no underlying substance; the mind is not an entity, but a *function*. There can be no division between object and subject, for both are interrelated.

In many ways. Dewey completed the work of Francis Bacon. Like Bacon, Dewey was concerned primarily with the *functional* aspects of knowledge, which could bring about a new renaissance of culture.

In modern culture Dewey finds four pronounced changes from medieval ideals:

First, there is the transfer of interest from the eternal and universal to what is changing and specific, concrete—a movement that showed itself practically in carrying over of attention and thought from another world to this, from the supernaturalism characteristic of the Middle Ages to delight in natural science, natural activity and natural intercourse. Secondly, there is the gradual decay of the authority of fixed institutions and class distinctions and relations, and a growing belief in the power of individual minds, guided by methods of observation, experiment and reflection, to attain the truths needed for the guidance of life. The operations and results of natural inquiry gained in prestige and power at the expense of principles dictated from high authority.

6. *Reconstruction in Philosophy*, p.26 .

Consequently principles and alleged truths are judged more and more by criteria of their origin in experience and their consequences of weal and woe in experience, and less of criteria of sublime origin from beyond everyday experience and independent of fruits in experience. It is no longer enough for a principle to be elevated, noble, universal and hallowed by time. It must present its birth certificate, it must show under just what conditions of human experience it was generated, and it must justify itself by its works, present and potential. Such is the inner meaning of the modern appeal to experience as an ultimate criterion of value and validity. In the third place, great store is set upon the idea of progress. The future rather than the past dominates the imagination. The Golden Age lies ahead of us, not behind us. Everywhere new possibilities beckon and arouse courage and effort. The great French thinkers of the later eighteenth century borrowed this idea from Bacon and developed it into the doctrine of the indefinite perfectibility of mankind on earth. Man is capable, if he will but exercise the required courage, intelligence and effort, of shaping his own fate. Physical conditions offer no insurmountable barriers. In the fourth place, the patient and experimental study of nature, bearing fruit in inventions which control nature and subdue her forces to social uses, is the method by which progress is made. Knowledge is power and knowledge is achieved by sending the mind to school to nature to learn her processes of change.[7]

Applying this viewpoint to science, Dewey believed that philosophers had not paid enough attention to scientific progress. They still believed in fixed ideas and they still adhered to a priori theories. However, science disclosed a universe which was neither fixed nor closed, but which revealed unlimited possibilities. Furthermore, science had a new respect for material facts. This implies that philosophers likewise had to adopt a new perspective which stressed experimentation and control, rather than a static contemplation of nature.

Such an experimental viewpoint was an expression of Dewey's

7. *Ibid.*, pp. 47-49.

democratic tendencies. He disliked static realities; instead, he favored change. In fact, his universe almost reminds us of Heraclitus in its dynamic pattern. Feudalism believed in fixed classes and in an absolute order; in philosophy it was represented by traditional idealistic theories which relied upon the fixity of species. Dewey's instrumentalism, however, stressed the reality of the individual and tolerated no absolute patterns. It believed in the future rather than in the past, and it had immense faith in the possibilities of man.

In this way, Dewey echoed the American spirit. Had not the pioneer negated the limitations of the Old World? Was not progress the watchword of American culture? Was not growth a constant feature of American city life? The buoyant, energetic spirit of America is revealed in Dewey's technical philosophy.

Being a follower of the empirical tradition, Dewey stressed the importance of sensation. However, he did not follow Locke completely, for Dewey also emphasized the importance of intelligence. It goes without saying that to him intelligence is not an abstract, hypothetical capacity; rather, its function is to make possible for man a better adjustment to his environment. We cannot speak any more of pure reason; rather, we must realize that man's reason is hypothetical.

This theory has important implications. It implies, first of all, that we must use our reason *concretely*. Education must come down to earth and contribute to the solution of man's social and political problems. Second, Dewey believed in tentative standards and hypothetical ideas: Reason has no exclusive key to reality. Our mind is not the gateway to the thing-in-itself; the standards of our generation should not necessarily guide the path of the following generation.

In the third place, our intelligence must be studied biologically since it evolved in the same way as all the other capacities of man. Dewey fought a perennial war against all those who tried to "deify" man's mind.

Like Machiavelli, Dewey was concerned with actuality rather than with abstract ideals. The philosophers who had pictured only a Shangri-la and who, like Royce, had appealed to the Absolute, had done serious harm to mankind, for they had divorced actuality from man's aspirations. To Dewey, ideals are not distant goals, but methods. They indicate our intellectual progress, and they must be applied to our daily life.

The philosopher of the future will not be concerned with a perfect realm. Nor will he seek to escape into a changeless reality; on the contrary, he will take part in the social strife of his time, and he will attempt to apply his ideals to the betterment of social institutions.

Our culture, especially poetry, art, and religion, cannot be sustained by relying upon the traditions of the past, but only by anticipating the trends of the future.

> Poetry, art, and religion are precious things. They cannot be maintained by lingering in the past and futilely wishing to restore what the movement of events in science, industry and politics has destroyed. They are an out-flowering of thought and desires that unconsciously converge into a disposition of imagination as a result of thousands and thousands of daily episodes and contact. They cannot be willed into existence or coerced into being. The wind of the spirit bloweth where it listeth and the kingdom of God in such things does not come with observation. But while it is impossible to retain and recover by deliberate volition old sources of religion and art that have been discredited, it is possible to expedite the development of the vital sources of a religion and art that are yet to be. Not indeed by action directly aimed at their production, but by substituting faith in the active tendencies of the day for dread and dislike of them, and by the courage of intelligence to follow whither social and scientific changes direct us. We are weak today in ideal matters because intelligence is divorced from aspiration. The bare force of circumstance compels us onward in the daily detail of our beliefs and acts, but our deeper thoughts and desires turn backwards. When philosophy shall have cooperated with the course of

events and made clear and coherent the meaning of the daily detail, science and emotion will interpenetrate, practice and imagination will embrace. Poetry and religious feeling will be the unforced flowers of life. To further this articulation and revelation of the meanings of the current course of events is the task and problem of philosophy in days of transition.[8]

Artistic Ideals and Education

The progressive spirit of Dewey is revealed in his esthetic theories. An excellent summary of them is contained in *Art as Experience* and in chapter IX of *Experience and Nature*.

To Dewey, art has, above all, a *social* significance. Thus, Phidias represents the Greek ideal of life, and the Ionic style of architecture was best suited to the Greek taste. Roman art specialized in engineering and was especially concerned with public buildings. Here again the artist mirrored the mood of his society.

In the same manner Dewey gave a social interpretation of the medieval cathedral. The Gothic style of architecture gave a functional expression of medieval ideals. It was the product of a social experience that believed in supernaturalism. However, artistic goals are not static; they change just as much as political and economic ideals.

Dewey was not an enthusiastic supporter of medieval culture; we cannot go back to the age of Faith. Dewey had no use for Gothic architecture in modern America. It may have had its use in the Middle Ages; in a scientific civilization it is outmoded.

Art, according to Dewey, must be *dynamic*. Hence, he welcomed the new styles in painting and architecture. The artist who dwells in the past absorbs a one-sided perspective, for he becomes isolated and is unable to contribute to the progress of culture.

Art, Dewey asserted, has a utilitarian function. It cannot be divorced from life. Thus, he felt that there should be a clear

8. *Ibid.*, pp. 212-13.

connection between the industrial and fine arts. Esthetic principles are to be utilized not only in the museum, but in the home, school and factory.

In art education Dewey's influence was widespread. He showed that children often have a more adequate appreciation of art than adults. The teachers who tried to formalize the esthetic habits of children had been extremely shallow in their approach; for children, according to Dewey, are not to be trained in stereotyped esthetic patterns; rather, their individuality is to be encouraged.

The Reformer

As a political philosopher Dewey expressed progressive ideals. In many ways he influenced the New Deal. He maintained that a laissez-faire concept of freedom is inadequate, and that freedom and social security go together. The experimental method must be extended to politics if man's condition is to be improved. This, again, demands a real reconstruction of our institutional system. In politics, as in philosophy and in religion, Dewey maintained an open mind and a flexible attitude.

Absolutism can best be prevented through voluntary organizations:

> Associations of mathematicians, chemists, astronomers, business corporations, labor organizations, churches are trans-national because the interests they represent are worldwide. In such ways as these, internationalism is not an aspiration but a fact, not a sentimental ideal but a force. Yet these interests are cut across and thrown out of gear by the traditional doctrine of exclusive national sovereignty. It is the vogue of this doctrine or dogma, that presents the strongest barrier to the effective formation of an international mind which alone agrees with the moving forces of present day labor, commerce, science, art and religion.

> Society, as was said, is many associations, not a single organization. Society means association; coming together in joint inter-

course and action for the better realization of any form of experience which is augmented and confirmed by being shared. Hence there are as many associations as there are goods which are enhanced by being mutually communicated and participated in.[9]

Contributions

Dewey's contributions to philosophy and education may be summarized briefly as follows:

1. He gave a logical explanation of pragmatism and tried to divorce logic from metaphysics. To him logic was a *naturalistic* discipline.

2. In his philosophy of instrumentalism he stressed the importance of change and opposed static ends and static ideals.

3. In his methodology, he showed how the scientific method could be applied to all realms of inquiry. He stressed that the knowledge of the future must be functional, experimental, and subjected to the rigorous tests of the laboratory method.

4. In his ethical system he was a meliorist. Rejecting both pessimism and optimism, he used the concept of growth as the standard of ethical evaluation.

5. In religion he opposed all types of dogmatism and tried to develop a common faith which regards God as a unifying ideal and which uses scientific knowledge in religion.

6. In education he emphasized the importance of the learner. A trenchant critic of traditional liberal education, he influenced the development of vocational education and the adoption of a student-centered curriculum.

7. In esthetics he stressed that art is a progressive discipline and that it must be correlated with life. Thus he did not accept the Victorian ideal of art for art's sake.

8. In his outlook on philosophy he was antimetaphysical. He approached intellectual problems from the viewpoint of biology rather than of theology.

9. *Ibid.*, p. 205.

9. In his social philosophy he was consistently liberal; he rejected all forms of authoritarianism.

10. In his political views he was a pluralist. He did not favor concentration of governmental power; rather, he favored voluntary cooperation of a variety of groups, such as churches, labor unions, business corporations, and scientists, who would work together for the common good.

In Dewey, the voice of the pioneer, the stirring energies of the reformer, the patient method of the scientist, and the faith of the teacher are united in a search for a new education through which man can survive in a chaotic age.

27. Gandhi

Oriental Ideas in Perspective

Eastern thought has frequently encouraged *regressive* social trends. Thus, Hinduism has been the supporter of the caste system; Mohammedanism has encouraged feudalism; and Shintoism has emphasized emperor worship. Confucianism in China was a stumbling block in the achievement of adequate educational reforms and in the introduction of new ways of life and new methods of government.

Social progress in the Near East and in the Orient has often been delayed because the common people have been too docile and too lethargic. This attitude is largely caused by educational and religious teachings that encourage the spirit of fatalism and resignation. Obedience to God and to secular authorities is emphasized as the cornerstone of life. Furthermore, the time perspective of the Orient is so vast that the present does not matter, for life on earth is regarded as a minor incident. Especially disturbing is the condition of the outcasts in India, who often live in a more deplorable condition than animals, although in the twentieth century determined attempts have been made to better their social and educational status.

Social regression has been intensified by the traditionalism of

327

Oriental education. Very often the past is the criterion of evaluation. This tendency is especially strong in Confucianism, which felt that in ancient days a real utopia prevailed and that we can learn from the piety and virtue of the ancient Chinese rulers. In Confucianism, family relationships were regarded as fundamental, and rebellion on the part of children was not encouraged. While this attitude caused an elaborate code of manners, it did not promote change and educational progress. The spirit of traditionalism was even stronger in Shintoism than in Confucianism, for Shintoism taught that the gods were born in Japan, and that they bestowed upon the Japanese people unique insight and a unique code of morality.

It has often been charged that Eastern thought has a basic antiscientific attitude. Thus, we find that in Hinduism the highest stage of knowledge is intuition, and that in Taoism there is an intense contempt for reason. Again and again it is pointed out in the Upanishads that the enlightened sage becomes almost as naïve and simple as a child, relying upon a spontaneous insight into reality.

What matters most in Eastern thought is *peace of mind,* not scientific progress.[1] In fact, almost all Oriental philosophies have a contempt for technology. Yet it appears that without an adequate technological system no real advancement can be made by the common man. Of course, the disciple of Eastern ideals will point out that technology is not an unmixed blessing; in fact, that it may be the decisive factor in the disintegration of Western culture.

Furthermore, it has often been charged by the West that Eastern thought is *negativistic.* Thus, in Hinduism, Buddhism, and Taoism, spiritual education implies a loss of all individuality. Nirvana itself stands for the extinction of personality. Practically, such a spirit symbolizes a fatalistic resignation to the events of life. The individual is regarded as insignificant; in fact, his

1. See C. Moore (ed.), *Philosophy—East and West.*

mortal life is of minor importance. This means, especially in Hinduism, that the events of this world are to be disregarded. Everyday happenings should not distress the sage who seeks for a total perspective. When he sees suffering, he is not distressed, for he regards it as part of a vast cosmic cycle, and as the result of the law of Karma.

The detachment of Eastern thought widens the gulf between the saint and the common man. The former often tries to escape from society and, as in Hinayana Buddhism, is primarily concerned with his own salvation. The common man, however, is surrounded by a veil of superstition, and he makes little effort to achieve spiritual insight.

However, all these charges against Eastern thought are only partially valid. For, to some extent, Eastern ideals do not support an outworn social system, are not dominated by tradition, are not antiscientific, and do not reflect the spirit of negativism. The greatness of Eastern education and religion is probably best reflected by the teaching of Buddha. Certainly he fought with all his might against social discrimination. Buddha, like Dewey, was intensely positivistic. He was not interested in metaphysical disputes, and he refused to rely upon supernatural aid. Nor can we regard this teachings as being basically negativistic. It is true that he looked upon life as a sorrowful process, but he made it clear that there is a way, the Eight-fold Path, to overcome man's sorrows.

Eastern thought and Oriental education are characterized by a spirit of peace and tranquillity. In the West we can benefit from such a spiritual perspective and cultivate an attitude of inwardness. It is also significant that the scholar in the Orient has a higher status than the Western scholar. There are many aspects of Oriental education that should be a guide to Western man in his quest for real education.

Real education in the twentieth century can give us a renewed faith in the dignity of the individual, the sacredness of human life, and the creativity of man's spirit. It can teach us a new respect for alien ideals and alien concepts; for we must learn how to get along, not only with our friends, but also with those who differ from us. As in the past, educational ideals appeal to us to disregard the petty, the superficial, and the transitory, and to concentrate instead on the perennial issues of life and reality. Genuine education, with its universality and social idealism, can be the unifying force for the Atomic Age and can thus aid in the survival of civilization.

Gandhi's Ideals

In many ways, Mahatma Gandhi (1869–1948) represents a climax of Oriental thought. His personality has evoked the admiration of both the East and the West. In every way he lived up to his ideals, and he demonstrated the perennial vitality of faith.

Born at Porbandar in Western India, Gandhi studied law in England. Later, he went to South Africa where he fought against racial discrimination. Upon his return to India, he protested against the oppressive acts of England, and in 1920, he officially started a policy of nonviolent noncooperation. He was sentenced to jail in 1922, for six years, but he was released two years later. As a leader of the National Congress, Gandhi had immense power, and he was the leading spirit in achieving Indian independence. He constantly urged peace between the Moslems and Hindus; when riots broke out after the granting of Indian independence, he personally started a campaign of penance. His pacifistic and moderate attitude infuriated his extreme followers, and he was assassinated by one of them on his way to a prayer meeting.

Romain Rolland has compared Gandhi with Jesus, and there are many parallels in the concepts taught by both men. Like Jesus, Gandhi believed in the love of God and of humanity. Like Jesus, Gandhi had uncomplicated faith; he felt that it was primarily a matter of the heart; complicated theological systems were unnecessary if man was to be saved. Like Jesus, Gandhi had respect for all races and all nations. He believed in a universal God whose providence included all parts of the universe and, like Jesus, he taught by precept and example.

Gandhi made it clear that God's work was manifested in many different religions. He respected the insight and moral heroism of Mohammed; he was moved to tears by the sacrifice of Jesus; he had an abiding love and understanding for the teachings of Buddha. Nevertheless, Gandhi remained a Hindu and accepted its scriptures, although he protested against the abuses of its caste system.

Gandhi's moral status was fully revealed during his trial in 1922. The prosecutor had demanded the full penalty of the law, and pointed to Gandhi as the real culprit in causing armed resistance against British rule. Without hesitation, Gandhi accepted full responsibility. He stated that he could not dissociate himself from the acts of the Indian people, and that he should have realized that his speeches and publications would inflame their passions. He did not defend the crimes and outrages that had been committed, because violence outraged his soul. He ended his speech not by pleading for mercy, but by saying that he deserved the full penalty of the law.

Even when he was in solitary confinement, his spirit did not break. He used his time in prison to study Western writers, especially Thoreau, Emerson, Ruskin, and Tolstoy. He found new inspiration in the *Bhagavad-Gita,* particularly in the concept of *Bhakti,* which means unconditional love of God. Gandhi was certain that man's spirit was more important than his body, and that religion and education could aid him in creating a knowledge and an awareness of man's basic spirituality.

All his life Gandhi believed in the power of prayer. He did not pray for selfish advantages or for supernatural rewards, nor for the destruction of his enemies; rather, he prayed that he might be faithful to his ideals and that his life would add to the goodness and harmony in the universe. To Gandhi, education without prayer was a futile process.

Religion, according to Gandhi, was not a compartmentalized activity. It was not a separate and isolated activity. It was not a vocation for the spiritual aristocracy; on the contrary, to him, life and religion were one. A life without faith would be utterly meaningless and sterile; while religion that was not adjusted to man's daily existence, and that only appealed to a few, was utterly worthless.

Gandhi did not have much faith in scientific education. He did not feel that science had created permanent happiness. Around him he saw the evil effects of science, especially the instruments of destruction and mass murder that man's ingenious brain had devised. Furthermore, science had made man skeptical. Gandhi felt that faith in God was all-important, and that faith, therefore should be the center of educational instruction.

Like Tolstoy, Gandhi preached against modern materialism. There could be no real progress when man paid so much attention to his physical comforts and neglected the demands of his soul. Gandhi realized that the temptations of materialism and spirituality were often the same. Did not most denominations stress quantitative expansion? Did not the struggle of the various religions represent a basic atheism? Was there not a frequent union between Western religion and Western imperialism?

True spirituality, according to Gandhi, meant a constant search and an unending quest for perfection. There was no time for a feeling of smugness or superiority. Gandhi believed that the saint shared the imperfection of the sinner, and that the work of the saint was never finished. So long as war, disease, and poverty prevailed in society, the saint had not accomplished his mission. The saint, as a spiritual teacher, could not rest upon his laurels; his task was to re-educate mankind.

While Gandhi had many wealthy followers, he was at home with the poor of India. He found that poverty was the most meaningful prelude to spirituality. The rich man was too dependent on his possessions; he was a slave to convention; his values were superficial because they were dominated by social approval. The poor man, on the other hand, was close to nature. The poor man suffered, he toiled, and he knew how to appreciate life.

In his moral ideals, Gandhi, above all, stressed the importance of the good motive. In every way he opposed the teachings of Machiavelli, for he contended that the end does not justify the means. For example, if the caste system created misery and oppression, there was still no justification for its violent overthrow and for a bloody revolution against all those who believed in it. For Gandhi thought that a victory, achieved in this manner, would ultimately become a defeat. Once a policy of bloodshed is adopted, it becomes the dominant technique, and thus it undermines the fruits of conquest.

Like Buddha, Gandhi felt that all life is sacred; not only the life of mankind, but also of animals. To destroy life was to sin against creation. He attacked Western man for his insensibility regarding the life of animals. Of course, this was only an overture to the imperialistic policy of the West, which, throughout its history, had shown little respect for the sacredness of life.

Gandhi believed in a universal religion which included all denominations, all prophets, and all the various revelations of mankind. He believed in one God, but he thought that He was manifested in many different ways. Thus, the Hindus would have an impersonal concept of God, while the Christians would pray to a personal deity. The educated scholar would formulate a theological system of God, while the man on the street would express a spontaneous and emotional view of the Supreme Being.

Gandhi was certain that God was not a distant force, unconcerned with mankind, but that He was constantly creative and that His spirit was forever active. God could best be found in the silence of meditation, when man becomes conscious of his divine origin and divine destiny. The man who dedicated himself to God, who gave up all comfort and all worldly goods, would find an abiding meaning in life and he would thus achieve, while still in this existence, a vision of true immortality.

In regard to education, Gandhi was not a theorist, but a teacher who believed in action. Knowledge and action had to be combined, for Gandhi's ideal was the development of all-around excellence for the individual. Like John Dewey, Gandhi believed that we learn by doing and that book knowledge is less important than practical experience. Literary education should be based on our knowledge of crafts; self-control and discipline—including celibacy for young students—were indispensable tools for the achievement of real wisdom.

He wanted better libraries, more laboratories, and more research institutions for India; they were to be open to all people with the necessary qualifications. But his real love, the education of villagers, was based upon the ideal of self-sufficiency and the promotion of basic crafts. He did not neglect the arts and music, for to him they were essentially spiritual activities.

Gandhi wanted no narrow theological training; rather, he favored ethical education. We teach morality best, he affirmed, by being examples in our conduct. An enemy of narrow nationalism, he maintained that "no culture can live, if it attempts to be exclusive." Culture, to him, represented a living synthesis of the past and the present, of physical, moral, and spiritual qualities. Man could only progress when he combined the love of society with the love of truth. Moral principles were to be applied to the schoolroom as well as to society.

Gandhi was neither traditional nor progressive in his concept of education. We can learn valuable lessons from the past; at the same time, we cannot be guided by its necessities. The true teacher, he maintained, needs an international perspective, and should see life under the aspect of eternity.

Education, according to Gandhi, could either impede or advance the cause of humanity. If education only cultivated our analytical powers, it could have negative consequences for man. Scholarship alone was not enough; what mattered was the development of a spiritual attitude, whereby ideas had a living reality and became part of our daily existence.

Thoreau had a fundamental impact upon Gandhi's educational ideas. Like Thoreau, Gandhi believed in the simple life of nature, and that time "was something we could go fishing in." Like Thoreau, Gandhi believed that the intellect was a cleaver, unable to penetrate the core of reality. Like Thoreau, Gandhi wanted to simplify education so that only essentials would be taught. Like Thoreau, Gandhi was opposed to mere technological education, and urged instead the virtues of the contemplative attitude.

Silence and meditation are the centers of education, according to Gandhi. We have a divine source of knowledge within ourselves. Thus, the teacher stirs the innate capacities of students and he reminds them of their essential self. "Know thyself and know God" are the bastions of Gandhi's educational thought.

Gandhi thus opposed a purely rationalistic system of education. The teacher could not neglect the wisdom of the heart. Ultimately, religion and education mean the same. Both aim at the true knowledge of God and the universe.

As for evil, Gandhi thought that, metaphysically, evil is unreal. To be sure, we cannot overlook the oppressions of mankind and the ravages of nature and the imperfections of the institutional system; yet, in the final analysis, only goodness counts. Gandhi asserted that goodness could transmute evil, and that the time would come when evil would be completely conquered. All this could be accomplished through education, which would teach man the importance of compassion.

The universe, according to Gandhi, represents a moral order. The law of cause and effect operates as much in the moral as in the physical realm. Thus, the evil man does not gain a lasting victory, and he eventually creates his own hell. At the same time, goodness is never in vain, for it creates the seeds for a truly meaningful and universal existence. The evil man only lives for himself and inevitably isolates himself from others; the good man, who is truly educated, is never alone, and he is never without comrades. *His dwelling-place is eternity and his soul is in humanity.*

Gandhi accepted the reality of the mystical experience. The ultimate spiritual stage could not be defined intellectually; it could only be felt and experienced. To the mystic, intellectual ideals were secondary; only the union between man and God was of real importance. Such a union produced in Gandhi a feeling of complete peace and serenity. Education and religion thus end in mysticism, which creates a feeling of oneness, turns us away from materialism, and teaches us the virtue of detachment.

To achieve this condition, Gandhi disciplined his body; often he would fast; sometimes he would eat only milk and fruit—he was certain that this asceticism strengthened the resources of his soul. Real insight, he believed, could not be achieved without abstinence from sensuality.

His love was unconditional—it included his friends and enemies; by his love he overwhelmed even his prosecutors. Evil was not to be resisted by violent means—it was to be overcome by compassion and kindness. To Gandhi, *nonviolence was the basis of education and spirituality.* As he stated:

> For me the law of *Satyagraha,* the law of love, is an eternal principle. For the past thirty years I have been preaching and practicing Satyagraha. The principles of Satyagraha, as I know it today, constitute a gradual evolution. . . .
>
> The term Satyagraha was coined by me in a demonstration of its permanence and invincibility. It can be used alike by men, women and children. It is totally untrue to say that it is a force to be used only by the weak so long as they are not capable of meeting violence by violence. It is impossible for those who consider them-

selves to be weak to apply this force. Only those who realize that there is something in man which is superior to the brute nature in him, and that the latter always yields to it, can effectively be Satyagrahis. This force is to violence, and therefore to all tyranny, all injustice, what light is to darkness.[2]

Since Gandhi had little faith in modern industry, he urged a return to a simple peasant economy. Together with political self-rule, he believed in home production. However, his followers, including Nehru, realized that the industrialization of India could not be delayed and that it contributed to the emancipation of man.

Gandhi's contribution to philosophy and education should not be minimized. His ideals may be the basis of a union between East and West; they remind modern man of the transcendent significance of the life of faith. For all those who treasure idealism, Gandhi's philosophy is a *tribute to man's creative spirit,* a milestone in man's search for emancipation, and a symbol of the universality of genuine education.

2. *Satyagraha.*

28. Kilpatrick

Progressive education is the product of both European and American ideas. Rousseau, Pestalozzi, and Froebel contributed to its development. In America, James, Peirce, Parker, and Hall stimulated its growth. The progressive movement in politics had educational implications, for it held that free schools are the bastions of democratic living.

The Progressive Education Association was established in 1919. At first, under the impact of Kilpatrick, it emphasized individualistic ideals. After the Depression in 1930, through the ideas of John L. Childs, George Counts, V. T. Thayer, and Boyd H. Bode, it turned more to the consideration of social issues. After World War II, the movement lost impetus. This was due to a shift of interest. Reconstructionism, as championed by Theodore Brameld, gained new adherents. It made social reform the primary concern of educators. The conservative reaction in politics had educational consequences, and thinkers like Russell Kirk criticized the assumptions of progressivism and urged a return to tradition. Neo-Scholastics pleaded for the type of unity represented by the medieval church. Robert Hutchins and Mortimer J. Adler advocated the Great Books as the center of the

339

curriculum. Essentialists attacked the neglect of discipline in progressive education. James Conant in his report on the American high school recommended a subject-centered emphasis, and urged the study of solid material rather than concentration on experimental projects.

Still, the progressive movement has attracted able proponents in our time. Among them mention should be made of Ernest Bayles, Lawrence G. Thomas, H. Gordon Hullfish, George Axtelle, Frederick C. Neff, and Bruce Raup. Their concern is with the experimental foundations of knowledge, and they regard the traditional view of education as obsolete.

Progressive educators believe that subjects should not be taught in isolation. They feel that planning should be cooperative on the part of teachers, administrators, and children. Learning involves no preconceived goals, but implies a constant reconstruction of the ideas and ideals of students and teachers. Mere reflection is inadequate, for it leads to unending abstractions. There is an emphasis upon activity. Learning becomes a theory of inquiry; knowledge becomes active participation. Specific ideas rather than general concepts are stressed. This means that a specific project—for example, the city in modern life—may become the subject of extended investigations in the school.

Freedom and cooperation govern the progressive school, which objects to traditional controls. Freedom implies that no dogmas are allowed and that indoctrination is shunned. Thus, progressive educators have fought against loyalty oaths and against other types of thought control. Progressive eduction is interested in evidence, not in static beliefs. Cooperation implies that the students learn best when they share ideas and experiences. The progressive educator feels that competition leads to anxiety, which vitiates a genuine educational experience.

The teacher in such a system has a unique role. His task is not that of a disciplinarian. He works with children so that mutual goals are achieved and creative capacities are actualized. The progressive administrator does not impose his ideas upon the school; rather, he encourages his associates, who are regarded as equals in the educative process, to think for themselves.

Education in this way becomes an experience in relatedness. The school becomes a miniature democracy, where the interests of all are safeguarded. The effectiveness of the school is measured not by its capacity to transmit knowledge, but by its ability to develop constructive attitudes and motivations so that cooperation and freedom may prevail and all forms of discrimination may be abolished.

Kilpatrick and Education

The most influential of the progressive educators was William Heard Kilpatrick (1871–1965). His influence was felt at every level of education and extended to adult and vocational education. The various state departments of education often gave voice to his ideas. In the 1960's, especially in California, a reaction took place. In fact, Max Rafferty in California viewed the ideas of Kilpatrick as false and as leading to a superficial education. Admiral Rickover charged him with being the champion of an overemphasis on methodology, which, according to the admiral, is the real roadblock to educational advancement.

Educated in Georgia schools, Kilpatrick attended Mercer University, eventually becoming its acting president. In 1909 he went to Teachers College at Columbia University, where he soon became its most famous teacher. After his retirement in 1938 he continued his lecturing and writing.

Among his books, special note should be made of his *Foundations of Method* and *Philosophy of Education*. The latter is the climax of his mature thinking and is an eloquent defense of the progressive educational philosophy.

Kilpatrick was especially influenced by Darwin. Life is an evolving process; man is an organism who survives by adjusting himself to new environments.

The scientific method, Kilpatrick held, can be extended to all areas of inquiry. It stands for an open mind and free inquiry; it is the foe of all forms of dogmatism and avoids absolutes.

Science means rigorous honesty. Kilpatrick challenged the conservatism that prevailed at Mercer University, and was promptly accused of heresy. He felt, however, that the logic of evidence is stronger than the logic of faith, and that, if necessary, the educator should be a martyr for his beliefs.

Kilpatrick had great admiration for both Peirce and James. Peirce he respected for his stress upon fallibilism and his opposition to determinism. William James he admired because James had discerned the intimate connection between philosophy and psychology. Like James, Kilpatrick was certain that there could be no advance in philosophy without an adequate theory of learning. Philosophy is not an expression of eternal truths, but rather a struggle for social welfare, an intellectual expression of man's search for the good life.

John Dewey became the main guide for Kilpatrick. Like Dewey, Kilpatrick regarded education as a democratic process, and he stressed the belief that learning involves experience and the reconstruction of our environment; like Dewey, he believed in group action and favored a child-centered program. Kilpatrick especially championed the activity method, which appeals to the interests of children.

Kilpatrick attacked the evils of traditional education, which he called an "Alexandrian conception of learning." Ancient Alexandria represented a decline in culture because it imitated Greek learning and was book-centered.

Kilpatrick had little use for the Great Books. They may have been of some value during the period in which they were produced, but now they are mostly obsolete. Book learning is authoritarian; it leads the student away from the real conflicts of life to a conservative view of society.

The prevailing emphasis on liberal education was rejected by

Kilpatrick, who felt that it creates only snobbery on the part of the ruling class. Liberal education was less important than vocational education, which involved direct experience and democratic participation. Professors in the liberal arts promptly charged Kilpatrick with an overemphasis on methodology and with a consequent proliferation of the curriculum.

Man's social nature, Kilpatrick emphasized, is more important than his intellectual traits. The intellect cannot exist in isolation; it should not be trained through grammar and memorization; rather, it should be used to solve the conflicts of our time. Religion, if it was to be taught anywhere, would have to be subjected to critical analysis and would have to submit to scientific evidence.

Kilpatrick was a strong supporter of reforms in government and in better social legislation. Education cannot be separated from social action. As long as war and poverty threaten the survival of mankind, the educator cannot be passive. His aid is needed in protecting the public interest and in advancing humanitarian causes. Kilpatrick was interested in adult education, and in improving the lot of the Negro and in ending segregation in both the South and the North.

Like Dewey, Kilpatrick believed that life is a process of flux and that there can be no absolutes in ethics, politics, or religion. Religion represents a positive attitude toward one's greatest value; it needs no supernatural exemplification. To Kilpatrick, a liberal religion has positive consequences, for it aids man in his concerns in this life, while a conservative religion obscures the real problems and the real conflicts of man.

To Kilpatrick, both American materialism and Russian materialism represent perverted religions and false values. American materialism reduces human values to property standards, and emphasizes efficiency over human happiness. It creates a soulless and mechanized culture. Russian Marxism, on the other hand, subordinates man to a political party and stifles free inquiry. It creates an absolutism of conformity and denies the value of democracy. It overemphasizes the economic factors in history. It inhibits education, because in Marxism the teacher becomes the tool of the state.

To Kilpatrick, education fails if it does not provide real experience for children. Education is not the prelude to adult existence; rather, the school is an autonomous center designed for democratic living. Mere study, mere discipline are secondary devices that enhance the prestige of the institution but often have no genuine educational value.

Kilpatrick believed that such ideals as cooperation and personal happiness cannot be postponed until adult life. The student has to learn how to share, how to work as a member of a group, and how to cooperate with others, but his integrity must be protected; no artificial discipline may be imposed upon him.

Kilpatrick was certain that democracy failed so often because of the distance between theory and action. We preach freedom; yet we enact authoritarianism in the classroom. We stress the individual; yet we regard him as a statistic. We belive in the equality of all, and at the same time we develop a scholastic hierarchy. Let the schools, said Kilpatrick, become centers of cooperative learning in which the project method prevails. Let learning be not merely an intellectual process but one that involves the totality of one's reactions. Let memorization be abandoned; let examinations be regarded as obsolete devices; let there be no static curriculum. Above all, let the teacher and the student plan the curriculum together. Let the teacher be a friend, a resource person rather than a stern taskmaster. Let the schools become laboratories for our society; then a new civilization will emerge.

Kilpatrick in this way emphasized the child rather than the teacher, concomitant learning rather than subjects, experience rather than study, action rather than intellectual training, and—

most important, perhaps—interest rather that effort. The project method is central in his philosophy. It involves common planning; children pursue their own interests and learn to cooperate with the group. In this way learning is made vital and relevant.

Kilpatrick believed that specific subjects are far less important than general education. There is to be no specialization on the elementary level and not very much in high school. Even in college, core courses, which involve activity and participation, should be emphasized. To Kilpatrick, general education means something other than it means to Hutchins. It is not the study of books, it is not an exploration of theory, it is not a study of the past; rather, it involves projects that explore the dilemmas of the present and that bridge the gap between school and community.

Kilpatrick, as can be expected, was no supporter of traditional discipline, which, he believed, develops submissive, hypocritical human beings. Integrity cannot be legislated, standards cannot be coerced by administrative pressures. The school can frame certain elastic rules of conduct, but they will not work if the students do not support them and make them part of their own philosophy of life.

"We learn what we live" is the keynote of Kilpatrick's philosophy. Participation rather than contemplation is to govern our school system.

Impact

The impact of Kilpatrick was furthered by his unusual personality. He had an unbounded faith in democracy and in the possibilities of education. Even after he retired he spoke at countless gatherings and held seminars at his home. He corresponded with educators throughout the world, and in his eighties maintained a schedule that might have exhausted a younger man.

When he spoke, he sounded like an ancient prophet. With this author he addressed an education seminar at New York University in 1952. Kilpatrick had just recovered from a major illness. At first his voice was faint; then, as he proceeded with his talk, his intensity mounted. He told how the world had been governed by superstition, how the aristocracy had prevailed, how wars had conspired against human progress. He was certain that universal education would usher in a new period in which real democracy would prevail. Theological students questioned him about his religious beliefs. He answered with complete sincerity that he did not believe in a religion of dogmas, but only in one that gave support to ideal values and that went beyond denominational barriers.

When he finished his discourse, there was a moment of silence; then there was prolonged applause. Even those who opposed his ideas were impressed by his sincerity and his missionary fervor for education.

As a teacher, Kilpatrick had the ability to lecture with eloquence and at the same time be a most stimulating discussion leader. He made education relevant to the issues of our time. His classes were so popular that many students had to stand. His audience included parents, political leaders, and businessmen. To Kilpatrick, progressive education was not a movement, it was a cause, which had to prevail or democracy would be endangered.

In his classes, Kilpatrick emphasized the importance of questions. He did not try to give final answers; rather, he stressed more penetrating inquiries. He was not trying to build a system of philosophy, for he wanted to develop the personal understanding of the student.

He was a most proficient counselor. When students experienced psychological problems, they found him to be extremely understanding. When they needed a letter of recommendation, he would oblige, taking time out to advance their careers. His kindness was unfailing. His home was open to all: freshmen were received with as much attention as graduate students.

He was certain that freedom would fail if the schools adhered to authoritarian philosophies. He wanted to emancipate parents, children, teachers, and administrators from the old form of education. Parents were to become better counselors; they were to safeguard the interests of the child. Youngsters were to develop without the rigid standards of the adult world. Teachers were to find a new dignity in their vocation. Administrators, who were to open the door to significant educational experimentation, were to welcome new ideas and aid genuine educational advancement.

Kilpatrick was certain that our theory of learning has vast consequences for education and society. If we regard learning as an abstract process, if we view it as a theory of books, we shall create a second-rate civilization, one which imitates and is bound to be eclectic. Like Alexandria, it may produce magnificent buildings and libraries and laboratories, but it will create no sound educational growth, which depends on shared experiences and active participation.

A theory of learning that involves participation and situations that are relevant today produces individuals who can work together, who have faith in their originality, and who will face the future without having recourse to the obsolete views of the past.

29. Robert Hutchins

If the main task of the thinker is to provoke thought and controversy, Robert Hutchins must rank among the great teachers of
world history. Certainly no one can deny the brilliance of Robert
Maynard Hutchins (1899———), who became dean of Yale Law
School while still in his twenties and president of the University
of Chicago at the age of thirty. Even more impressive are his
achievements in his mature years. When he felt that civil liberties were threatened, he started the Center for the Study of Democratic Institutions in Santa Barbara—an organization that has
made important contributions to the understanding of Western
ideals. It is the ambition of Hutchins to create an institution that
will rival Plato's Academy. Like Plato, Hutchins feels that education is a total process and that it fails unless it can change man's
institutional relationships.

Hutchins speaks and writes in a provocative manner. If, as
Whitehead indicates, style is the ultimate morality of man,
Hutchins indeed must rank high. His sentences are crisp and
clear. He is a master of irony and his sense of humor is penetrating.

Few have fought more vigorously for academic freedom than

349

Robert Hutchins. This means to him not merely protection of the rights of those who agree with him, but tolerance even of those who disagree in a most violent manner. He has never succumbed to the expediency of the moment; instead, he has concentrated upon the long-range objectives of education.

While Dewey and Whitehead stress the unitary aspects of knowledge, Hutchins upholds fundamental dualisms. In his system there is a conflict between theory and action, education and training, wisdom and knowledge, philosophy and science, and permanence and change. The true scientist, Hutchins asserts, will be concerned with general principles. The lesson of science is not, as Dewey thought, flux and change; rather, it is the permanence of life. Does not Darwin speak about species? Is not human nature everywhere the same? Do not all men search for wisdom, truth, and justice? Are there not great books without which education is hopelessly incomplete?

Hutchins is engaged in a warfare against utilitarianism. College courses in typewriting and home economics are anathema to him. He scorns the cult of athletics. The purpose of education is intellectual; talk about educating the whole child is mere sentimentalism. Universities are no substitutes for the finishing school, the Salvation Army, the Boy Scouts, or the home environment. They should be independent centers of thinking. They should be concerned not with usefulness but with the cultivation of reason.

Hutchins has great faith in the powers of rationality. While Dewey looked upon reason as an activity, Hutchins regards reason as an end. The man who cultivates his reason, according to Hutchins, will be effective in any activity. Reason is disciplined by grammar and logic. Without fundamental skills our entire education will be an adventure in chaos.

With vigor Hutchins directs his attacks upon naturalism. To identify experience with nature is inadmissable. The true naturalist, Hutchins states, is concerned with the nature of things, not with our valuation of them. Nature as such is blind; to understand nature we must go beyond it.

Dewey's naturalism, according to Hutchins, has helped to undermine the unity of the curriculum. Instead of time-honored subjects, trivial inquiries are conducted. Instead of being concerned with the problem of the good, students now try to learn about cosmetics or the intricacies of population statistics.

The idea that nothing is true unless it works is received with scorn by Hutchins. Does this not lead to an emphasis upon utilitarianism? Does this not imply a worship of technology? Is this not materialism in a new disguise?

Hutchins makes a sharp distinction between knowledge and opinion. Opinion is relative, whereas knowledge is absolute. We can disagree regarding matters of opinion, but when it comes to knowledge we should be guided by the expert. Hutchins charges that the progressive educator reduces all knowledge to opinion, and thus makes relativism supreme in education.

With irony and scorn, Hutchins speaks of the higher learning in America. He attacks especially three evils: (1) the emphasis upon professionalism, (2) the stress upon scientism, and (3) the prevalence of anti-intellectualism. Hutchins has little use for professional and vocational education. Universities should stress the great books and the liberal arts. Specialization, especially in science, leads to the narrow mind and creates the man with vast knowledge and little education. The universities have become social and athletic centers. Hutchins wants them to become centers of independent thinking and interdepartmental inquiry.

Hutchins has outlined the university of Utopia. It would consist of three departments: natural sciences, social sciences, and metaphysics. Controversial subjects would be welcomed; complete freedom of inquiry would prevail; professors and students would be engaged in the discussion of timeless subjects.

All this does not imply that Hutchins is uninterested in social issues. He has been one of the leaders in the movement seeking to establish a world government; he has served on a commission studying the freedom of the press; he has fought consistently for racial equality; he has defended political diversity; and he has resisted the attempts of political organizations to dominate the affairs of educational institutions.

Hutchins has the vision of one world. This world, he believes, cannot be established by force or by military power, but only through the cultivation of reason. He hopes that the educational curriculum everywhere will ultimately stress the great books and the great ideas of mankind. Imbued with a sense of the past, Hutchins feels that the study of previous cultures and civilizations will give to modern man a broad perspective, which he desperately needs if he wants to survive.

The philosophy of Hutchins is summarized by the famous statement: "Education implies teaching. Teaching implies knowledge. Knowledge is truth. The truth is everywhere the same. Hence education should be everywhere the same."

It is easy to criticize this statement on semantic grounds. Stuart Chase in *The Tyranny of Words* has attacked the semantic fallacies involved in the view that education should be everywhere the same. But, in a deeper sense, this statement is based on a fundamental vision. To understand a thinker the verbal meaning is less important than the symbolic significance involved in his views. The word, after all, is only a reflection of experience; it stands for an underlying faith, a basic world view.

Hutchins believes that truth is eternal and that education should give us a concept of absolute truth. Education should train the intellect; all other goods are subordinated to the cultivation of reason, which exists as an end in itself. Once we accept this premise, the particular aspects of education appear to be insignificant compared with its universal mission: to train man in the life of reason.

Still, the weaknesses of the philosophy of Hutchins cannot be overlooked. Hutchins has too much faith in reason. Our rational capacities cannot be separated from our emotional drives. Reason is not an entity, but a process. It is cultivated best not by the discipline of grammar or by the study of the Aristotelian syllogism, but by scientific experimentation, by esthetic experience, and by realizing the problematic nature of knowledge.

To Hutchins, the intellectual experience is the highest form of knowledge; yet the intellectual life suffers when it is aloof from society. To be more concrete, a work experience for a college student can be as significant as the study of the great books. Knowledge without action leads to intellectual isolation; action without knowledge leads to social sterility. Both extremes are undesirable in education.

This certainly does not eliminate the need for the reading of the classics. But they must be accepted in a more critical spirit, not as absolute guides to knowledge, but as points of reference showing both the similarities and contrasts between modern and ancient ideals of knowledge. The great book, as Descartes points out, is the book of the world. Its study should be our supreme task and vocation.

Yet, despite these reservations, we must acknowledge Robert Hutchins as one of the truly great educational thinkers of Western civilization. He has helped to clarify our problems; he has demolished some of our most cherished idols; he has strengthened the foundations of liberal education. In an age of conformity his is the voice of vigorous dissent and valiant individualism.

30. Teaching in Action

The great teachers indicate that education without activity is a contradiction in terms. Too often in the educative process students and instructors are essentially strangers. The instructor sees a multitude of faces in front of him and he feels obliged to cover so much material per lecture hour. He speaks mechanically, using the same notes over and over again. The student, on the other hand, listens with apathy and occasionally makes notes so he can pass the examination. He reacts on a reflex level; he does not really think creatively during the class.

When education becomes creative it is like a drama in which there are no spectators. Now the student assumes a new role: he does not sit passively; rather, he feels personally involved in the educative process. His questions have a sense of urgency. When the hour is over he feels that only a few minutes have passed. The material that has been covered has a personal significance.

Whitehead once remarked that the tragedy of education is its preoccupation with inert ideas. This is an extremely important observation. Inertia is always an enemy of culture, which demands effort. Mere activity does not imply genuine education, but without activity education is only a useless form of ornamentation.

Ultimately, in the educative process the teacher becomes unessential. This is a process that leads from dependence to autonomy. There comes the time in life when we have to be independent, when we have to make our own mistakes, and when we cannot accept anyone else's opinions. Only those ideas are truly valuable which we discover for ourselves.

What is important, then, is that we develop a feeling about ideas. We have to become intense. As long as we remain neutral we are in a limbo of insignificance, and we shall never make real intellectual discoveries.

A man can be defined by the things that matter to him. What really matters most in our civilization? If we are completely frank, the answer is money and social approval. As for education, it is an activity that is merely endured by many. And many students feel that ideas have no real meaning in their own lives. Why bother with abstractions? Why be interested in abstruse theories? Why worry about basic research? To them, only the cash values of knowledge matter.

We shall never have a great culture until we develop a passion for wisdom. The Athenians made an immortal contribution to culture because to them reason was a way of life, and intellectual curiosity was man's most important trait. The dramatic performances were not reserved for the few, but were for all: the wise and the ignorant, the rich and the poor. Art was not confined to the museum but was a part of their everyday living. Philosophy was not a classroom activity, but a lively undertaking that excited the minds of Athens, and it dealt with problems that have a timeless significance. The teacher in Athens taught young and old, and his classroom was everywhere.

We have made the mistake of institutionalizing education and of confining the teacher. We say we believe in beauty; yet most of our cities are incredibly ugly. We maintain that art is a way of life; yet the poet has no audience. We praise the role of reason, but reason is seldom used in the discussion of social and political issues.

We say that we want education for all, but in practice it often becomes a form of mass-conditioning. We believe in complete freedom of thought, except in times of crisis and hysteria. We speak about love and creative human relations; yet we have many prejudices when other nationalities and races are involved.

A critic might say that our condition is hopeless and that we are bound to live an unexamined life in a utilitarian culture. But he would be wrong, because we are entering upon a new age. Our students are not materialists; they do not want conventional answers; they do not desire easy success. Many are like Larry in *The Razor's Edge,* with a boundless capacity for idealism. What strikes me most is their sincerity. They really want to know, they want to investigate and to ponder profoundly.

Never before has the teacher had such a grave responsibility. In an isolated civilization, false ideas could only create limited havoc; in a world civilization without real frontiers, false ideas and false values can create total havoc.

Nothing can be really taught that is not lived. Wisdom is never an isolated theory, but knowledge applied and utilized. Only an awakened teacher who feels the urgency of his mission can meet the challenge of our time.

Prelude to Creativity

As teachers, we need a new sense of humility. Let us never forget that the most important accomplishments cannot be tested objectively. How can we test a student's appreciation of Van Gogh? How can we measure our feelings about a symphony by Beethoven? How can we measure our ability to converse in a profound manner? How can we test in an objective way what our real interests are?

Undoubtedly we are living in an age of quantification. We like to categorize and in this way achieve order in our intellectual life. But categories are only conventional postulates; what matters most is not attainment but subtle growth.

In China many centuries ago, Lao-tze maintained that the universe represents a subtle essence, and he found an identity between the infinite and the infinitesimal. Real knowledge, he maintained, could not be defined; it could only be felt and experienced. Bergson, in more recent times, spoke of the power of intuition, which to him was the source of real progress and real enlightenment. Does not an over-reliance upon analysis paralyze our power to act and to appreciate? To Bergson, life was movement, and knowledge, which relied on static categories, could never explore the inner structure of human existence.

Thus, any test is at best a superficial device. Just as man in his emotional life remains a mystery, so his mind cannot be described completely in mathematical terms. What is important is to stress our senses so that we become aware of the kingdom of the mind, and so that we find the identity of the object and the subject, of nature and the self. Study nature and study thyself, was the advice of Emerson and this counsel has perennial meaning. The more we undertake this activity, the more we find an underlying unity. How wise were the authors of the *Upanishads* when they maintained that the external essence—Brahman—is the same as man's essential self—Atman. Knowledge thus leads from pluralism to monism, from separateness to unity.

The great teachers of the past indicate that knowledge alone is not enough. More important than theory is involvement; more significant than intellect is the compassion of the human heart. Thus, education is measured by its impact. Its aim is to change individuals and societies so that a permanent enlightenment is achieved and so that peace becomes a universal reality.

Other Great Teachers

LAO-TZE (c.604–531 B.C.)

An opponent of Confucianism, Lao-tze believed in the cultivation of intuition, and did not favor intervention in the political and social affairs of his time. As a philosophical anarchist, he fought against conventional education and regarded nature as the guide for man. The task of the teacher, he asserted, is to spread an attitude of humility so that the pretensions of formal knowledge can be overcome.

CHUANG-TZU (fl.4th century B.C.)

A follower of Lao-tze who developed the idea of paradox in philosophy and education. He opposed the artificial life of the aristocracy and admired the intuitive wisdom of the common man. Education, according to Chuang-tzu, leads to an acknowledgment of the limitations of man's knowledge. He pointed to the fact that nature goes beyond good and evil, and that moral judgments are only human devices that have no cosmic reality. He maintained that we achieve a sense of unity through the *Tao*, which stands for unity amidst apparent diversity.

HIPPOCRATES (460?–?377 B.C.)

The great ancient pioneer physician, termed the Father of Medicine, who gave an empirical account of disease. Before him, disease was regarded as divine punishment. His power of observation was keen and he gave a systematic account of man's anatomy. He had a pragmatic type of mind, and thus was mainly interested in practical remedies that would alleviate the illnesses of mankind.

ISOCRATES (436–338 B.C.)

An eloquent Greek orator who believed that the public speaker needed a penetrating philosophy of education, and who regarded communication as the essence of liberal thought. He advocated better organization of the schools so that they could have a wide impact on public affairs.

PROTAGORAS (c.480–c.410 B.C.)

A Greek Sophist of Abdera who attracted a wide following, and who believed that man is the measure of all things. An opponent of absolutism, he pointed to the shifting currents of thought. He contributed to the study of the humanities in Greek civilization. Protagoras was so successful as a teacher that he ended as a millionaire.

ZENO (c.336–c.264 B.C.)

A great Greek philosopher who developed the main ideals of Stoicism. He believed in self-control, reason, and resignation as the fundamental values of life. He stressed his belief that philosophy had an ideal function, and that the wise man in his tranquility was an example for the multitude.

ERATOSTHENES (c.275–c.195 B.C.)

Librarian at Alexandria, who believed that the knowledge of books is more significant than any other form of intellectual experience. He developed the study of geography and expanded the world view of his time. An encyclopedist, he was interested in both the sciences and the humanities.

CICERO (106–43 B.C.)

He was active both in politics and literature. As a leader of Rome, he opposed the policies of Julius Caesar. His works include *On Good and Bad Ends* (*De Finibus Bonorum et Malorum*) and *On the Nature of the Gods* (*De Natura Deorum*). Essentially, he was an eclectic who tried to synthesize the main currents of ancient thought. In education he emphasized the study of Greek thought and the significance of moral ideals in social life. Wisdom, to Cicero, demanded a commitment to action, whereby the teacher attempted to improve the moral values of civilization.

PLUTARCH (A.D. 46?–?120)

Best known in education by his treatise *On the Education of Children* in *Moralia,* his collected essays. As a moralist, he favored strict discipline, for he believed that children learn best by example. Only teachers with the highest personal values were to be selected, and parents were to check the wayward impulses of their youngsters. A note of puritanism prevailed in the educational philosophy of Plutarch.

EPICTETUS (b.A.D. c.60)

One of the most revered teachers of Rome, Epictetus, a Stoic, believed that man must seek inner fulfillment. He believed that education should be concerned not with science but with moral perfection. Man was to appreciate his status in the universe and accept his fate without fear and anxiety. His philosophic teachings as set forth in the *Discourses* of his pupil Havius Arrian, became famous both in education and in philosophy as a symbol of the Stoic spirit.

MARCUS AURELIUS (A.D. 121–180)

A Roman emperor, he yearned for the solitude of philosophy. His *Meditations* are an expression of his search for tranquility amidst the changing political currents of his time. To Marcus Aurelius, education is an exercise in self-control whereby man becomes conscious of the divinity within himself, and whereby he triumphs over all forms of externality.

ALCUIN (A.D. 735–804)

English scholar in charge of the Palace School under Charlemagne. Later, became Abbot of Tours. He combined a knowledge of the sciences, arts, and theology. He emphasized his teaching that secular studies are only preludes to divine wisdom. He attempted to improve the standards of instruction among both laymen and clergy. His student Rhabanus Maurus, Abbot of Fulda, helped to perpetuate Alcuin's intellectual endeavors.

AVICENNA (A.D. 980–1037)

An Arabic philosopher who sought to combine the philosophy of Aristotle and Moslem thinking. He contributed to medicine by his exact observations and by his empirical spirit. He urged more tolerance in intellectual controversies and favored an educational system based on the liberal arts and the natural sciences.

IRNERIUS (1050?–?1130)

He made the study of Roman law a basic discipline at the University of Bologna. An expert on the laws of Justinian, Irnerius collected the legal ideas of the famous Byzantine emperor. Irnerius believed that the study of Roman law was not merely a technical occupation but also a fundamental part of education, and that its structure would lead to a revival of medieval learning.

AVERROËS (1126–1198)

Moslem thinker who believed in a liberal interpretation of his religion. He maintained that a principle may be valid in philosophy but may not apply to religion. He followed Aristotle in denying the possibility of personal immortality. An eloquent teacher, he viewed philosophy as man's most significant study.

MAIMONIDES (1135–1204)

Jewish rabbi, physician, and philosopher, among whose works is *Guide of the Perplexed.* He tried to combine Greek philosophy and Jewish wisdom and maintained that education should produce individuals who have an immediate awareness of God. He was active both in religion and in medicine. He was certain that the sciences are less important than the study of theology, which brings man closer to God.

THOMAS AQUINAS (1225?–1274)

One of the Fathers of the Church, Saint Thomas Aquinas made a synthesis of the ideas of Aristotle and the Church. His *Summa Theologica* has become the major work in world theology. Aquinas stressed the spiritual functions of the teacher, who was to be a loyal son of the Church and who was to fight all forms of heresy. In education he wrote a treatise, *On the Truth* (*De Veritate*), that stresses the significance of reason in the life of man and that views learning as an actualization of intrinsic intellectual potentialities.

ROGER BACON (1214?–1294)

Bacon, English philosopher and scientist, opposed the education of his time and urged the cultivation of the sciences instead of scholasticism. His *Opus Majus* and *Opus Minor* predict the structure of modern science. He believed that mathematics was the key to nature and that experimentation would widen man's power over the external world. A bold innovator, he opposed the traditionalism of the medieval scholars and their reliance on ancient authorities.

PETRARCH (1304–1374)

He contributed to the spirit of humanism and opposed the tone of medieval scholarship. He believed in exact knowledge and regarded Cicero as the model for modern man. His ideal scholar would not live an existence of isolation but would apply his knowledge to improve the social institutions of man. He stressed the cult of individualism both in literature and in education.

VITTORINO DA FELTRE (1378–1446)

He championed the study of Latin as a basic discipline. His school at Mantua became famous for its level of scholarship and its humanistic spirit. He stressed both the intellectual and physical training of his students. To Vittorino, the study of ancient history was an example for the civilization of his time, which was to strive for artistic and intellectual excellence.

JOHN COLET (1467?–1519)

Founder of one of the great humanistic centers in England, St. Paul's, where the classics were stressed, Colet believed in the cultivation of Greek philosophy and opposed the spirit of scholasticism. He admired the Italian schools of his time, which he contrasted with the traditionalism of English education. Greek and Latin, he asserted, are the keys to liberal education.

DESIDERIUS ERASMUS (1466?–1536)

He was the most famous humanist who used satire as a method of educational reform. His *In Praise of Folly* constituted an attack on all forms of authoritarianism. He opposed war and urged moderation and conciliation. To Erasmus the authentic teacher was the leader of civilization. Like Colet, Erasmus stressed the study of the Greek and Roman civilization and regarded the classical languages as basic tools for modern man.

MELANCHTHON (1497–1560)

He contributed to school organization by his *Report,* which urged a better utilization of educational resources. He tried to apply Luther's ideas to the school system and thus made much of moral instruction. Influential in the spread of secondary schools, he championed the use of the humanities and of ancient languages. Like Luther, he urged the expansion of libraries for the instruction of the average man.

FRANÇOIS RABELAIS (1494?–1553)

He opposed the spirit of asceticism in intellectual life and, instead, urged individualism and the pursuit of pleasure. He regarded the schools of his time as veritable intellectual roadblocks, and anticipated the spirit of progressive education in his high regard for the integrity of the student. His *Gargantua* is a satire on the follies of orthodox religion and education, and represents an eloquent plea for an educational system based upon humanism.

JOHANN BUGENHAGEN (1485–1558)

Contributed to the development of German education by his advocacy of schools for the common people. A follower of Luther, whom he helped in translating the Bible, he stressed the spiritual responsibilities of the teacher. He helped to reorganize the University of Copenhagen. He taught at Wittenberg, where he was admired for his pedagogic skill.

THOMAS ELYOT (1490?–1546)

Best known for his work on the *Governour,* which outlines the training of the English gentleman. Elyot was not a proponent of scholastic education; rather, he favored sports and hunting. The gentleman, he emphasized, should be interested in all parts of life, and should excel in the enjoyment of the social graces.

JUAN LUIS VIVES (1492–1540)

Among his sigificant works we find *Concerning the Teaching of the Arts, On a Plan for the Study of Youth,* and *Concerning the Mind.* He believed that women should be educated as well as the lower classes. He favored a reform in educational methodology so that theory would be supplanted by concrete experiences and so that learning would be universalized.

JOHANNES STURM (1507–1589)

Active in the educational life at Strasbourg, where he was in charge of a famous secondary school, Sturm believed that education should develop a sense of piety in the students and masters. He emphasized the importance of Latin and Greek and made much of oratory in his scheme of instruction. He contributed to careful school organization and to better pedagogic skills. His weakness lay in a one-sided stress in education, for he omitted physical education as a basic subject.

JOHN CALVIN (1509–1564)

A famous theologian, Calvin was concerned with education as a preparation for religious life. He emphasized the instruction of the common man, who was to study both secular and religious works. According to him, the goal of education was a life dedicated to God. He made much of Greek in instruction and favored physical punishment for wayward students. His *Institutes of the Christian Religion* has become the major foundation of Presbyterianism.

ROGER ASCHAM (1515–1568)

Ascham's treatise *The Schoolmaster* became a basic text in English education. As tutor to Queen Elizabeth, his influence was felt on all levels of English culture. He favored the humanistic way of life and had a high regard for modern languages. Unlike Calvin, he advocated a compassionate view of discipline and regarded interest as the foundation of learning.

PETRUS RAMUS (1515–1572)

He opposed the world view of Aristotle and favored an inductive approach to knowledge. In the curriculum he stressed the creative role of literature, which was to expand the horizon of man. He believed in a practical and utilitarian approach to learning.

RICHARD MULCASTER (1530?–1611)

He urged a fundamental reform in education which was to stress the total development of man. He felt that the schools ought to be student-centered and that pedagogy ought to make education a truly dramatic experience. Favoring instruction in the modern languages, he encouraged the study of the arts as well as the sciences. He recommended that institutions be established for the training of new teachers, who were to be examples in their fervor for dynamic education.

MICHEL DE MONTAIGNE (1533–1592)

A skeptic, he opposed traditional scholarship and viewed education as an aid to leisure. He recommended an objective study of the world and was enthusiastic about travel as a device for new ideas and ideals. He was opposed to specialization; instead, he favored general knowledge which would synthesize the arts and the sciences. To Montaigne, education was concerned with the conduct of life and with the achievement of tranquillity amidst the shifting currents of man's fate.

FRANCIS BACON (1561–1626)

Bacon believed that knowledge is a power that has to be applied for a reconstruction of man's social institutions. In such works as *Novum Organum, New Atlantis,* and *Advancement of Learning,* he outlined a new curriculum that would stress the sciences instead of theology, and that would overcome the idols of man. Opposing scholasticism, he favored the inductive method of knowledge. He predicted the structure of the modern university and anticipated many inventions of our time.

WOLFGANG RATKE (1571–1635)

Best known for his *Methodus Nova,* which is based upon an empirical approach to education, Ratke favored nature as the guide for the teacher. He believed that excessive memorization blocks the progress of the student. He favored more individuality in instruction and maintained that learning depends on a careful organization of subject matter. His approach to discipline was based on the view that the student can control his impulses and that he needs no artificial coercion.

RENÉ DESCARTES (1596–1650)

He developed the method of doubt in philosophy and education. He felt that mathematics should replace scholastic logic. His main works, *Discourse on Method* and *Meditations,* have created the basis for modern thinking. Descartes emphasized methodology in education, which, he asserted, should emulate the clarity and objectivity of science.

JOHN MILTON (1608–1674)

In education Milton produced his *Tractate of Education,* which was to spread a wider knowledge of the liberal arts. Milton was not an enthusiastic proponent of Greek and Latin; instead, he urged a more careful study of the English language. He was a humanist in stressing the application of knowledge and in his concern for the contemporary relevance of scholarship.

BARUCH (BENEDICT) SPINOZA (1632–1677)

Best known for his *Ethics,* which gives an account of man and his relationship to God and the universe. Spinoza championed the intellectual love of God and determinism, and he set forth a pantheistic account of life. He stressed freedom of inquiry and refused a professorship at Heidelberg because he could not have complete liberty in expressing his views. His ideal for the educated man was "to see life under the aspect of eternity."

ABBÉ JEAN BAPTISTE DE LA SALLE (1651–1719)

The Counter Reformation influenced the educational ideals of Abbé de la Salle, who in 1684 at Rouen established the institute of the Brothers of the Christian Schools (the Christian Brothers). This institution was based on advanced concepts of instruction and favored secular as well as religious subjects. He was concerned with the education of the lower classes, for he felt that all are eligible for the kingdom of learning. He believed that the teacher should have a deep knowledge of motivation and that he should set a moral example for his students.

FRANÇOIS DE SALIGNAC DE LA MOTHE-FÉNELON (1651–1715)

A pioneer in the education of women, Fénelon believed that their intellectual powers were to be intensified. His work *On the Education of Girls* was based on progressive ideals. He favored less discipline and more interest as the basic motivation for learning. Education was to develop wise individuals who would be interested in lifelong learning, and who would feel a responsibility for the improvement of mankind.

AUGUST HERMANN FRANCKE (1663–1727)

A pioneer in the training of teachers, Francke favored a better organization of school life. He believed in the education of the poor, who were to be taught utilitarian subjects. A pietist, he felt that intellectual knowledge is less important than an emotional awareness of God, and that religion is the most significant concern of man.

JULIUS HECKER (1701–1768)

He was interested in the science of pedagogy, and in 1738 he established a training institution for teachers. To Hecker, education was a utilitarian endeavor that would improve all occupations, especially business life. He achieved fame as head of the *Realschule* in Berlin, established in 1747. This school spread popular enlightenment in Prussia and attracted some of the best teachers of the age.

BENJAMIN FRANKLIN (1706–1790)

Benjamin Franklin is an eloquent representative of the liberal tradition. Statesman, scientist, and educator, he reflected a progressive viewpoint and a pragmatic philosophy of life. He implemented the academy movement in the United States and his *Proposals Relating to the Education of Youth in Pennsylvania,* published in 1749, represents a landmark in American educational history. He urged the cultivation of modern languages and stressed the centrality of history in the educative process.

JOHANN BERNHARD BASEDOW (1724?–1790)

A pioneer in popular education, Basedow attempted to improve textbooks as vehicles of instruction. He believed that all classes ought to be educated and that children should be treated in a compassionate way. He established the Philanthropinum at Dessau, a model school for children, and wrote important such works as *Book of Method,* which would make education more functional so that it would have greater impact in reforming society.

IMMANUEL KANT (1724–1804)

Kant attempted to indicate the limits of reason in such works as *Critique of Pure Reason, Critique of Practical Reason,* and *Critique of Judgment.* He was interested in pedagogy and stressed the need for discipline and the improvement of morality. To Kant, education has a cultural significance, and he felt that without authentic education man remains a savage. He urged the establishment of experimental schools that would improve the level of teacher training.

JOHANN GOTTLIEB FICHTE (1762–1814)

Fichte contributed to German nationalism by his emphasis on the superiority of the German spirit. To him, the teacher is the leader of civilization, who has to be a man of action and whose vocation is the betterment of civilization. Fichte was influenced by Pestalozzi; thus, he urged that new schools be established that would improve vocational as well as liberal education.

WILHELM von HUMBOLDT (1767–1835)

He helped to establish the basis of Prussian education. As head of the Department of Public Instruction in Prussia, he improved the standards of the teaching profession. He developed greater centralization in curriculum methods and pedagogy. Exact provisions were made by him for the structure of elementary, secondary, and higher education.

PHILIPP EMANUEL von FELLENBERG (1771–1844)

He was a friend of Pestalozzi and helped to expand the basis of vocational education. He believed that man learned best when he used his hands, and that farming was an essential part of education. His ideas influenced the development of vocational education in the United States, and they contributed to a utilitarian view of the school system.

JOSEPH LANCASTER (1778–1838)

Lancaster was especially concerned with the education of the lower classes in the United States and England. He used students as teachers and his monitorial method became very popular in the first half of the nineteenth century. As a Quaker, he favored a humanitarian method of discipline and respected the integrity of the student.

SAMUEL READ HALL (1795–1877)

Concerned with the preparation of teachers, Hall, in 1823 in Concord, Vermont, opened the first school for the training of teachers. This institution anticipated the normal school and gave impetus to new methods of instruction. Regarding education as a moral discipline, Hall felt that the future of the United States depended on the excellence of its teachers.

JAMES GORDON CARTER (1795–1849)

Carter was the pioneer of popular education in Massachusetts. He was interested in teacher training and helped to establish the second normal school in the United States. He influenced the American High School in Boston, which was established in 1827. He regarded a sound education as the foundation of progress and as the basis of enlightenment.

MARY LYON (1797–1849)

She was the founder of Mount Holyoke Seminary for Girls (1837). She maintained that the education of women had been neglected in the United States and that this condition had contributed to a second-rate culture. She believed that the liberal arts should be cultivated at

Mount Holyoke and that women should be models in learning and in virtue. The curriculum that she established was strict, demanding both intellectual and moral discipline.

MARK HOPKINS (1802–1887)

He was professor of philosophy and rhetoric at Williams College, where he later was President. His course in moral philosophy was regarded as the most inspiring part of the curriculum of the college. His philosophy of education was idealistic. He wanted to create a spiritual reform in his students so that learning would become a way of life and so that moral ideals would be applied to all aspects of man's development. President Garfield remarked that the ideal educational situation would be Mark Hopkins on one end of a log and a student on the other, discussing philosophical issues.

JOHN STUART MILL (1806–1873)

He contributed to philosophy, economics, and education through such works as *Essays on Liberty, Principles of Political Economy, Three Essays on Religion,* and his *Inaugural Address,* which he gave as Rector of St. Andrew's University. He emphasized a knowledge of the past as well as of modern issues, and he affirmed the need for intellectual freedom. To Mill, experimental science was the foundation of education, for it created logical minds and a utilitarian basis for reasoning.

HENRY BARNARD (1811–1900)

Contributed to educational scholarship as editor of the *American Journal of Education.* His outlook on education was cosmopolitan; he felt that American teachers could learn a great deal from Europe, especially from Germany. He contributed to the spread of popular education in Massachusetts and Rhode Island, and as the first U.S. Commissioner of Education improved the standards of teacher preparation. He was less liberal than Horace Mann and thus pointed to the conservative function of the U.S. school system.

HERBERT SPENCER (1820–1903)

Spencer opposed an educational system that emphasized the classics; instead, he urged the cultivation of science. The goal of education, he stated in *Education: Intellectual, Physical and Moral,* was the unfolding of life in all its aspects. He stressed the social duties of teachers and viewed constructive citizenship as an important basis of all instruction.

EDWARD T. SHELDON (1823–1897)

Sheldon, superintendent of schools at Oswego, New York, helped to popularize the ideas of Pestalozzi. Like Pestalozzi, Sheldon believed in the cultivation of manual as well as intellectual skills and felt that democratic ideals should be applied to the school system. He contributed to the improvement of science teaching, and he made geography a dominant subject in the curriculum. Education, he stressed, was not merely a factual study, but also demanded the capacity to evaluate and to apply moral ideals to daily life.

THOMAS HENRY HUXLEY (1825–1895)

A follower of Darwin, Huxley popularized the knowledge of his time. He not only gave instruction to the educated classes but also contributed to adult education, especially to the training of workers. He opposed the classical curriculum as being too narrow; instead, he urged more scientific knowledge. He felt that education should create a spirit of debate and inquiry rather than blind obedience to established institutions and authorities.

WILHELM WUNDT (1832–1920)

Wundt believed in the close relationship between psychology and education. In 1878 he established the first experimental psychological laboratory at Leipzig. He emphasized the role of introspection in psychology and also contributed to the study of folk psychology. Wundt's viewpoint in psychology is called structuralism, which stresses the role of consciousness in man's emotional processes.

CHARLES WILLIAM ELIOT (1834–1926)

Eliot contributed to the development of the junior high school and favored a more elastic curriculum. Believing in the elective system, he stressed scientific skill rather than classical knowledge. As President of Harvard, he expanded the function of the university and emphasized the significance of contemporary studies.

WILLIAM TORREY HARRIS (1835–1909)

He stimulated the development of the kindergarten in the United States and popularized the ideas of German idealism. He stressed the role of discipline and inspiration in education. As Commissioner of Education of the United States, he urged better professional preparation of teachers and more public support of education. To William T. Harris, Hegel was the ideal educator and philosopher; like Hegel, he championed the demands of society over the privileges of the individual.

FRANCIS W. PARKER (1837–1902)

He anticipated the main ideas of progressive education. He urged a humanitarian concept of discipline and was especially interested in the development of the social sciences. He opposed all forms of nationalism and militarism and believed that the schools ought to be beacons of enlightenment. As principal of the Cook County Normal School in Chicago, Parker encouraged vigorous experimentation, especially in the study of geography.

SIGMUND FREUD (1856–1939)

His views in psychology, which emphasized the struggle between the super-ego (man's cultural and inhibiting drives) and the id (man's animal passions) greatly influenced the development of modern educational ideas. Freud stressed the centrality of man's sexual drives and pointed to the significance of subconscious motivations. His view of psychoanalysis has both psychiatric and educational implications, for it leads to the belief that education has a therapeutic as well as an intellectual function.

RABINDRANATH TAGORE (1861–1941)

In 1901 Tagore founded a noted school at Santiniketan which emphasized progressive principles. A Nobel prize winner, he celebrated the virtues of India and looked to education for enlightenment and emancipation. He believed that we can learn best in close contact with nature, and that the goal of instruction is creativity rather than the imitation of the past.

EDWARD LEE THORNDIKE (1874–1949)

He was professor of psychology at Teachers College, Columbia University, and made outstanding contributions to educational psychology and methodology. His masterwork *Educational Psychology* is divided into three volumes. Volume 1 deals with the foundations of learning; volume 2 treats the laws of learning; and volume 3 discusses individual differences. Thorndike felt that exact research should govern the discipline of education and that subjects like Greek and Latin have little transfer value.

MARIA MONTESSORI (1870–1952)

This distinguished educator and physician was the first women to receive a medical degree in Italy. She devoted herself to underprivileged and defective children. When she died, her fame was worldwide and schools dedicated to her method could be found on all continents. She emphasized the importance of sense perception and the significance of the prepared environment. She favored both discipline and creativity. Stressing the natural capacities of children, she encouraged a compassionate form of instruction. To her, education was man's ultimate hope.

ALFRED NORTH WHITEHEAD (1861–1947)

Whitehead was lecturer and professor of mathematics in England; in the United States he was professor of philosophy at Harvard University (1924-36). In addition to gaining fame in mathematics and philosophy, he contributed a major work to education entitled *The Aims of Education*. In this work he pleads for active participation in culture and for the application of progressive ideas to social issues. He favored scientific instruction as the basis of knowledge and as the foundation of progress.

BERTRAND RUSSELL (1872————)

Noted for his work in philosophy and in mathematics, Russell with Alfred North Whitehead wrote *Principia Mathematica,* a classic in symbolic logic. His contribution to education is contained in *Education and the Good Life,* in which he pleads for the modern spirit and attacks Victorian ideas in instruction. He makes much of intellectual courage—a trait that he exemplified in his own life. In 1950 he won the Nobel prize in literature. A realist in his technical philosophy, Russell is concerned with social causes, especially with disarmament. His aim is to reform education so that it will become a tool of peace.

JAMES BRYANT CONANT (1893————)

Conant was a brilliant professor of chemistry at Harvard and President of Harvard University from 1933 to 1953. He contributed to the expansion of general education, and his reports on the American high school and teacher training led to higher standards of public education. Concerned with the social implications of science, he has demanded a greater depth of scientific knowledge for all American citizens. He also urges the improvement of education in urban centers so that democracy will become a living ideal in our time.

JEAN-PAUL SARTRE (1905——)

The major work of Sartre is *Being and Nothingness*, which was published in 1943. He has gained wide fame through his essays, novels, and dramas, and especially through his *No Exit*. The high priest of existentialism, Sartre points to man's subjectivity and his need to make meaningful choices. In education he stresses the significance of literature and the importance of self-definition and self-examination on the part of the teacher.

Selected Bibliography

Adams, Fay, *Educating America's Children*. 2nd ed. New York, The Ronald Press Company, 1954.

Adler, Mortimer J., *Art and Prudence*. New York, Longmans, Green and Co., 1937.

Adorno, T. W., and others, *The Authoritarian Personality*. New York, Harper and Brothers, 1950.

Aikin, W. M., *The Story of the Eight-Year Study*. New York, Harper and Brothers, 1942.

Allport, Gordon, *Becoming*. New Haven, Conn., Yale University Press, 1955.

American Council on Education, Committee on Religion and Education, *The Function of the Public Schools in Dealing with Religion*. Washington, D.C., The Council, 1953.

Anshen, Ruth Nanda (ed.), *Freedom; Its Meaning*. New York, Harcourt, Brace & Company, 1940.

————, *Moral Principles of Action*. New York, Harper and Brothers, 1952.

Aquinas, (Saint) Thomas, *Basic Writings of Thomas Aquinas*. Edited by Anton C. Pegis, New York, Random House, Inc., 1945.

Ashley-Montagu, Montague Francis, *Darwin, Competition and Co-operation*. New York, Henry Schuman, Inc., 1952.

————, *The Direction of Human Development*. New York, Harper and Brothers, 1955.

Bagley, William C., *Education and Emergent Man*. New York, Thomas Nelson & Sons, 1934.

Ballou, Richard B., *The Individual and the State: The Modern Challenge to Education*. Boston, Beacon Press, 1953.

Bantock, G. H., *Freedom and Authority in Education*. Chicago, Henry Regnery Company, 1953.

Bertocci, Peter Anthony, *Introduction to the Philosophy of Religion*. Englewood Cliffs, N.J., Prentice-Hall, Inc., 1951.

Bestor, Arthur, *The Restoration of Learning*. New York, Alfred A. Knopf, 1955.

Bettelheim, B., *Love Is Not Enough*. New York, The Free Press of Glencoe, 1950.

Cole, Luella, *Education from Socrates to Montessori*. New York, Rinehart and Co., 1950.

Cole, Percival R., *A History of Educational Thought*. New York, Oxford University Press, 1931.

Conant, James B., *Education and Liberty; The Role of the Schools in a Modern Democracy*. Cambridge, Mass., Harvard University Press, 1953.

Curtis, S. J., and Boultwood, M. E. A., *Short History of Educational Ideas*. London, University Press, Ltd., 1951.

Dewey, John, *Art as Experience*. New York, Minton, Balch & Co., 1934.

————, *Characters and Events*. New York, Henry Holt & Company, 1929.

————, *A Common Faith*. New Haven, Conn., Yale University Press, 1934.

————, *Democracy and Education*. New York, The Macmillan Company, 1916.

————, *Education Today*. New York, G. P. Putnam's Sons, 1910.

————, *Experience and Education*. New York, The Macmillan Company, 1938.

————, *Experience and Nature*. LaSalle, Ill., The Open Court Publishing Company, 1925.

————, *Human Nature and Conduct*. New York, The Modern Library, Inc., 1930.

————, *Interest and Effort in Education*. Boston, Houghton Mifflin Company, 1913.

————, *My Pedagogic Creed*. Personal Growth Leaflet, No. 19, Washington, D.C., National Education Association.

————, *The Quest for Certainty*. New York, Minton, Balch & Co., 1929.

————, *Reconstruction in Philosophy*. New York, Henry Holt & Company, 1920.

Dobson, J. F., *Ancient Education and Its Meaning to Us*. New York, Longmans, Green & Company, 1932.

Eby, F., *Early Protestant Educators*. New York, McGraw-Hill, Inc., 1931.

Eliot, T. S., *The Idea of a Christian Society*. New York, The Macmillan Company, 1935.

Farrington, Benjamin, *Francis Bacon, Philosopher of Industrial Science*. New York, Henry Schuman, Inc., 1949.

Frank, Jerome, *Fate and Freedom; a Philosophy for Free Americans*. New York, Simon and Schuster, Inc., 1945.

Freud, Sigmund, *A General Introduction to Psychoanalysis*. New York, Liveright Publishing Corporation, 1920.

Hans, Nicholaus A., *New Trends in Education in the 18th Century*. New York, Grove Press, Inc., 1951.

Hart, Joseph K., *Mind in Transition*. New York, Philosophical Library, Inc., 1949.

Heidbreder, Edna, *Seven Psychologies*. New York, D. Appleton-Century Company, 1933.

Henderson, Stella, *Introduction to Philosophy of Education*. Chicago, University of Chicago Press, 1947.

Herskovits, Melville, *Man and His Works*. New York, Alfred A. Knopf, Inc., 1948.

Hertzler, Joyce O., *The History of Utopian Thought*. New York, The Macmillan Company, 1926.

Horne, Herman H., *The Democratic Philosophy of Education*. New York, The Macmillan Company, 1932.

———, *The Philosophy of Christian Education*. New York, Fleming H. Revell Company, 1937.

Horney, Karen, *The Neurotic Personality of Our Time*. New York, W. W. Norton and Company, Inc., 1937.

Horkheimer, Max, *The Eclipse of Reason*. New York, Oxford University Press, 1947.

Hutchins, Robert M., *Education for Freedom*. Baton Rouge, La., Louisiana State University Press, 1943.

———, *The Higher Learning in America*. New Haven, Conn., Yale University Press, 1936.

Huxley, Aldous, *The Perennial Philosophy*. New York, Harper and Brothers, 1945.

Huxley, Julian, *Man in the Modern World*. London, Chatto & Windus, 1947.

Jaeger, W., *Paideia: The Ideals of Greek Culture*. New York, Oxford University Press, 1939.

James, William, *The Meaning of Truth*. New York, Longmans, Green & Company, 1909.

———, *Pragmatism*. New York, Longmans, Green & Company, 1907.

———, *The Principles of Psychology*. 2 vols. New York, Henry Holt and Company, 1890.

———, *Talks to Teachers on Psychology*. New York, Henry Holt & Company, 1900.

Jones, Howard Mumford, *Education and World Tragedy*. Cambridge, Mass., Harvard University Press, 1946.

Kallen, Horace M., *The Education of Free Men*. New York, Farrar, Straus & Company, 1944.

Kilpatrick, William H., *Education and the Social Crisis*. New York, Liveright Publishing Corporation, 1932.

———, *Foundations of Method*. New York, The Macmillan Company, 1925.

Kohn, Hans, *The Idea of Nationalism: A Study in Its Origins and Background*. New York, The Macmillan Company, 1944.

Langford, Howard D., *Education and the Social Conflict*. New York, The Macmillan Company, 1936.

Laski, Harold, *The American Democracy*. New York, The Viking Press, Inc., 1948.

Lauterpacht, H., *An International Bill of Rights of Man*. New York, Columbia University Press, 1947.

Lindsay, A. D., *The Essentials of Democracy*. New York, Oxford University Press, 1935.

———, *The Modern Democratic State*. New York, Oxford University Press, 1943.

Livingstone, Richard, *On Education*. New York, The Macmillan Company, 1944.

Lodge, Rupert, *Philosophy of Education*. New York, Harper and Brothers, 1947.

Lovejoy, Arthur O., *The Revolt Against Dualism*. LaSalle, Ill., The Open Court Publishing Company, 1930.

Lynd, Robert S., *Knowledge for What?* Princeton, N.J., Princeton University Press, 1939.

Malinowski, Bronislaw, *Freedom and Civilization*. New York, Roy Publishers, Inc., 1944.

Mannheim, Karl, *Diagnosis of Our Time*. London, Kegan Paul, Trench, Trubner & Co., 1946.

———, *Ideology and Utopia*. New York, Harcourt, Brace & Company, 1936.

———, *Man and Society in an Age of Reconstruction*. New York, Harcourt, Brace & Company, 1936.

Maritain, Jacques, *Art & Poetry*. New York, Philosophical Library, Inc., 1943.

———, *Art and Scholasticism*. New York, Charles Scribner's Sons, 1933.

———, *Christianity and Democracy*. New York, Charles Scribner's Sons, 1945.

———, *Education at the Crossroads*. New Haven, Conn., Yale University Press, 1943.

Matthews, Roderick R., and Akrawl, Matta, *Education in the Arab Countries*. Washington, American Council on Education, 1949.

Mayer, Frederick, *A History of Ancient and Medieval Philosophy*. New York, American Book Company, 1950.

———, *A History of Modern Philosophy*. New York, American Book Company, 1951.

———, *Education and the Good Life*. Washington, D.C., Public Affairs Press, 1957.

———, *Philosophy of Education for Our Time*. New York, The Odyssey Press, Inc., 1958.

Meyer, Adolph E., *The Development of Education in the Twentieth Century*. Englewood Cliffs, N.J., Prentice-Hall, Inc., 1949.

Miles, D. W., *Recent Reforms in French Secondary Education*. New York, Teachers College, Columbia University, 1953.

Monroe, Paul, *Source Book of History of Education*. New York, The Macmillan Company, 1923.

Moore, Ernest C., *The Story of Instruction: The Beginnings*. New York, The Macmillan Company, 1936.

———, *The Story of Instruction: The Church, the Renaissance and the Reformation*. New York, The Macmillan Company, 1938.

Mukerji, S. N., *Education in India Today and Tomorrow*. Baroda, India, Acharya Book Depot Opposite Jubilee Garden, 1952.

Mulhern, James, *A History of Education*. New York, The Ronald Press Company, 1946.

Plato, *The Dialogues of Plato*. Translated by Benjamin Jowett. 2 vols. New York, Charles Scribner's Sons, 1928.

Rader, Melvin, *Ethics and Society*. New York, Henry Holt & Company, 1950.

Randall, John H., Jr., *The Making of the Modern Mind* (Revised edition). Boston, Houghton Mifflin Company, 1940.

Rogers, A. K., *A Student's History of Philosophy*. New York, The Macmillan Company, 1907.

Rousseau, Jean Jacques, *The Social Contract*. New York, G. P. Putnam's Sons, 1906.

Russell, Bertrand, *Education and the Good Life*. New York, Boni and Liveright, 1926.

Tawney, R. H., *The Acquisitive Society*. New York, Harcourt, Brace & Company, 1921.

Thut, I. N., *The Story of Education*. New York, McGraw-Hill, Inc., 1957.

Tillich, Paul, *The Courage to Be*. New Haven, Conn., Yale University Press, 1952.

Toynbee, Arnold, *A Study of History*. New York, Oxford University Press, 1939.

Ulich, Robert, *Conditions of Civilized Living*. New York, E. P. Dutton & Co., 1946.

———, *History of Educational Thought*. New York, American Book Company, 1945.

———, *Human Career*. New York, Harper and Brothers, 1957.

Van Doren, Mark, *Liberal Education*. New York, Henry Holt & Company, 1943.

Wahl, Jean, *A Short History of Existentialism*. New York, Philosophical Library, Inc., 1949.

Wahlquist, John T., *The Philosophy of American Education*. New York, The Ronald Press Company, 1942.

Ward, Barbara, *The West at Bay*. New York, W. W. Norton and Company, Inc., 1918.

Warner, W. Lloyd, Meeker, Marcia, and Eells, Kenneth. *Social Class in America*. Chicago, Science Research Associates, 1949.

Whitehead, Alfred North, *The Aims of Education and Other Essays*. New York, The Macmillan Company, 1929.